From Author to Text

From Author to Text

Re-reading George Eliot's *Romola*

Edited by

CAROLINE LEVINE and MARK W. TURNER

Ashgate

Aldershot • Brookfield USA • Singapore • Sydney

Published by
Ashgate Publishing Limited
Gower House
Croft Road
Aldershot
Hants GU11 3HR
England

Ashgate Publishing Company
Old Post Road
Brookfield
Vermont 05036-9704
USA

British Library Cataloguing-in-Publication Data

From Author to Text: Re-reading George Eliot's *Romola*.
   (The Nineteenth Century series)
   1. Eliot, George, 1819-1880, *Romola*.
   I. Levine, Caroline. II. Turner, Mark W.
   823.8

Library of Congress Cataloging-in-Publication Data

From author to text: re-reading George Eliot's *Romola* / edited by
   Caroline Levine and Mark W. Turner.
      (The Nineteenth Century series)
      Includes bibliographical references and index.
      ISBN 1-84014-258-8 (alk. paper)
      1. Eliot, George, 1819-1880, *Romola*. 2. Savonarola, Girolamo, 1452-
   1498—in literature. 3. Eliot, George, 1819-1880—Knowledge—Italy. 4. English
   fiction—Italian influences. 5. Florence (Italy)—in literature. I. Levine, Caroline,
   1970-   . II. Turner, Mark W. III. Series: Nineteenth Century (Aldershot,
   England).
      PR4668.F76   1998
      823'.8—dc21   98-8699
                                                                              CIP

ISBN 1 84014 258 8

This book is printed on acid free paper

Printed and bound in Great Britain by MPG Books Ltd, Bodmin, Cornwall

Contents

CONTENTS

The Nineteenth Century
General Editors' Preface

The aim of this series is to reflect, develop and extend the great burgeoning of interest in the nineteenth century that has been an inevitable feature of recent decades, as that former epoch has come more sharply into focus as a locus for our understanding not only of the past but of the contours of our modernity. Though it is dedicated principally to the publication of original monographs and symposia in literature, history, cultural analysis, and associated fields, there will be a salient role for reprints of significant texts from, or about, the period. Our overarching policy is to address the spectrum of nineteenth-century studies without exception, achieving the widest scope in chronology, approach and range of concern. This, we believe, distinguishes our project from comparable ones, and means, for example, that in the relevant areas of scholarship we both recognize and cut innovatively across such parameters as those suggested by the designations 'Romantic' and 'Victorian'. We welcome new ideas, while valuing tradition. It is hoped that the world which predates yet so forcibly predicts and engages our own will emerge in parts, as a whole, and in the lively currents of debate and change that are so manifest an aspect of its intellectual, artistic and social landscape.

Vincent Newey
Joanne Shattock

University of Leicester

List of Figures

Acknowledgements

Romola fanatics, we have discovered, have been hiding their passion for too long. Spanning three years and two continents, work on this collection of essays has revealed more secret *Romola* enthusiasts than we had ever imagined. Our project began with a conference in 1995, 'Reviving *Romola*', which brought an audience twice the expected size. Since then, we have run into *Romola* zealots at conferences and in cafés, on the web and in the library—some of whom have since added their contributions to this volume.

We are thrilled with the results, and have many to thank. First of all, we are grateful to the University of London's Centre for English Studies and its head, Warren Chernaik, who hosted 'Reviving *Romola*'. And we want to extend our special thanks to the Centre's Rebecca Dawson, whose able and cheerful assistance not only made this project possible, but also enjoyable. We are indebted, too, to Andrew Sanders, whose Penguin edition of the novel did so much to revive interest in *Romola*, and whose support and enthusiasm for the project were invaluable. Jane Pringle, at Roehampton Institute London, provided essential technical support. And the institutions which have actively sustained our work on the project include the Birkbeck College English Department, the University of Luton, Leighton House, the Roehampton Institute London and the Wake Forest University English Department.

We would like to thank Yale University Press for permission to print Chapter One, 'George Eliot v. Fredric Leighton: Whose Text Is It Anyway?' a version of which is forthcoming in *Frederic Leighton: Antiquity, Renaissance, Modernity,* eds Tim Barringer and Elizabeth Prettejohn (New Haven and London: Yale University Press, 1998). And we are grateful, too, to Joanne Shattock, our series editor at Ashgate, who showed such an unstinting interest in our project.

Finally, among our friends, we would like to thank Caterina Albano, John Allen, Corin Bennett, Jan Caldwell, Morena Capovilla, Deedee and Joe Levine, Jon McKenzie, Lisa Sternlieb, and Margaret and Wayne Turner for countless acts of Romola-like generosity.

Editors' Note

All of the contributors have relied on the same edition of *Romola* for this volume. Page numbers in parentheses in the text refer to Andrew Brown's fine critical edition of *Romola* (Oxford: Clarendon Press, 1993).

All citations of George Eliot's letters come from Gordon Haight's nine-volume collection, *The George Eliot Letters* (New Haven: Yale University Press, 1954-78), These references are cited as *Letters* in parentheses, followed by the volume and page number. The volumes are as follows: vol. 1 1836-1851—vol. 2 1852-1858—vol. 3 1859-1861—vol. 4 1862-1868—vol. 5 1869-1873—vol. 6 1874-1877—vol. 7 1878-1880—vol. 8 1840-1870. Supplementary letters—vol. 9. 1871-1881. Supplementary letters. Addenda and corrigenda.

Introduction

CAROLINE LEVINE AND MARK W. TURNER

The end of George Eliot's *Romola* is no conventional conclusion. In place of the happily married couple, prepared to carry on the family name, we are surprised to find the angel in the house paired with her *alter ego*, the fallen woman, working together to raise a pair of illegitimate children. Oddly, this unconventional ending does not seem to have rattled the Victorians at all, if the reviews are anything to go by. Few critics in the 1860s even bothered to notice the epilogue. But by 1924, readers had altered: in the film adaptation of *Romola*, starring Lillian Gish, director Henry King changed the novel's ending—silently, of course, like the film itself. In this version Tessa drowns herself, and Romola closes the narrative alone. It is all too easy to speculate about the reasons for this transformation: the female-headed household that concludes George Eliot's novel hints at women's independence and power, perhaps even the pleasures of lesbian love. Too threatening for the Hollywood audience of 1924, the novel's ending curiously looks more radical to the roaring 20s than it did to its own contemporaries.

The difference between Victorian tranquillity and the sexual anxieties of the 1920s should prompt us to ask some questions about the historical nature of reading. Do our ways of interpreting the text tell us more about ourselves than they do about George Eliot and her contemporaries? Or is it true that we manage to be more 'knowing', more sophisticated, more *right* about meaning than our Victorian counterparts? Is the epilogue 'really' innocent because nineteenth-century readers failed to mark it, or is it 'really' subversive because the twentieth century has ferreted out its revolutionary messages? And what kinds of presuppositions underlie such questions?

The essays collected in this volume urge us to move beyond the opposition between Victorian innocence and postmodern knowingness in order to construct a richer set of relationships between critical methods and nineteenth-century texts. Indeed, this book represents an argument for theoretical pluralism, seeking to demonstrate the genuine compatibility and fecundity of multiple, overlapping—and even opposing—readings. Some of the interpretations in this book begin with nineteenth-century contexts, others with later critical paradigms, but together they compel us to confront and compare a variety of interpretative criteria, and thus to recognize the wide array of conceptual paradigms that can legitimately inform the study of texts.

Our emphasis is of course unusual—a little-known text by a celebrated author, a writer unequivocally established in the Victorian canon and in the history of the novel. It is a text that had a curious, troubled reception in its own time. Hailed by a number of reviewers as one of the highest achievements in Victorian fiction, 'the author's greatest work',[1] it was also criticized for its 'instructive antiquarianism'[2]—or 'recherche excessive', as a French reviewer put it[3]—which readers found laborious and deadening. George Eliot herself explained that she never meant the novel to reach a broad cross-section of the reading public: 'Of necessity, the book is addressed to fewer readers than my previous works, and I myself have never expected—I might rather say *intended*—that the book should be "popular" in the same sense as the others' (*Letters* IV, 49). As it turned out, she was right about her audience: though never 'popular', the novel was recognized by the élite as a remarkable literary accomplishment, even a *tour de force*.[4]

If *Romola* was a problem text for its nineteenth-century readers, it has encountered difficulties in the twentieth century for a rather different set of reasons. In this volume, we seek to persuade readers that it has been the hegemony of a *single* critical principle—the author-function—that has both shaped twentieth-century readings of the novel and relegated this particular text to comparative obscurity. Despite the celebrated 'death of the author' and her more recent resuscitation, most literary critical studies for the past hundred years have remained organized around the principle of the single author. Biographies abound, and discussions of writers, renowned and forgotten, have been the daily fare of academic literary studies. And in the context of author and *oeuvre*, *Romola* has for years revealed only deficiencies—likened unfavourably to George Eliot's other works on formalist and psychological grounds. 'The book is, in comparison with *Adam Bede, The Mill on the Floss*, or *Middlemarch*, a failure', writes Joan Bennett. 'To read *Romola* is a fascinating exercise of the mind rather than an imaginative experience'.[5] Barbara Hardy accounts for her disappointment in the characters of *Romola* by arguing that, unlike *Middlemarch*, the earlier novel tells more than it shows.[6] And more recently, Harold Bloom's sample of the 'best criticism available on the novels of George Eliot', does not even include an article on *Romola*, preferring to mention the novel only in passing.[7]

But it is our contention that it is only when set in the unitary context of George Eliot's *oeuvre* that the novel disappoints, drawing criticism, most emphatically, for failing to resemble the author's other novels. Readers have looked for the integrated web of *Middlemarch* and have been frustrated to find the generic puzzle of *Romola*. In this century, then, George Eliot scholars and readers have too often overlooked the rich historical complexity of *Romola* as Victorian *tour de force*, its fascinated concern with the subtleties of gender, identity, representation, history and ethics. And the central claim of this volume is that given a pluralist criticism—with a wide-ranging attention to multiple contexts and textualities—the novel shows itself extraordinarily fertile in issues both literary and political.

But to devote a whole collection to a single, uncanonical text may still seem to require some justification. Typically, the single texts that have shaped critical book-length studies in the past have been the most inflexibly canonical 'masterworks'. If a text has been consecrated by the critical establishment, then a volume of essays may focus attention on it. But *Romola*, always seen as a pivotal text, midpoint in George Eliot's *oeuvre*, is perceived as both too flawed and too transitional to merit a study of its own. In part, then, *From Author to Text* deliberately challenges critical assumptions about the status of both the *oeuvre* and the 'masterwork' by choosing just such an uncanonical text. Does *Romola* merit attention despite its 'failures'? Are those failures themselves contingent on particular ways of reading, on changing historical standards? This volume suggests that a range of readings reveals not only new meanings, but also new *values*—new criteria for critical judgement.

In fact, it is this attention to critical practice itself that forms the second significant aim of this project. This collection of essays proposes—polemically—that the most forceful case for theoretical pluralism emerges from a reading of a single text. In 1995, the editors organized a conference at the University of London's Centre for English Studies, called 'Reviving *Romola*'. It was here that we first witnessed the movement away from George Eliot and her *oeuvre*, and allowed ourselves to think through a whole set of new contexts for *Romola* which pushed us beyond the parameters of the author's life. In the essays collected here, we see the novel placed in a range of contexts: for example, in the periodical *Cornhill Magazine*, among novels of martyrdom, alongside twentieth-century psychoanalysis and through the lenses of contemporary feminism. Thus to set aside the author-function as one way of reading among many is both to re-read *Romola* for its complex abundance, and to confront the vast array of *ways of thinking* about the text. By staging a deliberate interpretative pluralism, we have sought not only to focus attention on the rich resources of this text, but also on criticism itself—and particularly on relationships among critical schools and traditions. After all, differing critical aims and intentions are at their most intelligible when critics of various persuasions come together to discuss a single object. Theoretical eclecticism, when focused on a common reference point, necessarily opens out into a dialogue among critical and interpretative models. *Romola* throws light on theory, just as theory throws light on the novel.

Roland Barthes, in his famous essay, 'From Work to Text', distinguishes between the finite, physical object that can be held in the hand—the work—and 'the methodological field'—the text.[8] The fundamental distinction, here, is not between kinds of objects, of course, but between ways of reading. And to read texts rather than works, Barthes suggests, is to move away from fixing classifications, meanings and conventions, and to focus instead on the movement of language itself. Unlike the bounded work, the text does not stop with the covers of the literal book; it is fundamentally *plural*—cutting across individual works and generic categories, allowing us to think about language and meaning in all of their complexity. In the spirit of Barthes, our volume asks not what *Romola* means, but how it can generate multiple, compatible and irreducible meanings under the lenses of different reading practices. We posit not one work, but a range of different 'texts'—*Romola* within the network of nineteenth-century cultural artefacts, *Romola* as both visual and verbal text, *Romola* as plotted narrative, as history, as music.

In our own shift *from author to text*, then, we urge a plural reading of a single text as not only liberatingly fertile but also as belated, as long overdue. Any unitary reading or way of reading will determine a text's boundaries, and if we are to become self-conscious, as critics, about the partial, incomplete nature of those boundaries, we must set a number of readings side by side to see how we might truly draw numerous different maps of the 'single' text. Again, the plural reading invites us to recognize that reading the author as authority—as 'father'—has historically closed down both the interpretative abundance of this novel and the self-consciousness of critics and scholars. Barthes himself moves us away from authors in 'From Work to Text', claiming that the author of a text is not privileged, paternal, original, but rather 'inscribed in the novel like one of his characters, figured in the carpet'.[9] We, in turn, invite readers to refuse the apparent fixity of the body of George Eliot the author—her biography, her intentions, her 'complete' works—in order to allow the single text to become multiple and rich, a 'network' rather than an 'organism'.[10] Only then do we invite George Eliot to come back into the text. In our volume, she comes, as Barthes would say, as a 'guest'.[11]

From Author to Text is divided into three sections, each of which prompts radically new readings of *Romola*. The first, 'Rethinking the Text', asks us to consider the many material transformations of the literary text. The second, 'Rethinking the Heroine', investigates the enigmatic 'central' character—who has not always seemed so central—and invites us to think through the woman's quest for identity, power and independence in the context of psychoanalytic and feminist critical models. The final section, 'Rethinking Authority', asks a more general question about interpretation, challenging readers to become self-conscious both about the ways in which the text shapes itself into an authority and about the authorities that mould our own reading practices.

Rethinking the text

The first question posed in this collection concerns the boundaries of the 'text' of *Romola*. Having become accustomed to reading the novel as a work—bound in paper, cloth or leather on the library shelves—readers are urged to think past the boundaries of bindings. Our volume begins by asking not, 'What does the text mean?' but rather, 'Which text?' This opening section asks how we define the text given its many material transformations, and how an attention to those transformations alters our ways of reading.

In 'George Eliot v. Frederic Leighton: Whose Text Is It Anyway?' Mark Turner reads the novel in the context of its serial publication in *Cornhill Magazine*, and suggests that by reading the serial text, we are forced to confront a new set of questions about what constitutes the text of the novel. He focuses on the relationship between word and image, by 'reading' Frederic Leighton's illustrations for the serial alongside George Eliot's words. He looks closely at the highlighting of domesticity in the visual text and focuses particularly on the ways that Leighton's illustrations both enrich and challenge George Eliot's conceptions of gender. In effect, there are two texts interacting at the site of reading in the serialized version of the text, George Eliot's novel and Leighton's illustrated version of her novel.

In 'The Texts of *Romola*', Andrew Brown, the editor of the fine Clarendon edition of the novel, confronts the impossibility of fixing the text in a modern edition as George Eliot herself intended it. He discusses the ways that George Eliot's manuscript of *Romola* was mediated and revised over the many early editions and forms in which the novel was published. In particular, Brown uncovers the vast number of transformations in punctuation—from George Eliot's breathless, comparatively comma-less prose to the stilted standards of Victorian editors—and contends that such differences are not 'neutral' when it comes to reading. Thus he draws our attention both to the mediating processes of cultural production and to the complexities of deciding what exactly constitutes an 'authoritative' text.

Rethinking the heroine

If the materiality of the text emerges as shifting and generatively uncertain, so too does our reading of the novel's heroine. This volume's emphasis on Romola herself is something of a critical departure from what has often been seen as the novel's central interest, the characterization of Tito. In an appreciative and insightful review of the novel, R. H. Hutton remarked that 'there is not a more wonderful piece of painting in English romance than this figure of Tito'.[12] And other critics at the time concurred that in Tito,   George Eliot had created a

masterful study in fear and duplicity. In his recent survey of the secondary
criticism on George Eliot, Graham Handley asserts that 'there is little doubt that
Tito is the triumph of *Romola* for the modern reader'.[13] But our contributors
suggest otherwise, and it is about time that the eponymous heroine is given her
due.

Particularly in the wake of contemporary feminist criticisms, a new
generation of George Eliot readers find in Romola a revealing way of
unravelling the complexities of female identity in the novel. In 'Mapping
Romola: Physical Space, Women's Place', Shona Elizabeth Simpson addresses
'the problem of the intellectual woman's relationship to love', by exploring the
ways gendered physical space—for example the construction of internal and
external boundaries—are related to Romola's attempt to define her own place as
an intellectual woman in the world around her. It is only through the negotiation
of male and female spaces that Romola is able to challenge the definitions of
'woman' and 'intellectual'. Romola's struggle with her internal, irrational self is
also the focus of Julian Corner's '"Telling the Whole": Trauma, Drifting and
Reconciliation in *Romola*'. Romola's 'search for an idea, by which she may
"thread" her life together', Corner suggests, 'is a cycle of hope and despair'. He
draws on the psychoanalytic theories of D. W. Winnicott and the philosophy of
Søren Kierkegaard to understand Romola's—and George Eliot's—impulse to
reconcile traumatic events. With links to both Simpson and Corner, Susan M.
Bernardo sees Romola's struggle for independence in relation to spatial politics
and psychological displacement. In 'From Romola to *Romola*: The Complex Act
of Naming', Bernardo argues that only through the renegotiation of social space
and the active use of spoken language can Romola achieve a form of stable
identity. It is in Romola's 'eventual appropriation of naming' that we see her
begin to establish an autonomous self.

These three chapters intersect, overlap and finally enrich one another.
Though not all explicitly feminist, all three pieces are informed by a critical
context in which feminism has become a basic foundation for inquiry and
research. Corner's investigation of the woman's psyche might not openly favour
a political programme, for example, but it is impossible to imagine his rich
consideration of the novel without feminism as a background. Importantly, then,
these three articles demonstrate there is no single feminist reading, or way of
reading; rather, there are feminisms—feminist ways of approaching and
considering the literary text, which emerge as various and complex.

Indeed, this trio of chapters invites us to compare and question the grounds of
political readings more generally. For Simpson, *Romola* falls short of achieving
a truly liberating model of the intellectual woman, free from the roles of the
nurse, Madonna and mother; while for Bernardo, Romola takes powerful control
of both spoken language and meaning by the end of her narrative. We can use
these chapters, then, to think about the interpretative claims of two important

traditions of feminism—the materialist focus on work and the psychoanalytic emphasis on language and identity. Are these mutually exclusive, or should they rather be wielded together? How does each throw light on the limitations of the other? If the relationship between gender and power is multivalent and complex, then both *must* have a place in theoretical discourse, if only to determine the relative importance of their claims. In part, we want to make the case that both psychoanalytic and materialist traditions produce persuasive, legitimate readings of *Romola*; and thus divergent feminisms turn out to be compatible at the very least as equally enriching ways of reading a literary text.

Yet faced with apparently opposing feminist interpretations, how should we determine the political force of *Romola*? Is it, finally, a radical or a conservative text? This volume suggests that the search for a 'final' political reading is itself misleading, since it ignores the ways in which a text like this one can be both radically unsettling and frustratingly conservative. Any politicized reading of a text depends upon the critical framework of the reader—focusing our attention on different articulations, uses and sources of power; and the differences among the critics' interpretative perspectives can therefore help us to sort out the novel's subtle and conflicting political messages. In fact, it is part of the very perplexity and stimulation of a difficult text like *Romola* that it resists simple categorization and demands to be *read*.

This brings us to articulate the purpose of advocating a theoretical pluralism. Arguing for the simultaneity of critical arguments is not to suggest that all readings of a text are equally valid, for such an approach leads ultimately to an uncritical relativism. Rather, it is through an attention to intersections and departures across critical approaches that political readings become dialectical, dynamic and generative rather than fixed and programmatic. Our volume, with its focus on the single novel, therefore asks readers to think about these disparate feminist perspectives together, and thus to ask how each is convincing, how each case seeks to intervene politically, how we might weigh the claims of one against the other.

Rethinking authority

New schools of criticism have made it possible to attend to Romola as a focus for the text which bears her name, and we have seen, in this context, that the critical tradition of feminism both enlarges our interpretative possibilities for the novel and reveals *itself* as richly eclectic and provocative—rather than, as is sometimes charged, restrictively and deadeningly ideological. We now shift to an even broader critical category—that of *authority*—a term which is as complex, ambiguous and dialogic as the literary text itself.

How might we locate interpretative authority? Does it belong with the 'author', whose own title would seem to demand it? Or, in the context of a historical novel, should we doubt George Eliot's authority—the tenuous status of her own fiction in relation to historical fact? Ought we to attend, instead, to the almost obsessive concerns with authority within the novel itself, the critique and subversion of the figures within the text who seek to usurp interpretative authority? Or does authority 'really' rest with generic forms and traditions—with cultural contexts rather than individual minds or characters? Does it belong, in the end, with the contemporary critic, who can 'see' the novel through the apparently translucent historicizing lenses of the late twentieth century?

It is in the context of these questions that our volume makes its most forceful argument for theoretical pluralism. Our collection makes the case that critics inevitably rely on one or another version of authority for any reading—whether it be a version of authorial intention, a focus on the interpretative voices within the text itself, or the persuasive force of a critical or cultural tradition. And if the essays collected here convince the reader of the legitimacy and compatibility of these variations, fixing 'authority' authoritatively emerges as impossible. Thus we must acknowledge that critics are not compelled, but rather *choose*, one of many 'authoritative' starting-points for our own readings. We suggest that it does not make sense, on political grounds, to dismiss authority out of hand, but that we must instead become self-conscious about the relationship between 'authorities' and critical practices. In this section of the volume, authority turns out to be not univocal, rigid and complete, but rather multiple and productive.

The chapters in the final section of this volume thus allow us to consider a network of possible and plausible authorities. In 'George Eliot Martyrologist: The Case of Savonarola', David Carroll argues that George Eliot sought to render the profound and mysterious character of Savonarola more effectively than contemporary historians had done—and thus suggests that the historical novel has more authority, when it comes to character, than conventional history-writing or historical fiction. Carroll reads George Eliot's novel as a deliberate, secularizing revision of the profusion of popular historical novels about Christian martyrdom—Charles Kingsley's *Hypatia* and John Henry Newman's *Callista*, among others. For Carroll Savonarola is a martyr who dies witnessing the destruction of his own beliefs. And ultimately, we are led to recognize an equation of his martyrdom with the human condition itself. Revising two genres at once, George Eliot critiques their authority and seeks to establish her own, secular humanist model in their place.

Writing the historical novel might involve wresting authority from both the historians and the novelists, but there is of course a another set of questions about authority attaching to the figure of Savonarola. How is it that a single man can seize both moral and civic power and then lose it again in the space of a few tumultuous years? In 'Power and Persuasion: Voices of Influence in *Romola*', Beryl Gray offers us a wholly new response to this question by uncovering

George Eliot's emphasis throughout the novel on Savonarola's *voice*. She contrasts the thrilling power of his commands and entreaties with the liquid, melting tones of the perfidious Tito, making a compelling claim for the centrality of speech as an index of character. And the voice not only tells; it also transforms.

If Gray helps us to contemplate the shaping of authority *within* the novel, Caroline Levine examines the overarching form of *Romola*, interrogating the persuasive power of plotted narrative. In 'The Prophetic Fallacy: Realism, Foreshadowing and Narrative Knowledge in *Romola*', Levine argues that suspense and foreshadowing urge a *resistance* to conventional authority, and both reader and protagonist learn to challenge authority through plotted doubts and experiments. But, paradoxically, plot is a form which is inherently authoritative. We learn from plotted 'snares' to be sceptical, but Levine shows how that very scepticism can be turned back on the plot itself to reveal the ideological investments of the novel's own conclusions. Thus the plot contains the seeds of its own critique. Setting George Eliot's fiction in the context of John Ruskin's *Modern Painters*, this chapter pairs the patterns of plotted suspense with the aims of Victorian realism, arguing that *Romola* is a quintessentially realist novel—and one that reveals the very limits of realism.

Chris Greenwood shares Levine's interest in the plotted impulses that push the narrative of *Romola* forward, focusing on the suspenseful act of seeing in the novel. In 'An Imperceptible Start: The Sight of Humanity in *Romola*', Greenwood looks closely at the moments when Tito's 'dark past breaks into view', and he shudders, starts or blushes at mentions of lost fathers and guilty secrets. What Greenwood notices is that the other characters fail to interpret such moments correctly; invariably they generate interpretations that reflect their own self-absorbed concerns. But the narration itself can 'see' clearly, which illustrates both that the truths of 'human nature' are in fact visible, available for discovery, and that we can discern these truths if only we learn to see disinterestedly. Greenwood exposes a 'hierarchy of observation', in which the relationship between the eye and the will is one of power. The less political and social power a character has, the less he or she can perceive. In this context, the narration emerges as 'authoritarian', and Romola takes on her 'quiet authority' only towards the end, when she shapes herself into the visual spectacle of the 'Blessed Lady'.

Like Greenwood, Leonee Ormond investigates the novel's emphasis on visual and pictorial details, but her focus shifts to the authority of iconographical tradition. Closing the volume with her 'Angels and Archangels: *Romola* and the Paintings of Florence', Ormond looks at George Eliot's quest for historical accuracy in visual details, and particularly her reliance on pictorial authorities for her own vision of fifteenth-century Florence. But the novelist also *invents* her own picture gallery for *Romola*, generating portraits, allegories and symbols.

Most importantly, Ormond shows that Tito is repeatedly pictured as Saint Michael in George Eliot's invented images. There is an irony, here, since he is 'not a rescuer but a destroyer', and Ormond reveals the novel's subtle attention to Tito's transition from angel to 'fallen angel'. Like David Carroll, Ormond reveals George Eliot's rewriting of religious tradition to establish her own more secular authority.

Authority emerges, then, as the whole range of shaping interpretative and material forces rather than as a single, monolithic power. There is authorship itself, a seizing of authority from other texts and a refashioning of old ideas and generic patterns for a new literary manifesto. In this context, George Eliot's erudite authorship reveals itself as both resistant and productive, transforming long traditions of thought and belief to forge new values and ideas. But authority is also moulded and challenged within the text itself, and to investigate the different structures of power mapped and fostered by the narrative is to discover that we may wish actively to contest the text's own version of authority. Finally, there is the authority of critical paradigms, the set of concerns that authorize reading itself—our interpretative starting-points in character, form, language, context and culture.

Convergences

We have repeatedly urged that the chapters in this volume can help us to reflect on the relationship among critical traditions and premises. Finally, then, we want to point to some of the ways in which the chapters here converge. In particular, we seek to draw attention to the episodes from the novel that appear more than once in our volume, treated differently in the context of disparate critical paradigms.

Take, for example, the scene of Romola's 'drifting away' to the plague-stricken island. This scene appears with startling frequency in these chapters. In previous generations, scholars have found this episode disturbingly illegible. Anti-realist and formally inelegant, it has been seen as an unseemly breach in the narrative.[14] In our volume, however, the 'drifting away' scene gathers significance, becoming a crucial site of interest. It is interpreted variously here— as the moment of Romola's sanctification, as the appropriation of her own story, as the end of narrative suspense and as a telling shift to the unconscious mind, to give just a few examples. Thus our contributors demonstrate that the critical agenda for reading has changed: the faultline has ceased to be faulty, and has become instead intriguing, revealing and pivotal.

What these chapters share, most importantly, is the idea that Romola's drifting away crowns or completes her development, and that its very strangeness is a clue to its importance within the narrative. The interpretative emphasis on this scene testifies, on the one hand, to a transformation in critical perspective in the past few decades, from a privileging of formal coherence to a focus on gaps, breaks and experiments; and on the other hand, critical attention to the episode bears witness to the richness of a text that can fruitfully bear eight—and no doubt more—readings of a single scene.

Since these convergences form part of the pleasure of reading multiple interpretations, we want to close simply by gesturing to some themes and scenes which appear more than once in this volume—and which have barely been a focus of critical attention before. For example, Tessa, the surprisingly innocent fallen woman, takes on a new interest in the context of a recent emphasis on complex constructions of gender and domesticity. Her very childlike innocence, once considered a failure in terms of character,[15] becomes worthy of attention in the eyes of critics concerned to understand cultural formations of gender and power. In another instance, critics in the past have dismissed *Romola* as unrealistic, condemning it for its minute archeologizing and its profusion of prophetic voices. Until recently, therefore, the text has not been allowed to take its place in the complex, many-sided discourse of realism alive in its own time, which was certainly self-conscious about the difficulties of matching language and the world. As several chapters here reveal, George Eliot, herself vocally engaged in this discussion, can be seen to rethink realist conventions in the experimental *Romola*. Furthermore, a number of the chapters in the volume also depart from past treatments of the novel in concentrating on its renegotiations of motherhood and domestic space. They help us to think about the relationships between public and private realms, between mothers and stepmothers, between material spaces and textual margins, and between masculine freedoms and feminine prisons.

These are just a few of the overlapping themes and concerns gathered in this volume. The reader will no doubt discover any number of other intersections among these chapters, and we are thrilled to imagine the range and richness of these discoveries. Most importantly, we hope that readers will think of these chapters *together* for their power to generate both a new respect for this novel and a new—and engaging—self-consciousness about the activity of interpretation.

Notes

1. *Westminster Review* **80** (October 1863), p. 344. R. H. Hutton wrote that *Romola* was the 'greatest [George Eliot] has yet produced', in the *Spectator* **36** (18 July 1863), p. 2267.
2. *Saturday Review* **16** (25 July 1865), p. 124.

3. E.-D. Forgues, *Revue des deux mondes* **48** (December 1863), p. 945.

4. G. H. Lewes wrote that *Romola* 'has been flatly received by the general public though it has excited a deep enthusiasm in almost all the élite' (*Letters*, IV, 102). Anthony Trollope 'congratulated' George Eliot on her 'perfection of pen painting', especially in her depiction of Romola (*The Letters of Anthony Trollope*, ed. Bradford Booth [Oxford: Oxford University Press, 1951], p. 174). And Robert Browning famously wrote George Eliot a letter: 'to express my gratitude for the noblest and most heroic prose-poem I have ever read' (*Letters*, IV, 96).

5. Joan Bennett, *George Eliot: Her Mind and Her Art* (Cambridge: Cambridge University Press, 1962), p. 140. Jerome Thale sees *Romola* as such a disaster that he entitles his chapter, 'The Uses of Failure: *Romola*', and claims that 'Her art was at one of those stages of development where the preparation for real advances is often marked by retrogression. George Eliot's art had to get worse before it could get better'. *The Novels of George Eliot* (New York and London: Columbia University Press, 1959), p. 77.

6. 'One of the deadnesses of *Romola* comes from its life of unrelieved crisis which, except perhaps in Tito's case, does not allow motive and action to unfold slowly, and which is explained in exposition rather than revealed in dramatic and varied action'. Barbara Hardy, *The Novels of George Eliot: A Study in Form* (1959; reprinted New York: Oxford University Press, 1963), p. 61.

7. In his introduction to the volume, Bloom affirms that '*Romola* is rightly forgotten'. *George Eliot: Modern Critical Views*, ed. Harold Bloom (New York and Philadelphia: Chelsea House Publishers, 1986), p. 4.

8. Roland Barthes, 'From Work to Text', in *Image, Music, Text*, trans. Stephen Heath (London: Fontana Press, 1977), pp. 156-7.

9. Ibid., p. 161.

10. Ibid.

11. Ibid.

12. *Spectator* **36** (18 July 1863), p. 2267.

13. Graham Handley, *State of the Art of George Eliot: A Guide through the Critical Maze* (Bristol: The Bristol Press, 1990), p. 9.

14. The *Westminster Review*, for example, complained that the episode 'is strangely disconnected' from the rest of the narrative: 'The pestilential village and its call upon [Romola's] sympathies is another of those extravagantly fortuitous circumstances of which the author makes such free use. All sense of probability is here sacrificed for a moral effect, which yet jars upon us like an isolated light that does not harmonize with the rest of the picture'. *Westminster Review* **80** (October 1863), p. 351.

15. Leslie Stephen complains that Tessa is 'so much of a kitten that she approaches very nearly to be an idiot'. *George Eliot* (London and New York: Macmillan, 1902), p. 139. And more recently, Juliet McMaster writes: 'The most simply physical beings among [George Eliot's] characters are simply called animals [...] Tessa is a 'pigeon', and a 'puss-faced' minx', and she makes companions of young goats'. See Juliet McMaster, 'George Eliot's Language of the Sense', in *George Eliot: A Centenary Tribute*, eds Gordon S. Haight and Rosemary T. VanArsdel (Totowa, NJ: Barnes and Noble Books, 1982), p. 20. And entirely overlooking Tessa's role in the novel, Jerome Thale argues that one of the great failures of the novel is that Romola has no double: 'She exists in a kind of splendid isolation'. Thale, p. 82.

PART ONE

Rethinking the Text

CHAPTER ONE

George Eliot v. Frederic Leighton: Whose Text Is It Anyway?

MARK W. TURNER

Romola, serialized in the popular monthly *Cornhill Magazine*, was the only novel by George Eliot to be accompanied by illustrations in its first form. In his drawings for the serial, Frederic Leighton, now best remembered for his large paintings of classical and Renaissance themes, undertook the task of bringing fifteenth-century Florence alive for readers. It is the interface between Eliot's written text and Leighton's visual depictions that I will discuss here, to indicate ways the illustrations form a parallel text—a text that actually highlights the domestic conflict in the novel. Broadly, I argue that the relationship between word and image in Victorian serials is far more complicated than has been acknowledged, challenging our ways of reading visual images and our ways of understanding nineteenth-century serial fiction.

Illustrating fictions

Founded in 1860, *Cornhill Magazine* was unique among the most popular 'high' literary monthlies for the inclusion of illustrations in each issue, which added to the magazine's tremendous initial popularity. Unlike other popular magazines such as *Fraser's*, *Blackwood's*, *Temple Bar*, or *St James*, *Cornhill* commissioned quality wood-block engravings to supplement serial fiction and some poetry; although some middle-class monthlies and many weeklies were liberally illustrated, notably *Good Words* and *Once a Week*, none approached *Cornhill* in the early 1860s for the quality of fiction and of drawings.[1] As Simon Houfe observes, illustrating for *Cornhill* was the '*sine qua non* of having reached the zenith as an illustrator'.[2] Gradually throughout the nineteenth century, as technological improvements made reproductions of drawings cheaper and as visual images became increasingly prominent in public (through posters and billboards, for example), illustrations became more frequent in print journalism.[3] Reactions to the proliferation of illustrations were not uniform; in 1870 the *Gentleman's Magazine* welcomed illustrated papers, calling the phenomenon 'a new mania in journalism',[4] but it was not always thus. William

Wordsworth, condemning similar publications twenty years earlier, writes in a sonnet,

> Now prose and verse sunk into disrepute
> Must lacquey a dumb Art that best can suit
> The taste of this once-intellectual Land.
> A backward movement surely have we here,
> From manhood—back to childhood; for the age—
> Back towards caverned life's first rude career.
> Avaunt this vile abuse of pictured age!
> Must eyes be all in all, the tongue and ear
> Nothing? Heaven keep us from a lower stage![5]

For the old and by now deeply conservative poet, the popular language and images of newspapers were unmanly, regressive and anti-intellectual. He did not recognize the irony of such anti-popular railery coming from a poet whose aim in *Lyrical Ballads* a half-century earlier had been to champion the language of the common man. Wordsworth, who wrote the poem in the mid-1840s, was doubtless reacting against such new publications as the *Illustrated London News* which was launched in 1842. Between the time of Wordworth's poem and the *Gentleman's Magazine* proclamation of a new 'mania' was the revolution in wood-block illustration in the 1860s which can be witnessed in the pages of middle-class shilling monthlies throughout the decade.

In 1864, in time for the Christmas season, Smith, Elder published the *Cornhill Gallery*, a collection of the magazine's illustrations, including many of Leighton's drawings for *Romola*, presented as works of art. It cost one guinea and could be purchased as one volume, elegantly bound with gilt edges, or as a portfolio with separate pictures, presumably suitable for hanging. The *Athenaeum* praised the 'Art-value of the designs' and in an advertisement, we learn that both the *Observer* and *Morning Star* called it a wonderful drawing-room book.[6] Later in the 1860s, other publishers followed suit with collections of drawings from their magazines.[7] That such books were published attests to the public interest in periodical illustrations and the worth of the drawings apart from their literary source. And the inclusion of full-page illustrations and vignettes in *Cornhill* owes as much to the publisher's seemingly endless financial support of the magazine as to the technological and economic factors in the printing trade which increasingly made mass-produced illustrations financially viable.

The ways readers viewed the illustrations which accompanied serial novels will of course have been as varied as the readers. We are not able to determine exactly how the illustrations in magazines functioned visually for particular viewers. As twentieth-century viewers, our perception of a nineteenth-century drawing will necessarily be different from Victorians, and we read into the works retrospectively and with different assumptions about visual images and visual culture. As John Berger writes, 'today we see the art of the past as nobody saw it before. We actually perceive it in a different way'.[8] And the way we actually 'see' or consume a drawing depends on how, when and where we encounter it. For example, illustrated magazines may have been especially suited to rail travel because the drawings could provide a centre of focus during a rattling and often uncomfortable journey.[9] Or, as noted in the advertisement for the *Cornhill Gallery*, a collection of serial drawings might become a 'monument of many agreeable tales',[10] implying that drawings could somehow commemorate the experience of serial reading. Furthermore, the way images are remembered is itself culturally specific, so that the way we process and recall Victorian illustrations is necessarily different from the Victorians; memory and the relation between perception and cognition are not innate.[11] Wolfgang Kemp has argued for the need to question how the transmission of images between eras operates to discover the difference between the 'utterance' and the 'remembrance'.[12] I will not pretend to tackle the breadth of Kemp's suggestion here, but it is important to accept—to remember—our distance from mid-Victorian periodical illustrations and the gap between the representations offered and our understanding of them.

Almost no work has been done on the ways periodical illustrations in the nineteenth century were consumed. While there is an ever-increasing body of work on Victorian images, there is little work that theorizes ways for twentieth-century viewers to encounter nineteenth-century visual culture. Serial illustrations in periodicals come with their own set of particular questions. To articulate a few: how do these drawings relate to the literary text? How do they relate to other visual images within the magazine? How does each individual image stand apart from the series?

Leighton's method of producing wood engravings placed an unavoidable distance between the artist and the reader-consumer. In fact, such mediation is perhaps part of the process of all cultural production.[13] Leighton's drawings for *Romola* for *Cornhill* meant that he drew chalk sketches on gray paper which were then recast in pen on the wood blocks. The publisher George Smith arranged to have photographs taken before turning the wood blocks over to the engravers, Swain and Linton. The engravers cut away those areas intended to appear white in the final print and left in relief those areas to be black. The blocks were locked into the printer's form and inked at the same time as the type.[14] The actual printing process puts the final product which the magazine reader consumes at several removes from the initial visual representation of the artist, and often the engravers' interpretation of the ink drawing was at odds with the image envisioned by the artist.

Despite the distance between reader and artist, effective illustrations might narrow the gap between image and words, and act as the reader's entrance into the literature. In his book on *Victorian Novelists and their Illustrators*, John

Harvey calls serial drawings a 'valuable aid' 'for a public which did not easily imagine what it read'.[15] While it is risky to presume that the Victorian public had difficulty imagining fiction, it may be reasonable to assert that, considering some serials lasted over 18 months or two years, the importance of an effective illustration to the reader is as a reminder of fictional events which may have occurred months or years before. Furthermore, a drawing could become a point of discussion about a magazine; family circle reading was one way readers encountered the serial and introduced elements of the novel and its drawings into open discourse.[16] An article about the British artist Abraham Solomon appearing in the March 1862 number of the *Art Journal* describes how 'the walls of our exhibition rooms teem every year with pictures illustrating the pages of the standard novel, or poem, or drama'.[17] The article goes on to mention that 'the constant repetition of subjects' with which every one is familiar 'had become tiresome and wearying'.[18] Whether or not book illustrations had become iconographically staid may be a matter of some debate, but it is certain that some drawings were available in a middle-class public forum, the art gallery, and were likely to remind readers and gallery viewers of a similar, shared literary experience.[19] It is worth mentioning here that even though middle-class magazine readers had become familiar with a set of drawings over the period of serialization, and despite the common exhibition of illustrations in public galleries, reviewers of illustrated novels subsequently published in book form rarely mentioned the drawings. To be fair, the *Publishers' Circular* made special mention of Leighton's drawings in their literary intelligence section on 1 July 1862, and a few months later they credit *Cornhill* with the development of quality wood engravings (8 December 1862); but, as a trade journal, the *Circular*'s audience was specific and limited.

Illustrations have a relation to the text, but the nature of that relationship is more complicated than one of direct correspondence. Often the author's idea of images varied from the artist's, as happened with George Eliot and Leighton over the depiction of Romola in the very first drawing, 'The Blind Scholar and His Daughter' (Fig. 1.1). But the argument about accuracy is a moot one when considering that drawings are not merely extensions of the literary text, but exist within the context of the magazine and within visual culture in general. Harvey has written that serial novels are unique because 'they do show text and picture making a single art',[20] but his attempt to unify the two forms ignores the contextual complexity of the illustrations which exist physically in a collective of fiction, poetry, advertisements, non-fiction and other illustrations. The drawings, like the novels, can be examined together with those other variables which constitute the context to expose a multiplicity of textual responses. As Lynda Nead has observed in her study of representations of Victorian women,

> the meaning of a given image is never simply a question of its content
> alone. There will always be other conditions and contexts which will affect

the way in which a picture is understood at a specific historical moment and it is these broader historical considerations which have to be identified in order to discover the ways in which visual images produce meaning.[21]

The variety of complex responses to periodical reading demonstrates how the visual text may or may not have collaborated with other texts to produce meaning within a cultural formation. My interest in studying periodical illustration is not primarily in determining the fidelity of a drawing to the fiction, but in understanding how illustrations enter into the discourse of a magazine and, specifically, how they engage in the ideology of a domestic ideal based upon the separation of gender-defined spheres.

Leighton's version of *Romola*

According to separate spheres ideology, which has been widely discussed elsewhere,[22] the gendering of separate spheres in mid-nineteenth century middle-class culture naturalized women as the moral safeguard of society whose proper place is in the domestic sanctuary. The serial illustrations to *Romola*, however, do not promote the uncomplicated, conventional view of Victorian domesticity that we might expect of an extremely popular, middle-class periodical like *Cornhill*.

Although *Romola* is an historical novel, George Eliot makes clear in the Proem that it is as much a story about mid-Victorian England as Renaissance Florence. She insists on 'the same great needs, the same great loves' and the 'sameness of the human lot, which never alters in the main headings of its history' (3), and, she adds, 'we still resemble the men of the past more than we differ from them' (3). It is in part because Eliot invites us so particularly to draw comparisons between the two periods that we are able to read *Romola* as a comment on her own day. A reviewer of the book edition of *Romola*, writing in the *Westminster Review* in October 1863, felt, like many readers and reviewers, that the historical setting was distracting, but he recognized how very like nineteenth-century figures Romola and Tito were.[23]

As her letters to the artist reveal, George Eliot was generally pleased with Leighton's drawings for her novel.[24] In his study, *George Eliot and the Visual Arts*, Hugh Witemeyer notes that Leighton was the right artist for the job because he had studied in Florence and had made Renaissance subjects an early specialty.[25] Eliot welcomed advice from him about particular points relevant to the novel's period, but took care to recommend scenes appropriate for illustration. Since Leighton worked on his drawings using the monthly page proofs for each instalment, he was not privy to the development of the novel as a whole, and his visual response to the novel was based upon his reading of the work in serial form.[26] In looking at the Leighton and Eliot collaboration, a term used advisedly, I will foreground the role of the domestic in both the novel and the illustrations and determine how the drawings construct a parallel text in relation to the novel.

The second drawing from the third instalment in August 1862, 'Under the Plane-tree' (Fig. 1.2), a scene recommended to Leighton by Eliot, shows Tito asleep in the lap of Tessa, the innocent peasant girl who will become his mistress after he marries Romola. Tito has just rescued Tessa from a conjuror in a Florentine square, and Tessa has fallen in love with this handsome nobleman who is all kindness to her. Throughout the story Tessa offers a haven for Tito away from his increasingly treacherous life. The drawing is the third consecutive illustration to feature Tito as the subject and, although he has already fallen in love with Romola, we have yet to see a depiction of the two together. The only drawing we have seen of Romola appeared as the first in the serial, which depicts her standing over the shoulder of her blind father (Fig. 1.1), the man who has so far dominated her life. In terms of the illustrations, the novel has been Tito's story, and 'Under the Plane-tree' shows us his weak side, his need to forget the lies he continues to tell. The chapter in which the scene appears is the last in the instalment, although this is not the final scene, and the kiss between Tito and Tessa after he awakes is guaranteed to be remembered because the visual image documents the love affair.

In contrast, the first illustration in the fourth instalment (September 1862) shows 'The First Kiss' (Fig. 1.3) between Tito and Romola. In fact, this scene does not occur until the second chapter of the instalment, but the drawing immediately responds to the sexual relationship in 'Under the Plane-tree'. The title, 'The First Kiss', is ironic, since the reader knows about, and has a visual reminder of, Tito's first kiss with Tessa. Tito left us in the previous instalment wondering whether Romola would ever kiss him as Tessa does, and the drawing answers that question before the written text has had a chance. In the same chapter in which the kiss occurs, Tito proposes to Romola, so the reader's knowledge of his other relationship, reinforced visually, becomes more illicit. The drawings depict early on the alternative sexual options, differentiated by class, which Tito has created, so any reference to Romola's domestic situation, from this point forward, will be measured against Tito's secret life. The differences between the illustrations are revealing: with Tessa, Tito is relaxed as he reclines between her legs in a natural, public setting; with Romola, Tito is upright, formal and must take the opportunity to kiss her in a small closet-like chamber. In Leighton's depiction of the room, a curtain has been pulled aside creating a stage for which the reader is a secret onlooker.[27] Tito holds Romola's hand and leans down to kiss her. Her head is lifted and her other hand hangs limply by her side. As Eliot describes it, the quick kiss was 'all the more exquisite for being unperturbed by immediate sensation' (123), but passionless may best describe Leighton's version. Thus the narrative formed by the serial drawings is unsettling. The only illustration of Tito and Romola together thus far, exhibiting their first and only moment of intimacy in the entire novel, is overshadowed by the earlier drawing of Tito and his mistress. Tito's treachery is reinforced because the reader has had time to reflect visually on the relationship with Tessa, so that the depiction of his kissing Romola immediately in the next instalment becomes that much more poignant. The man Romola loves and trusts is faithless, and we have the pictures to prove it.

The next and only other illustration of Romola and Tito alone together appears in the sixth instalment of December 1862.[28] In the time span of the novel, 18 months have elapsed and Bardo the blind scholar has recently died, leaving his daughter Romola hopeful for a new and happier life with Tito. 'Coming Home' (Fig. 1.4), the second illustration for the instalment, is extraordinary in depicting the 'narrative impulse'[29] which is the distance between husband and wife that Romola has been considering just before Tito's arrival:

> The next time Tito came home she would be careful to suppress all those promptings that seemed to isolate her from him. Romola was labouring, as a loving woman must, to subdue her nature to her husband's. The great need of her heart compelled her to strangle, with desperate resolution, every rising impulse of suspicion, pride, and resentment; she felt equal to any self-infliction that would save her from ceasing to love. (251)

She is resigned to being more appealing to Tito, but the words which describe Romola's resolution are violent; she will force herself into passivity and acceptance of Tito's secrets but only through desperation, denial and self-infliction. Eliot's description of Tito's return simply designates that 'there was a lamp hanging over the stairs, and they could see each other distinctly as he ascended', and that Romola has changed much more than Tito since they first met. Leighton's Romola is at the top of the stairs in the upper right of the drawing, not anxious at her husband's unexpected return, but 'subdued, less cold, more beseeching' (252). Tito, whose back is to us and whose figure is cut off at the waist, is ascending the stairs from the lower left. A series of s-curves holds the composition together—note how the drapery in Romola's dress and the curtains move into Tito's figure—but the illustration reinforces the separateness of the couple rather than any hoped-for union. There is a sexual feeling to the drawing, mostly expressed in Romola's languid, yielding pose as she leans and draws back the folds of the curtain. But, as the horizontal line in Romola's gown echoes the levels of the steps, Tito is cut off from Romola and on a lower plane than her morally.[30] In the novel, there are no moments of intimacy apart from the first kiss in the third instalment and not even veiled hints at any sexual relations between Romola and Tito. *Cornhill* prohibitions may have precluded any serious sexual innuendo, but

Witemeyer astutely comments that the drawn curtain is a motif also seen in
'The First Kiss',[31] as if what we are seeing is a scene from a staged marriage.

Later in the instalment, Romola reacts angrily to Tito's suggestion that
they leave Florence, and Tito's response is to lock her in the library and assert
his masculine power:

> In an instant Tito started up, went to the door, locked it and took out the
> key. It was time for all the masculine predominance that was latent in him
> to show itself. But he was not angry; he only felt that the moment was
> eminently unpleasant, and that when this scene was at an end he should be
> glad to keep away from Romola for a little while. But it was absolutely
> necessary first that she should be reduced to passiveness. (291)

The spatial distance in the drawing represents the sort of spiritual distance
described in this passage. The drawing, therefore, depicts not only the words of
Eliot's description of Tito coming home, but the significance of Tito's return
and its consequences. This is the last time Tito and Romola will be alone
together visually, and what we notice, especially in contrast to 'The First Kiss',
is just how far apart the two really are. 'Coming Home' is a poignant illustration
in its representation of the sexually impotent, spiritually distant nature of this
frustrated marriage. Romola, who early in the novel is a Miranda figure sexually
awakened by a shipwrecked stranger, never reaches sexual fulfilment in the
novel. And as 'Coming Home' was the final illustration in the December
instalment, readers would have this image of distance, of unchannelled sexual
energy, to consider until the following month.

The first drawing for January 1863 depicts Tessa holding up her baby by
Tito to Baldassarre (Fig. 1.5). The illustration shows clearly the sexual potency
of Tito's and Tessa's relationship, and therefore acts as a strong contrast to the
thwarted feelings in the earlier drawing 'Coming Home'. The second drawing in
the January instalment is 'Escaped' (Fig. 1.6), depicting Romola's first attempt
to disguise herself and flee her treacherous husband. The drawing of Tessa
holding her baby is, therefore, framed by images of the disintegration of
Romola's marriage. Interestingly, there are no drawings of Tessa that are not
either preceded or followed by a drawing of Romola. The structure of the visual
narrative draws attention to Tito's two families and reinforces the contrast
between the two domestic situations.

The images of Tessa are the more gentle and domestic. But at this point we
ought to remember that Tessa, despite her innocence and ignorance, is in fact
'the other woman', and as such is a fallen woman and a magdalene figure. Eric
Trudgill has demonstrated that by mid-century the figure of the magdalene was
ascending in her treatment by writers.[32] And certainly Eliot is careful not to taint
Tessa despite her status as mistress and unwed mother. She is shown among the
trees with her lover asleep in her lap, what in other circumstances would be a
comforting pastoral image. She figures as the proud mother who holds her baby

up for approval. And in May 1863, Tessa is depicted as the dutiful mother rocking her baby in its cradle. The May depiction, significantly called 'Tessa at Home' (Fig. 1.7) from the chapter 'The Other Wife', is in fact the most conventionally domestic image in the whole *Romola* series. We watch the scene from the same point of view as Romola, as a voyeur who has accidentally stumbled upon Tessa's quiet, peaceful domesticity. The irony, of course, is that Romola is looking at Tito's other family and is there to return Tessa's lost child to her. 'Tessa at Home' shows visually the cosy details of conventional domesticity that we never see in Tito's relationship with Romola—a sleeping baby, the deep interior of the home, a devoted and perhaps pregnant mother, the daily preparations for a meal. Significantly, we see Tessa's bed through the open curtains in the background. Moments later, in the course of speaking with Tessa, Romola recognizes a lock of Tito's hair and begins to suspect that the family is his, and the whole of Savonarola's teaching, which insisted on her loyalty to duty, is called into question:

> She was thrown back again on the conflict between the demands of an outward law, which she recognized as a widely-ramifying obligation, and the demands of inner moral facts which were becoming more and more peremptory [...]
> [...] All her efforts at union had only made its impossibility more palpable, and the relation had become for her simply a degrading servitude. The law was sacred. Yes, but the rebellion might be sacred too. (473-4)

The instalment ends with Romola resolving to live apart from Tito, and this conclusion signals an emotional—and subversive—break in the text. If women's extramarital affairs were typically cited as the reason for the collapse of households, here it is the man's sexual transgression that breaks up the marriage. In Romola's moment of sacred rebellion, then, Eliot actually reverses cultural norms of gender and sexuality. As Lynda Nead notes, 'male unchastity in itself was not believed to corrupt the home in the way in which female unchastity was believed to'.[33] However, Tito pays for his sins through his death, and Tessa the fallen woman survives. Although it is undoubtedly true that men's sexual behaviour was treated more permissively than women's, it is important to remember that there were calls for a more significant denouncing of male promiscuity than was common.[34] Seen in the context of Victorian sexual constructions, Romola's independent move to leave Tito becomes all the more powerful and wilful.

The illustration for the June issue is a visual response to the tensions experienced in the last chapter of the previous instalment, a pattern used in other of Leighton's illustrations. 'Drifting Away' (Fig. 1.8) depicts Romola in a boat setting off to sea, although the events which describe Romola's second escape do not appear until the final chapter in the instalment. However, if we read just the text of the illustrations, Romola has had a glimpse of Tito's secret, comforting domestic life ('Tessa at Home' in May) and has fled as a result ('Drifting Away' in June). In Eliot's words, 'there is no compensaton for the woman who feels that the chief relations of her life has been no more than a mistake' (507). Romola's drifting away is the necessary end for a woman who has found only disappointment from men and the negotiation between the public and private an impossible moral dilemma:

> She longed for that repose in mere sensation which she had sometimes dreamed of in the sultry afternoons of her early girlhood, when she had fancied herself floating naiad-like in the waters.
> The clear waves seemed to invite her: she wished she could lie down to sleep on them and pass from sleep into death. But Romola could not directly seek death; the fulness of young life in her forbade that. She could only wish that death would come. (509)

Romola's flight from Florence is a second attempt 'to be freed from the burthen of choice' (510) between public devotion to duty and self-sacrifice and personal devotion to an inner moral law. 'Drifting Away', which illustrates Romola's suicide attempt, is taken from the final chapter in the June instalment and readers would have to wait two months, not the usual one, until the August instalment to learn Romola's fate; presumably, the delay would have created greater suspense around Romola's story as well as allowing time to tie together various strands in the novel. Such breaks and gaps of time in the narrative, constructed by the author, are the hallmark of serial literature and are lost in reading in book form.

The depiction of Romola's attempted suicide would have had resonances with Victorian representations of fallen women who were most often depicted drowning.[35] The twist in Romola's fate is that her suicide attempt is not brought on by her own sexual promiscuity, but that of her faithless husband; unusually, the sexual sins of the husband have led to the disintegration of the family unit. However, Romola's oppressors do not go unchecked, and in the events of the July issue, Savonarola's mission is challenged and Baldassarre murders Tito: both men to whom Romola felt devotional attachment are made powerless through acts of violence.

Romola prefigures middle-class heroines around the turn of the century like Kate Chopin's Edna Pontellier (*The Awakening*, 1899) and Virginia Woolf's Rachel Vinrace (*The Voyage Out*, 1915) whose deaths, similarly described as suicidal drownings, result from the limitations faced by women who find themselves trapped by marriage. For Romola, Edna and Rachel, a rebirth through a sea-change is a necessary element of their female development and personal empowerment. Although both Rachel and Edna die, it can be argued that their suicides are self-chosen, deliberate, positive acts of will by women who are unable to accommodate themselves to the world's expectations. Romola's passage across the sea is like a baptism, an awakening to her personal identity and individual potential. Elaine Showalter has observed that 'water is the organic symbol of woman's fluidity: blood, milk, tears';[36] Romola, Edna and Rachel each realize self-worth and will in a female element.

Romola, described early in the novel as an Antigone confused by public and private duties, becomes a Madonna figure in book three of the novel. Trudgill claims that George Eliot was quite taken by 'the ideal of woman represented by the Virgin' and offers *Scenes of Clerical Life*, *Romola* and *Middlemarch* as examples of novels in which heroines are linked to Madonna images.[37] Use of the Madonna promotes a view of womanhood that is pure, self-sacrificing and, most importantly, virginal. After adopting Savonarola's teaching, Romola devotes herself to the sick of Florence's plague-stricken streets and feels an unconventional domestic pleasure in her public mission which diverts her attentions away from her wrecked marriage:

> The idea of home had come to be identified for her less the house in the
> Via de' Bardi, where she sat in frequent loneliness, than the towered circuit
> of Florence, where there was hardly a turn of the streets at which she was
> not greeted with looks of appeal or of friendliness. (379)

Gendered spheres have been inverted; the private has become public. Romola has become the Florence Nightingale of Florence, and found some of the comforts lacking in her marriage by taking on a philanthropic mission. Significantly, philanthropy was one of the few options available to middle-class Victorian women outside the home. As F. K. Prochaska has noted, charity work was not subject to the prejudices against women's employment, and 'it heightened women's self-esteem and gave them a sense of place and direction'.[38] Romola's movement into the realm of the holy is connected with what Victorian readers would have recognized as a legitimate sphere of public activity for women, the care of the sick. A reviewer of the three-volume book edition wrote in the *Saturday Review* that Romola's devotion to good works 'gives her character that air of softness which it would otherwise want';[39] philanthropy has made Romola more womanly. Leighton's drawing for the March 1863 instalment, called 'The Visible Madonna' (Fig. 1.9) after a chapter in which Romola is shown to be nursing Florence's needy, links Romola with Italian Renaissance Madonna iconography. As Andrew Sanders observes,

> the orphans in Florence, the plague-stricken villagers, a chapter title, and
> one of Leighton's original illustrations, insist that we should see her as the
> 'Visible Madonna' in contrast to the 'Unseen Madonna', the veiled image
> carried through the streets. Romola becomes a manifest Virgin Mary,
> fleshly, loving, and involved in mankind.[40]

She is seen surrounded by young children who are touched and comforted, as if being blessed by her hands. Nead confirms that 'the image of the Madonna and Child was a paradigm of maternal devotion and purity and during the nineteenth century the image could be drained of its associations with Catholicism and taken up within English ruling-class culture as a sign of respectable, Protestant values'.[41]

The domestic feelings which are thwarted in Romola's marriage are exalted and given a new life in her role as Florence's Holy Mother.[42] The Proem states somewhat sentimentally that 'the little children are still the symbol of the eternal marriage between love and duty' (9), and by adopting Florence as her family, Romola has reversed the barrenness of her marriage.[43] In 'The Visible Madonna' chapter, Florentines praise her as they would the Virgin, and 'all that ardour of her nature which could no longer spend itself in the woman's tenderness for father and husband, had transformed itself into an enthusiasm of sympathy with the general life' (389). When Romola visits Tessa at home in the May instalment, she is seen by the young mistress as the Holy Madonna and her image 'remained confusedly associated with the pictures in the churches' (468). The contrast between Tito's two families focuses on the two wives, and especially on the two mothers who represent the paradox between the sacred and the profane. Comparing the two illustrations of the mothers, 'The Visible Madonna' and 'Tessa at Home', Romola has adopted a public role as devoted, self-sacrificing mother of all children, while Tessa remains the dutiful mother whose proper place is in the home. Through philanthropy, Romola creates a public position for herself separate from her life with Tito. By the final third of the novel, both Romola and Tessa enjoy valid domestic duties, however much their roles may differ.

'At the Well' (Fig. 1.10), the final illustration for the serialization in August 1863, returns to the iconography of Romola as Madonna. She has survived her attempt to drift off to sea and has been helping plague victims in a distant village. The drawing shows Romola at the well from which the villagers are too frightened to drink. She is carrying a young sick child, and her pose is artificial, statuesque and unmistakably that of the Madonna.[44] We might notice similarities to Raphael's 'Sistine Madonna', particularly the stance, drapery and awe-struck onlookers.[45] In the final instalment, Romola has come to embody the virtues of the sacred mother, and that is the visual image which concludes the serialization.

George Eliot's Epilogue concludes the novel, however curiously, by trying to restore faith in the domestic hearth by providing a modified, matriarchal version of it. Tessa and her two children by Tito, Romola and her cousin Monna Brigida, all live together happily in Florence, several years after the events of the novel. Tito's two families have been united after his death, and Romola finally achieves a surrogate family and home. Romola's self-empowering independence is modified by returning her to the home, but as Lynda Nead recognizes, respectability for women 'was defined in terms of their location within the domestic sphere and their consequent sexual respectability'.[46] George Eliot, whose own unconventional life with Lewes caused her to be shunned by society for many years, would have been acutely sensitive to the matter of women's respectability. The Epilogue's picture of domesticity is radical in its unconventionality, but it returns the novel to what Jennifer Uglow has called its main theme:

> the way a passionate intellectual woman responds to being told what to do all her life by men, and ends by shaking herself free altogether to become the matriarchal head of a household of women, shaping a boy of the next generation of men according to *her* beliefs.[47]

It is an extraordinary household with no father figure and with two mothers from distinctly different classes. Like Uglow, although less emphatic, Andrew Sanders believes it is a domesticity 'which looks beyond the confinement which we normally associate with Victorian ideal homes'.[48] And undoubtedly this is true to an extent. However, it is worth noting that in the Epilogue Romola returns to the female sphere of the home, whether as head of household or not, and reinforces the domestic unit as the basis for women's role in society. Romola's compassion for Tessa, her husband's mistress, supports the notion resulting from the 1857 Matrimonial Causes Act which in effect stated that women ought to forgive their husband's adultery.[49] And as Nina Auerbach has asserted, 'reclamation of fallen women was one of the few respectable activities available to philanthropically minded Victorian spinsters'.[50] Granted, living with a fallen woman is rather different from offering charity. Still, to assert that the Epilogue finalizes Romola's feminist emancipation seems to ignore the ways in which Romola's return to the home, radically overhauled as it may be, is also a return to the domestic sphere.

It is possible that Eliot had in mind her *Cornhill* reader, mostly conventional and respectable women of the middle class, for whom a total rebellion against the domestic would not be a real consideration. And there is the problem of historical truth, both in Renaissance Florence and mid-Victorian England, neither of which would have granted Romola many opportunities outside of the home. *The Westminster Review*, reviewing the first book edition, found the depiction of the sexes too modern and Romola's aspirations too unlike the fifteenth century.[51] There are several separate but coexistent discourses running through the novel. Eliot allows the possibility for Romola to become matriarch of a home which transcends class and to enjoy domestic comforts. The family was the primary image of social unity and order in Victorian Britain,[52] and the Epilogue does not overturn the values which stem from a domestic sphere. The writer has found both the attraction to female independence and to the female sphere powerful.[53] Yet the return to the domestic hearth produces mixed and complicated reactions because the Epilogue both reasserts the basic social unit, the family, while fundamentally radicalizing its power structure. Like Romola, Eliot was learning to enjoy her own surrogate family in the form of Lewes and his boys, as a letter from Lewes to John Blackwood indicates:

> Mrs. Lewes is as *anxious* about them as if they were her own boys; and it would interest you to see her with the eldest who *worships* her, and thinks no treat equal to having her all to himself for an evening to make, and be made much of. Among the many blessings that have come to me late in life this of seeing the perfect love between her and the children is one of the greatest; perhaps because it was one of the rocks ahead. Having had no domestic life for many years I now have such domestic happiness as can be given to few. (*Letters* III, 421)

Lewes was well known for his unconventional marriage to his wife Agnes, and the two were supposed at the time to have been part of Thornton Hunt's radical 'phalanstery' in Bayswater.[54] Although George Eliot was unconventional in her own 'marriage' to Lewes, and was sensitive to social reaction against her mode of life, like her heroine she feels some comforts of a domestic role. The *Spectator* called the Epilogue 'feeble and womanish', but the *Athenaeum* saw in it a 'far better life'.[55] More radical than Romola's position in the Epilogue is Tessa's, the vindicated fallen woman, as Ruby Redinger asserts:

> Could Tessa [...] have appeared in one of the English novels? [...] Tito's mistress, she bears his children without a sense of shame or guilt, survives both his marriage to Romola and his death, and at the end of the novel is a happy mother with Romola at her side to help care for the bastard children.[56]

Unlike Hetty Sorrel in *Adam Bede*, Tessa has no secrecy or guilt.[57] In fact, various discourses converge in the Epilogue: reformism and domestic comfort; the Madonna and the magdalene stories. The presentation of Romola's domesticity in the final episode challenges our assumptions about the proper role of Victorian woman, but our reaction is determined by our ability to accept the symbolism of a complex convergence of competing discourses.

Unlike other monthly magazines, *Cornhill* did not include articles which questioned the role of women in a direct way. There are no pieces on the rights of women or on redundant women as in *Blackwood's* and *Fraser's*, respectively. In *Cornhill*, domestic ideology is constructed largely in the domestic fiction, the visual texts, and between the lines of the non-fiction. Were we to consider *Romola*'s treatment of the domestic together with other concurrent texts in *Cornhill*—Trollope's story of a jilted lover in *The Small House at Allington*; Anne Ritchie's *The Story of Elizabeth*, about a rebellious young woman made to conform; William Smith's poem 'Maladetta' which tells the story of a young fallen woman, illustrated with a depiction of her heartbroken parents; or, Harriet Parr's story 'Sybil's Disappointment' which describes how a woman's cruel treatment of her cousin whose marriage hopes are thwarted, leads to the cousin's death—all of these texts taken collectively show how the magazine's domestic ideology was even more complicated than we might expect. Leighton's visual text unsettles the readers' assumptions about the ideal domestic sphere by continually contrasting images of Romola with Tessa, complicating our response to the Madonna and magdalene figures, the role of woman and mother in the home and her responsibilities to the public and private realms.

George Eliot's *Romola*, Leighton's version of *Romola*, and the overlapping fiction and poetry, far from comforting the reader, continually challenge the Victorian domestic ideal. These texts question assumptions about the delicate position of women who, whether by choice or not, find that marriage is not an option. What is most interesting is that this fiction appeared in one of the most popular literary journals of the day, *Cornhill Magazine*. It is my contention, then, that *Romola* does not have the same unsettling power on its own as it does within the context of the periodical, where we realize how forcefully the fiction and illustrations together engage ideologically with the most controversial topics of the day.

Notes

1. See the *Publishers' Circular* **25** (8 December 1862), p. 588.
2. Simon Houfe, *Dictionary of British Book Illustrators and Caricaturists, 1800-1914* (Woodbridge, Suffolk: Antique Collectors' Club, 1978), p. 113.
3. On the proliferation of visual culture in the early nineteenth century, see Patricia Anderson, *The Printed Image and the Transformation of Popular Culture 1790-1860* (1991; reprinted Oxford: Clarendon, 1994).
4. 'Illustrated Newspapers', *Gentleman's Magazine* **4** n.s. (March 1870), p. 459.
5. William Wordsworth, *The Poems*, ed. John O. Hayden (New Haven and London: Yale University Press, 1977), vol. 2, pp. 900-901. 'Illustrated Books and Newspapers' was written in 1846 and first published in 1849-50.
6. *The Cornhill Gallery* (London: Smith, Elder, 1865) refers to the illustrations as works of art. The *Gallery* review appears in the *Athenaeum* **II** (26 November 1864), p. 713. The *Observer* and *Morning Star* comments are found in an advertisement in the same *Athenaeum* issue, p. 694.
7. Similar collections include: *Idyllic Pictures* (London: Sampson Low, 1866) and *Touches of Nature* (London: Strahan, 1866). Forrest Reid discusses these publications in chapter two of *Illustrators of the 1860s* (London: Faber & Gwynn, 1928; reprinted New York: Dover, 1975).
8. John Berger, *Ways of Seeing* (London: BBC and Penguin, 1972), p. 16.
9. Houfe writes that 'the illustrated magazine or novel was the natural companion for rapid transit where plates might hold the wandering attention in a way that prose could not'. Houfe, p. 108.

10. See the *Cornhill Gallery* advert in the *Athenaeum* **II** (26 November 1864), p. 694.

11. On the cultural specificity of images, see Susanne Kuchler and Walter Melion, 'Introduction: Memory, Cognition and Image Production', in eds Susanne Kuchler and Walter Melion, *Images of Memory: On Remembering and Representation* (Washington, DC and London: Smithsonian Press, 1991), p. 4 ff.

12. Wolfgang Kemp, 'Visual Narratives, Memory, and the Medieval *Esprit du System*', in Kuchler and Melion, p. 89. Note that I read both the notion of the utterance and the remembrance as plural, rather than single or unified.

13. See N. John Hall's discussion of the role of the engraver in *Trollope and His Illustrators* (New York: St Martin's Press), pp. 150-56.

14. Hugh Witemeyer, *George Eliot and the Visual Arts* (New Haven: Yale University Press, 1979), p. 158, describes the method of production for Leighton's *Romola* illustrations.

15. J. R. Harvey, *Victorian Novelists and their Illustrators* (London: Sidgwick and Jackson, 1970), p. 3.

16. Linda Hughes and Michael Lund discuss the community of magazine readers in *The Victorian Serial* (Charlottesville, VA: University Press of Virginia, 1991), pp. 10-11.

17. James Dafforne, 'British Artists: Their Style and Character, No. LIX—Abraham Solomon', *The Art Journal* (March 1862), p. 73.

18. Ibid.

19. Sally Mitchell describes the extent to which fiction reading was a shared experience for readers: 'Literally millions of people were provided with emotional experiences that they held in common because they read the same fiction'. See her *The Fallen Angel: Chastity, Class and Women's Reading, 1835-1880* (Bowling Green, OH: Bowling Green University Popular Press, 1981), p. 3.

20. Harvey, p. 2.

21. Lynda Nead, *Myths of Sexuality: Representations of Women in Victorian Britain* (1988; reprinted Oxford: Basil Blackwell, 1990), p. 16.

22. See for example Nancy Armstrong, *Desire and Domestic Fiction: A Political History of the Novel* (Oxford: Oxford University Press, 1987); Mary Poovey, *Uneven Developments: The Ideological Work of Gender in Mid-Victorian England* (Chicago: University of Chicago Press, 1988); Jeffrey Weeks, *Sex, Politics and Society: The Regulation of Sexuality Since 1800* (London: Longman, 1981).

23. [Justin, McCarthy], Review of *Romola*, *Westminster Review* **24** n.s. (1 October 1863), p. 348.

24. *Letters*, III, IV and VIII contain letters relevant to *Romola*.

25. Witemeyer, p. 157.

26. Ibid., p. 158.

27. Ibid., p. 168.

28. I agree with Witemeyer, who says that the two illustrations of Romola and Tito together represent 'before and after' images documenting the characters' growth, p. 168. Note that Romola and Tito are also in 'A Dangerous Colleague' (March 1863) in which Romola is depicted overhearing Tito's political machinations. The subject of this drawing again documents the distance between the two, but the two are not alone as in 'The First Kiss' and 'Coming Home'.

29. Geoffrey Hemstedt, 'Painting and Illustration', in ed. Laurence Lerner, *The Victorians* (London: Methuen, 1978), pp. 148-9.

30. In *Myths of Sexuality*, Lynda Nead discusses George Elgar Hicks's cycle of paintings, 'Woman's Mission', and describes how the woman's level in relation to the man's in each of the paintings is indicative of power structures within the family, p. 14. Similarly, Leighton's two depictions of Romola and Tito together contrast how Tito, who initially leans over Romola protectively, has been reduced to a baser level morally and is literally cut off in the second illustration.

31. Witemeyer, pp. 168-9.

32. Eric Trudgill, *Madonnas and Magdalens: The Origins and Development of Victorian Sexual Attitudes* (London: Heinemann, 1976), pp. 287-90. Trudgill generally describes the 1840s as a period when magdalene figures committed suicide and the 1850s as the period when attempts were made to rescue the magdalene (chapter 11, 'The Fortunes of the Magdalen').

33. Nead, p. 50.

34. See for example, John Baker Hopkins, 'Social Rights of Man', *Rose, Shamrock, and Thistle* (August 1862), p. 341: 'I do not want to see a social inquisition established; but is it unreasonable to demand the expulsion of men from respectable society who are living in open profligacy? I do not deny the imperative necessity of the sentence of outlawry against a fallen woman, no matter how cunningly she was dragged to ruin, or how sincere her repentance. It is a terrible necessity, but I repeat, I cannot gainsay it. Yet, on the other hand, having driven the victim from the pale of society, shall the victimizer be permitted to mingle with our wives and daughters?'

35. Nead, p. 170.

36. Elaine Showalter, *The Female Malady: Women, Madness and English Culture, 1830-1980* (London: Virago, 1987), p. 11.

37. Trudgill, p. 263.

38. F. K. Prochaska, *Women and Philanthropy in Nineteenth-Century England* (Oxford: Clarendon, 1980), p. 12. The introduction overviews the reasons

for women's move into philanthropy. See also Helena Michie, *The Flesh Made Word: Female Figures and Women's Bodies* (Oxford: Oxford University Press, 1987), chapter 2.

39. *Saturday Review* **16** (25 July 1863), p. 125.

40. Andrew Sanders, *The Victorian Historical Novel 1840-1880* (London: Macmillan, 1978), p. 189.

41. Nead, p. 26.

42. In her chapter on Florence Nightingale in *Uneven Developments*, Mary Poovey discusses how women turned to nursing as a compensation for thwarted love. See p. 177.

43. In *Women and Philanthropy*, Prochaska notes that 'the running of a philanthropic society could be compared to the running of a family', p. 17.

44. It has been suggested to me that the composition of the drawing also recalls the imagery of standard depictions of the 'Rest on the Flight into Egypt'. My thanks to Carter Foster for pointing this out to me. Also note that Granacci's 'Holy Family with St John' (Fig. 15) was also known as 'Rest on the Flight with Infant St John'.

45. It is interesting to note that Raphael's 'Sistine Madonna' was also George Eliot's favourite painting in the whole world; whether Leighton was aware of this or not I have yet to determine. See Witemeyer, p. 21.

46. Nead, p. 28.

47. Jennifer Uglow, *George Eliot* (London: Virago, 1987), pp. 159-60.

48. Andrew Sanders, 'Introduction' to *Romola* (London: Penguin Classics, 1980), p. 28.

49. Nead, p. 52 and Poovey, chapter 3.

50. Nina Auerbach, *Woman and the Demon: The Life of a Victorian Myth* (Cambridge, MA: Harvard University Press, 1982), p. 153.

51. [Justin McCarthy?], Review of *Romola*, in *Westminster Review* **24** n.s. (1 October 1863), 348. The ending was, perhaps, especially too modern given the debates over single women at this time.

52. In *Myths of Sexuality*, Nead observes that 'the family, then, was a sign of order; it was as perceived as the foundation of social stability and progress', p. 36. And in *The Fallen Angel*, Sally Mitchell states that 'the central image of Victorianism is the enclosed family [...] Yet the very image of the family as a social order was based on a paradox. Women were inferior to men and were therefore to be submissive, protected and supervised; women were superior to men—in moral and spiritual qualities—and were therefore to be deferred to', pp. 6-17.

53. Richard Barrickman, Susan McDonald, and Myra Stark, *Corrupt Relations: Dickens, Thackeray, Trollope, Collins and the Victorian Sexual System* (New York: Columbia University Press, 1982) observe that, 'even

writers like George Eliot and Charlotte Brontë who consciously set out to oppose oppressive stereotypes about women and sexual relations find the ideal of woman as the benign, all-suffering restorer of cultural values powerfully attractive', p. 12.

54. Rosemary Ashton, *G. H. Lewes: A Life* (Oxford: Oxford University Press, 1992), pp. 56-7.

55. *The Spectator* **1829** (18 July 1863), p. 2267, and 'New Novels', *Athenaeum* **II** (11 July 1863), p. 46.

56. Ruby V. Redinger, *George Eliot: The Emergent Self* (New York: Knopf, 1975), p. 452.

57. Ibid.

CHAPTER TWO

The Texts of *Romola*

ANDREW BROWN

In all probability, fewer than a dozen people have ever read *Romola* exactly as George Eliot herself wrote it, and without significant interventions by a succession of third parties. The purpose of this chapter is to indicate the nature and extent of the changes imposed upon her original manuscript, and to question whether any printed edition can be thought of as an appropriate representation of her own design.

Let us briefly consider the textual history of the novel.[1] George Eliot wrote *Romola* between 1 January 1862 and 9 June 1863. Her autograph manuscript (hereafter *MS*), preserved complete in the British Library, served as setting copy for the serialization in the *Cornhill Magazine* from July 1862 to August 1863 (hereafter *CM*). Most of the 14 monthly parts were dispatched to the printers around six weeks in advance of their scheduled publication, and George Eliot generally corrected proofs for each while at work on the next or next but one. None of these proofs are extant, but it is clear that she revised them extensively. In all there are *c.* 1 000 substantive changes between *MS* and *CM*. The large majority are plainly authorial and might be characterized as running repairs, or occasional adjustments made with a degree of hindsight, to a text written under unaccustomed and uncomfortable pressure:[2] she adds footnotes, changes chapter titles, translates Italian into English, corrects factual errors, alters descriptive details, revises narrative emphasis. Though a handful of changes might have resulted from a *CM* compositor misreading her script, and she then failing to notice this, for the most part the verbal changes between *MS* and *CM* can fairly safely be ascribed to George Eliot's own intervention at proof stage.

When we turn from substantives to accidentals, however, the strong presumption is that almost all the changes were made by the compositors. The manuscript copy supplied by George Eliot was shot through with all manner of orthographic irregularities and inconsistencies of presentation. For example, her underlining of Italian words seems almost entirely haphazard, and her use of initial capitals equally so. Still more erratic was the *MS* punctuation: often so light and informal as to render the sense ambiguous, and on numerous occasions plainly inaccurate or lacking altogether—most notably when she had altered the words of a sentence in *MS* but had failed to repoint accordingly. In all such instances the *CM* compositors sought to correct, compensate, or normalize as they saw fit and as they had been trained to do. There are around 7 000 changes to the accidentals between *MS* and *CM*, no fewer than 6 000 of them involving punctuation—almost always making it more formal and more precise. George Eliot had the opportunity of reviewing these compositorial changes on the proofs, but what evidence we have suggests that she concerned herself little with such matters, even when proofreading under less unfavourable circumstances. By and large, it seems that she was content to leave such matters to the judgement of her printers.

On 6 July 1863, less than a month after she had sent off the concluding episode of the serial, the complete novel was issued in three volumes by Smith, Elder, & Co., the proprietors of the *Cornhill Magazine*. Again George Eliot read proof; again the proofs have not survived. The text of the three-decker (hereafter *1*) shows some 250 substantive changes from that of *CM*, the majority of them clearly authorial—more translations of Italian, further adjustments to factual, descriptive and narrative details (in the very first sentence, for example, the distinctive adjective referring to the angel of the dawn as 'star quenching' is dropped)—together with *c.* 600 changes to the accidentals, mostly involving punctuation, and most probably introduced by the compositors as part of their self-determined normalizing brief.

In September 1865 Smith, Elder, & Co. published a one-volume 'Illustrated Edition' (in fact containing just four of Frederic Leighton's 24 engravings for the *Cornhill* serialization). The stereotype plates of this setting (less the illustrations) were subsequently used to print a 2*s.* 6*d.* 'New Edition' which, from its initial issue in June 1869, reprinted regularly throughout the 1870s and became the best-selling version of the text to appear during George Eliot's lifetime. Though we know from her journal that she read proof for it during the summer of 1865, the authority of this setting (hereafter *2*) is questionable. As I have indicated, it is generally possible to infer which of the changes between *MS*, *CM* and *1* were authorial and which were introduced by the printers. Of the 100 substantive changes between *1* and *2*, however, no fewer than 95 might reasonably be ascribed to carelessness or miscopying in the printing-house. Tenses and cases change for no apparent reason, singulars become plurals and vice-versa, contractions are opened out, phrases transposed, word-forms cosmetically altered or apparently normalized ('should' to 'would', 'philosophic' to 'philosophical', 'northerns' to 'northerners', etc.). The circumstantial evidence suggests that the overwhelming majority of verbal changes in *2* were introduced, without authority, by the printer. That George Eliot's proofreading was less than exhaustive is attested by the clutch of misprints which she failed to spot. A further 350 changes were made to the accidentals in *2*, again most likely by the printer.

This complication in the line of textual transmission is compounded by the fact that when, in February 1877, George Eliot agreed to *Romola* becoming the first of her novels to be issued in Blackwood's 'Cabinet Edition' (hereafter *3*) of her works, it was a copy of the 1869 'New Edition' that she marked up and supplied as setting copy. This setting copy has survived, and shows that she called for fewer than 150 changes in all, most of them relatively minor. She corrected a number of the literals in *2* but missed others, she translated a further dozen Italian words, made a few alterations to the punctuation (often reinstating the original *MS* reading), and tinkered with close details of phrasing. The proofs of *3*, which have also survived, incorporate all the changes she had marked on the setting copy together with several hundred she had not. Almost all these latter are the result of house-styling (for the first time by Blackwood's compositors rather than Smith's), notably concerning spelling (e.g. *ize* word endings to *ise*). The proofs also contain some two dozen miscopyings or misprintings of substantives—'creditable' for 'credible', 'old' for 'odd', 'lose' for 'loose', etc.—none of which George Eliot apparently noticed, though she did mark around 150 new revisions on her set. A further 250 or so changes (more house-styling, mostly to the punctuation and hyphenation) were introduced between the author-corrected proofs and the text of *3* as finally printed in two volumes in 1877-78. These probably derive from a duplicate set of proofs, or from revises read in-house only.

George Eliot read proof for neither of the remaining British editions to appear during her lifetime. The first of these, Blackwood's one-volume 'Stereotyped Edition' of 1878, was set from a copy of *3* and differs from it on a mere 100 occasions. Almost all the variants involve punctuation and hyphenation; most were probably deliberate revisions by the compositors, continuing the process of standardization to house conventions. Smith, Elder, & Co.'s lavish two-volume edition of 1880 (limited to 500 sets) was the last new setting to be issued before her death. Interestingly, it follows the text of the 'Stereotyped Edition' rather than one of Smith's own, earlier ones (most obviously *2*)—probably because the publishers wanted to use the most recent available printing.

Five American editions of *Romola* were published during George Eliot's lifetime, though she read proof for none of them. The first, set from a copy of *CM*, was issued in August 1863 by the New York firm of Harper and Brothers. This was followed by Fields, Osgood & Co.'s 'Household Edition' (Boston, 1869), Harper's 'Library Edition' (New York, 1869), Fields's 'Illustrated Library Edition' (Boston, 1870) and George Munro's 'Seaside Library Edition' (New York, 1877), squeezed into 80 triple-column pages, paperbound, at the remarkable price of 10 cents. The Tauchnitz Edition, published in Leipzig in 1863, and which reprinted regularly until the early 1930s, follows the first book-form edition (*1*), with a few idiosyncratic errors of its own—for example, in chapter 3, the Tauchnitz compositors, presumably missing Nello's erudite allusion to the dispute between the Greek and Roman Churches over the use of leavened or unleavened bread during the Mass, altered his remark to Tito, 'if you would just change your opinion about *leaven*', to 'if you would just change your opinion about *heaven*' (my italics) (37).

Most posthumous reprints derive from the text of the 'Stereotyped Edition'—even, so far as it goes, the crudely abridged 'Film Edition' (n.d. ?1925) with its colourized jacket illustration of Lillian Gish as Romola, in the silent film of 1924 (shot on location in Florence, directed by Henry King) which also featured Dorothy Gish as Tessa, William Powell as Tito and Ronald Coleman in the role of Carlo Bucellini, a character invented for the film.

Turning to 'editions' proper, rather than simple reprints, Guido Biagi's (Fisher Unwin, 1907) also follows the Stereotyped text; Rudolph Dircks's Everyman (1907) and C. B. Wheeler's (OUP, 1916), the latter printed from the same plates as Viola Meynell's World's Classics volume (OUP, 1913), both prefer that of the three-decker of 1863. Andrew Sanders's Penguin (1980) reproduces the Cabinet Edition. My own World's Classics volume (OUP, 1994) reprints the Clarendon text of the previous year, which was based on the *Cornhill* serialization. Dorothea Barrett's Penguin (1996) also follows the Cabinet Edition, but corrects obvious misprints in that text and reinstates a number of superseded readings from *MS* and *CM*.

To summarize, all bar one (the Illustrated Edition of 1865) of the four states for which George Eliot corrected proof have formed the basis of subsequent editions of the novel—as have several over which she herself exercised no direct control. The one version, however, that has never been printed is the one for which *George Eliot alone* was responsible, namely the autograph manuscript.[3] Bibliographically, this is unremarkable: the same is the case with George Eliot's other novels, and the majority of those of her contemporaries. Still, it is with *Romola* that this essay is concerned, so it falls to me, as the editor of the only critical edition of the novel, to defend my decision not to select *MS* as my base text. To put the issue in its starkest terms, why did I base the Clarendon Edition on a state of the text (*CM*) which there is every reason to believe includes several thousand non-authorial interventions?

First, let us be clear that the compositorial interventions in *CM* (like those in *1*, *2* and *3*) did not for the most part involve verbal changes to the text. Of the 1 500 or so separate substantive changes introduced over the 15-year period between *MS* and *3* (affecting a total of almost 10 000 words), the large majority were authorial revisions, marked on a succession of proofs and setting copy. The printers were independently responsible for fewer than 200 of them, mostly minor, and involving no more than 500 words in all. Most twentieth-century editions, following the Cabinet or Stereotyped texts, incorporate all these changes, including those made by the printers. The 1993 Clarendon

Edition (the first to be based on a collation of all relevant states) strips out the latter category and reconstructs a text comprised solely of George Eliot's own words—so far as they can be determined. I take it this is uncontentious, or at least that no editor in possession of this information would feel justified either in ignoring authorial proof revisions or, except for specified historical reasons, in including those made without authority by various printers.

It is when we turn from substantives to accidentals that the printers' contribution becomes more problematic, for now we are dealing not simply with miscopyings or misreadings, but also (indeed for the most part) with deliberate stylistic 'improvements' to the author's copy. The most significant category of these concerns punctuation, which is what I shall concentrate on here.[4] Between *MS* and *3* there are almost 8 000 changes to the punctuation of *Romola*. That amounts to an average of 13 changes per page in the Clarendon Edition, one every three lines. The available evidence, mostly circumstantial but powerful none the less, suggests that up to 95 per cent of these changes were made by the printers. On what grounds are such non-authorial revisions justifiable in a modern text?

To address this question let us consider the first and most crucial stage in the process of compositorial intervention—i.e. that between the original *MS* setting copy and the *CM* serialization. Let us recall the difficult circumstances of composition—writing piecemeal, in indifferent health and beset by the unaccustomed pressure of monthly deadlines, the extent of her own proof revisions indicating the provisionality of the copy she had submitted. As regards punctuation, the text of *MS* plainly required a measure of interpretative intervention before it could realistically be set before the public. As an experienced author, George Eliot knew that her printers would provide such a service, and there is no reason to suppose that she was any less prepared to delegate this task in the case of *Romola* than she had been with her previous novels. On the contrary, there is good reason to infer that under the circumstances she was unconcerned at supplying as setting copy the rapid, informal, and abbreviated system of punctuation that came most naturally as she wrote.

The case for preferring the punctuation of *CM* to that of *MS* is thus based on historical and material grounds: the *MS* version, lightweight throughout and occasionally lacking altogether, was simply a working draft; only as restyled and augmented by *CM*'s compositors did it reach a state appropriate for publication. Indeed, this appropriateness is why, for the most part, the additional changes made by the compositors of *1*, *2* and *3* may reasonably be rejected by the modern editor. The punctuation system of *CM* (unlike that of *MS*) did not actively *require* further modification in order to regularize sense and syntax, though naturally the changes marked by George Eliot herself on the setting copy and proofs of *3* must be respected, together with a handful of instances in *1* where the punctuation reverts to a distinctive *MS* reading. For example, Bardo's 'long white hand' in *MS* becomes his 'long, white hand' in *CM* (48); the *MS* reading is then reinstated in *1*, and one can reasonably surmise that it was George Eliot herself who deleted the extraneous comma on the proofs of the three-decker. By a similar token, there are cases where a change introduced in *CM*, though not subsequently overturned by George Eliot, seems to involve a misconstruction of what she had meant to signify. Take, for example, the particularizing reference to the younger of the Cennini brothers (proprietors of the family printing firm), which in *MS* runs 'Piero, the erudite, corrector of proof sheets, not Domenico the practical'. In *CM* the comma after 'erudite' is dropped, thereby changing the function of the word from an adjectival noun in apposition to 'Piero' to a simple adjective modifying 'corrector' (85). On balance (especially since by implication it also, and illogically, transforms the function of the word 'practical'), I believe this is a misrepresentation of the sense intended. In the Clarendon text, accordingly, the *MS* reading is reinstated. It was never my intention to impose the *CM* punctuation wholesale. Rather, each case is tried and determined on its particular merits. The default position of the Clarendon, however, in those several thousand instances where the *CM* reading differs from (modifies, interprets) but does not actively misrepresent the apparent sense of the shorthand *MS* version, is to prefer the more formal and compositorially 'normalized' system which George Eliot passed for publication. This was a case I argued at length in the introduction to the Clarendon Edition, and even in its brief reformulation here I find it largely persuasive.

Largely, but not entirely. An especially detailed review of the Clarendon Edition, by Dale Kramer in *Text: An Interdisciplinary Annual of Textual Studies*, has prompted me to reconsider my position, or rather to re-entertain doubts which I thought I had settled. Kramer reminds us that punctuation is not simply a set of neutral marks but one of precise rhetorical signs. It is only by the provision of punctuation that words acquire their exact weight and syntax its specific pacing. The pointing is an essential, meaning-bearing component of any given text. On what sound basis, therefore, should one elevate a printing-house style sheet, administered post facto by a team of compositors, over the spontaneous choice of the author in the process of creation? Why replace the author's own instinctive inclination by a set of generic or institutional rules imposed by disinterested third parties? How can a printer be better placed than the author to indicate the precise rhetorical shaping of the author's words? These are highly pertinent questions. My answer to them, as regards *Romola*, comes in three parts, corresponding to the three distinct categories of punctuation variance between *MS* and *CM*.

First, as I have already indicated, on numerous occasions the *MS* punctuation of *Romola* is simply missing. To reproduce *MS* exactly as it stands would lead to a text that does not make sense. This, at least, is undeniable, and its remedy is therefore uncontentious. If George Eliot failed to mark a full stop at the end of a sentence, or the inverted commas around direct speech, the function of the editor (whether in the 1860s or 1990s) is clearly to supply the basic markings which the author forgot. No argument between Kramer and myself on that head. Nor, indeed, as concerns the second category of variant, which occurs when authorial revisions to the words of *MS* are unmatched by corresponding changes to the original punctuation. For example, she initially wrote 'like one, in fact, who sins', but when she subsequently cancelled the words 'in fact' she scored through only the first of the two commas, leaving the syntactically incorrect reading (followed by the *CM* compositor) 'like one, who sins' (30). In this instance, and several others like it, I reject the thoughtlessly literal *CM* version, and reconstruct what there is better reason to suppose the author actually intended.

It is as regards the third, and most numerous category of *MS/CM* variants that Kramer quarrels with my practice in the Clarendon Edition. This category comprises those many thousands of occasions when the *CM* compositors decided that the punctuation of George Eliot's *MS* copy was in itself insufficient to establish the formal style and syntax which they had been trained to regard as appropriate to a printed text. On such occasions, accordingly, they repointed the setting copy as they saw fit: supplying marks where George Eliot had failed to do so, or 'normalizing' those of her own which they considered too informal or unconventional. The Clarendon Edition reproduces almost all these interventions by the *CM* compositors—on the grounds that since some degree of interpretative repointing of *MS* is required, historically it seems the most satisfactory course to settle on the version devised at the time and then approved for publication (even if only passively) by the author herself.

Opposing this view, Kramer contends that a modern editor should strip away the blanket of standardized punctuation imposed by rote by the contemporary printer, and reinstate the author's original version whenever possible. He cites the example of Peter Shillingsburg's Garland Edition of Thackeray, which addresses the problem of similar compositorial intervention by 'analyzing Thackeray's characteristic patterns of unconventional pointing, [and] emending the authorial punctuation only when mandatory to achieve sense or neutral conventionality'.[5] This may be an attractive course in principle, but in the case of *Romola* it tends to founder on the practical difficulty of determining any 'characteristic patterns' of *MS* pointing, however 'unconventional'. Consider the following passage from chapter 56, which in *MS* reads:

> Tessa who had hitherto been occupied in coaxing Ninna out of her waking peevishness, now sat down in her low chair near Romola's knee. (469)

The pointing is certainly unconventional (the *CM* compositor evidently thought it inadequate, and so added a comma after 'Tessa'), but is it characteristic in any sense more significant than characteristically careless? I don't believe so. On the previous page there is the reassuringly regular construction:

> Lillo, conscious that his legs were in question, pulled his shirt up a little higher. (468)

but later in the same chapter we find:

> Romola roused from her self-absorption, clasped the lad anew and looked from him to Tessa. (472)

Is this an idiosyncratic use of 'rouse' as an intransitive verb, or a momentary lapse of formal pointing? Surely the latter. The fact is that the punctuation of the *MS* of *Romola* is inconsistent. Sometimes it is punctiliously conventional; sometimes it comes up short of this formal mark, probably because in the moment of composition George Eliot was not immediately concerned with making unequivocally clear to her future readers the precise inflection of the words she could hear in her own mind.

Let us take another example:

> It was not long before Romola entered all white and gold more than ever like a tall lily. (201)

A striking sentence which one can imagine George Eliot writing rapidly and with feeling. I find it hard to credit, however, that she actively intended it to be read unpointed, as it is given (thus) in *MS*—any more so than she deliberately omitted the comma (supplied in *CM*, as were the hyphens) seven lines above in the phrase 'the half-pallid, half-sombre tints of the library'. Or again:

> He glanced cautiously round <,> to assure himself that Monna Ghita was not near, and then <,> slipping quietly to her side <,> kneeled on one knee <,> and said <,> in the softest voice, "Tessa!" (148)

Taken as a one-off example, and given the quicksilver action being described here, there is an almost plausible case that the omission of the pausing commas was deliberate, and that none of the five supplied by the *CM* compositor (enclosed above within angled brackets) should be included. On the other hand, it would be hard to read the sentence *un*inflected, which is presumably why the *CM* compositor added what he took to be the necessary, neutral and conventional marks of punctuation. And since it was George Eliot's custom to read passages aloud to Lewes at the end of a successful day's composition, we may assume that she was herself attentive to the spoken rhythms of her prose— and must have *heard* pauses in her own reading. A modern editor acting on the Kramer injunction might perhaps omit all but the comma after 'side', but I have to question whether this would represent George Eliot's own pacing of the sentence as she read it aloud to Lewes. One final example in this category:

> But the richest of all these [gifts] <,> it was said, had been given by a poor
> abbess and her nuns <,> who <,> having no money to buy materials <,>
> wove a mantle of gold brocade with their prayers, embroidered it and
> adorned it with their prayers <,> and <,> finally <,> saw their work
> presented to the Blessed Virgin in the great Piazza by two beautiful youths
> who spread out white wings and vanished in the blue. (382)

Certainly, this makes sense without the commas (in angled brackets) supplied
in *CM*. Indeed, it would probably make the *same* sense—since the reader
would very likely (at least on a second reading) infer most of the same pauses
that were formally indicated by the *CM* compositor. Put simply, the
intervention of the *CM* compositor was designed to obviate the need for a
second reading. Wilfully to prefer the *MS* version here would surely be a form
of bibliographic pedantry: 'authenticity' for its own sake, irrespective of its
potential for reader confusion.

On the other hand, it has to be acknowledged that to modern readers much
of the punctuation added in *CM* can seem unnecessarily fussy—as in the
following passage:

> [he] sat among his books and his marble fragments of the past <,> and saw
> them only by the light of those far-off younger days which still shone in his
> memory: he was a moneyless <,> blind old scholar—the Bardo de' Bardi to
> whom Nello <,> the barber <,> had promised to introduce the young Greek
> <,> Tito Melema. (47)

Here, while the first of the *CM* commas might be thought of as relatively
neutral in its effect, the following four are almost certainly redundant, perhaps
even obstructive to the natural flow of the narrative. By a similar token, in the
next example the *CM* compositor seems to have altered the intended pacing of
Tito's speech:

> There was strutting <,> and prancing <,> and confusion <,> and scrambling,
> [*MS* has a dash instead of a comma] and the people shouted <,> and the
> Cristianissimo smiled from ear to ear. And after that there was a great deal of
> flattery <,> and eating <,> and play. [*MS* has a colon instead of a full stop] I
> was at Tornabuoni's. I will tell you about it tomorrow. (256)

In this instance, none of the six commas added in *CM* is necessary to make
ready sense of the passage, while their cumulative effect is to remove from the
account the imitative vividness which George Eliot probably intended. Later,
when Tito gallops in to announce the providential lifting of the Emperor's
blockade, the breathless spontaneity of the moment is all but undermined by the
compositor's nit-picking intervention, which reduces the directest of speech to
the pace of a diplomatic transcript:

> I have to deliver to you the joyful news that the galleys from France <,>
> laden with corn and men <,> have arrived safely in the port of Leghorn <,>
> by favour of a strong wind <,> which kept the enemy's fleet at a distance.
> (384)

Less obvious in its immediate effect, though still significant in its general
tendency, is the weighing down by excessive pointing of the narrator's matter-
of-fact description in a passage such as the following:

> his plain cloth cap <,> with its *becchetto* <,> or long hanging strip of
> drapery <,> to serve as a scarf in case of need, surmounts a penetrating face,
> not <,> perhaps <,> very handsome, but with a firm <,> well-cut mouth. (4)

By modern stylistic standards, all but the last of the commas added in *CM* here
are strictly unnecessary. Their effect, however, together with those introduced
by the compositors on similar occasions *passim*, is to establish different
rhetorical patterns in the printed text from those of *MS*. So again (and finally)
why enshrine them in a modern edition?

My answer is that the alternative would on balance be less satisfactory, and
would place too precarious a responsibility on the editor. Kramer's advocacy of
the Shillingsburg-Thackeray method implies that it is founded on a systematic
assessment of objective criteria. I do not believe this is feasible in the case of
Romola. So often, and so unhelpfully to the editor at 135 years' distance, the
MS of *Romola* recalls a speaking voice, but one whose precise pacing,
inflection, and register is not always clear to third parties. There being no
characteristic pattern to the *MS* pointing beyond that of its inconsistency, the
modern editor who as a matter of principle rejected the *CM* overlay would in
effect have to reinterpret every single sentence afresh. I do not believe this
would be a sensible course. To turn Kramer's own argument back on itself, on
what grounds can a late twentieth-century scholar consider himself better
placed than a Victorian printing-house to repoint an (at least fitfully)
inadequate text by a Victorian author writing for a Victorian audience? Surely
there is no such thing as 'neutral conventionality' (to use Kramer's phrase)
independent of historical circumstances, whereupon the sparer, less formal, less
rhetorical pointing that a modern editor might be expected to settle on would
run the risk of falling into anachronism. That George Eliot herself punctuated
much of her 'draft' setting copy so irregularly is not in itself good reason to
reject the more formal system introduced by her contemporary printer, however
convoluted that may now seem on occasions. After all, she expected some such
system to be applied to her copy before it was put before the public, and she at
least had the opportunity of overturning changes or additions which she
considered inappropriate. What Kramer regards as the interference of the
printer was, I would argue, a necessary and mutually premeditated contribution
to the development of the text from private draft to public state.

A text of *Romola*, as by implication Kramer calls for, repointed only when the author's *MS* draft fails to make sense (to late twentieth-century readers) would be an exciting prospect in theory, but consider the practical problems that the editor of such a text would face. Critically, he would have to distinguish throughout between error and intention, lapses of concentration and deliberate though unconventional usage. Sometimes this would be relatively straightforward, as in Romola's proud statement to Bardo:

> Yours is a higher lot <,> never to have lied or truckled <,> than to have shared honours won by dishonour. (56)

Syntactically, this is so outlandish without the commas introduced by the *CM* printer that the modern editor would surely also have to supply them—unless perhaps he felt dashes were more appropriate. But what of the following passage:

> already the regrets for Lorenzo were getting less predominant over the murmured desire for government on a broader basis, [*MS* has a dash instead of a comma] in which corruption might be arrested <,> and there might be that free play for everybody's jealousy and ambition <,> which made the ideal liberty of the good old quarrelsome <,> struggling times <,> when Florence raised her great buildings <,> reared her own soldiers, drove out would-be tyrants at the sword's-point, and was proud to keep faith at her own loss. (83-4)

Like the example quoted above (382), this passage is just about comprehensible as written, at least on a second reading. So does one deem the *MS* pointing inadequate or not? Should the modern editor restrict intervention to a comma after 'raised her great buildings', and if so would the result be a more accurate rendition of how George Eliot expected the passage to be read? I simply don't know: indeed, in the case of the last question, how could anyone make a confident pronouncement? Further examples, similarly resistant to unequivocal answers, can readily be brought to bear:

> Politian was professor of Greek as well as Latin at Florence [...] but for a long time Demetrio Calcondila, one of the most eminent and respectable among the emigrant Greeks <,> had also held a Greek chair <,> simultaneously with the too predominant Italian. (95)

My own instinct would be to retain the first of the *CM* commas, but to omit the second. Others, of course, might react differently: after all, on what basis other than one's own critical (literary/stylistic) judgement can one determine exactly what constitutes inaccuracy on such occasions? For example, is the pointing of the second sentence in the following speech simply incorrect—or might it be a deliberate ploy designed to highlight the Italian idiom ('parlare a quattr' occhi') that Nello is using? (braces denote marks in *MS* that were dropped in *CM*):

> 'I will be mute', said Nello, laying his finger on his lips <,> with a
> responding shrug. 'But {,} it is only under our four eyes {,} that I talk any
> folly about her'. (93)

The next example is still more problematic, for here the *MS* pointing is characteristic of a locution (old-fashioned even in the 1860s) that George Eliot clearly favoured on occasions:[6]

> It would surely be an unfairness {,} that he <,> in his full ripe youth, to
> whom life had hitherto had some of the stint and subjection of a school,
> should turn his back on promised love and distinction. (98)

On the face of it, the adjustment in *CM* of the placing of the first comma is entirely logical, for the subordinate clause beginning 'to whom' plainly refers to the pronoun 'he' rather than to the noun 'youth'. I wonder, however, whether George Eliot may have intended the phrase marked off by *her* commas ('that he in his full ripe youth') as a single syntactical and conceptual entity—a composite pronoun at it were, a pronoun qualified by an adjectival phrase— whereupon the original *MS* pointing may be strictly correct. Whether it should therefore be preferred by a modern editor is another question. I am not sorry that my 'default' choice of *CM* as base text provided me with a ready and defensible rationale for rejecting the restoration of *MS* pointing on such tenuous grounds.

Under the circumstances, I have to hold by my decision to base the punctuation of the Clarendon Edition on that of the text which George Eliot passed for publication in 1862-63. At the very least, the result has the merit of being a text of its time, which I take it is what the textual bibliographer generally aims for. The 'Kramer' alternative, based on *MS*, would doubtless be closer to what George Eliot actually wrote, though not necessarily to what she expected to see printed. We should minimize the fact of authorial approval of the punctuation in *CM*. To be sure, the strong likelihood is that she concerned herself only casually with such procedural details, but the fact remains that she did correct proof for the *CM* serialization—as she could not for a newly reconstructed version—and that the *CM* text can therefore claim a historical authenticity beyond that of any contemporary revision. If one day an electronic edition of *Romola* is issued, with each relevant state from *MS* through *3* digitally encoded, a new generation of readers will be able to reconstruct their own versions according to their own (subjective) criteria. Until then, and while print technology restricts editors to a single state, I feel confident in defending the Clarendon and World's Classics texts as representing the closest historical approximation to how George Eliot agreed *Romola* should be published. On the other hand, of course, you can always go to the British Library and read the original.

Notes

1. For a more detailed discussion, see my introduction to the Clarendon edition of *Romola* (particularly l-lxi).
2. None of her previous full-length novels had been issued in serial form, and it is worth recalling that she turned down George Smith's initial offer (of £10 000) for the serial rights to *Romola* largely because he wanted to spread it over more monthly parts than she was happy with. In the event she preferred to accept a fee of £7 000 for a text of the same overall extent but divided (less commercially for Smith's purposes) into fewer episodes. Many years later, looking back on her experiences with *Romola*, she explained 'I have the strongest objection to cutting up my work into little bits', and that 'if I could gain more [money] by splitting my writing into small parts, I would not do it, because the effect would be injurious as a matter of art' (*Letters*, VI, 179).
3. My calculation that fewer than a dozen people have ever read the complete MS seems plausible. One can reasonably assume that Lewes read it during composition, and it is not unlikely that the publisher George Smith may also have done so. The MS setting copy, though, was divided up among several compositors in the *Cornhill*'s printing-house, with the result that none of them would have seen it in its entirety. Of the novel's later editors and commentators, only five show clear evidence of having consulted it in detail.
4. For details of the treatment of spelling, hyphenation, italicization and capitalization variants, see the Clarendon Edition (lxviii-lxx).
5. *Text: An Interdisciplinary Annual of Textual Studies*, vol. 9, ed D. G. Greetham and W. Speed Hill (Ann Arbor: University of Michigan Press, 1996), p. 380.
6. Earlier in the same chapter, for example, we find 'he wore that fortune so easily and unpretentiously {,} that no one had yet been offended by it' (96).

PART TWO
Rethinking the Heroine

CHAPTER THREE

Mapping *Romola*:
Physical Space, Women's Place

SHONA ELIZABETH SIMPSON

In *The Mill on the Floss* Maggie Tulliver refuses to finish Madame de Stael's *Corinne* because she does not want to read yet another book in which the fair woman rather than the intelligent one wins the man.[1] In so doing, she scrutinizes the rules by which we judge the success of women, even intellectual women like Corinne, and finds that they are those of the romance: the winner is the one who gets the man.

The problem of the intellectual woman's relationship to love—and sexual love at that—is, as Toril Moi describes it, one 'that George Eliot never ceased to work through'.[2] We see it perhaps most vividly in George Eliot's later novel *Romola*, where it is the child-like Tessa who comes nearest to winning Tito, not the exquisitely beautiful, educated and highly intelligent Romola. In none of Eliot's novels does the struggle of an intellectual woman to mark out her own space, especially in regard to love, appear more literally than in *Romola*, where Eliot's deliberate attention to the details of physical space negotiates the boundaries between male and female space to create—almost—a new, unmapped territory. In the process, Romola, who not only knows the ancient classics but also looks like a pre-Raphaelite Madonna, begins to redefine the terms 'woman' and 'intellectual'.[3] I say 'almost' and 'begins' because the experiment fails in the end, at least from a strictly feminist point of view: Romola ends up back inside the close walls and narrow streets of Florence, instructing Lillo, who is the son of Tessa and the 'perfidious yet disturbingly sexy' Tito.[4]

It is significant that Romola at one point longs to escape Florence in order to emulate Cassandra Fedele, the woman who is 'renowned throughout Italy for her Greek and Latin learning' and who is considered 'the most learned woman in the world' (327).[5] Romola actually leaves the city, planning to seek out this woman who had successfully 'invented a lot for herself [...] and ask her how an instructed woman could support herself in a lonely life' (327). Cassandra thus provides a possible alternative narrative for an intelligent woman's life, one against which Romola's actual narrative can be compared. For Romola never finds Cassandra Fedele, never even gets to search for her;

Savonarola forces her to turn back just as she is leaving the city gates. Romola certainly never discovers from Cassandra Fedele how an intellectual woman can live on her own, outside the confining walls of the city.

But the process of Romola's negotiation of space is itself one worth studying, and can help us better understand the connection between space and the intellectual woman. In this paper, I first examine the mapping of physical space in the novel and the gendering of that space. Deep ambiguities run like multiple fault-lines through the resulting pictures. A longing for walls and the protection those walls offer conflict with the sense of walls as a prison of obligation; thus, Bardo's library forms for Romola both a cradle of intellect (which Tito finds deeply disturbing) and a jail. The opposite inclination, for the freedom and independence found only outside of walls, takes shape first as a longing to be outside the home and finally outside the city, both of which have become sites of male dominance over Romola.

Eliot's careful descriptions of the piazzas, the markets, the stores and most of all the overflowing crowds detail for the reader the ambiguous sense of both open yet totally enclosed space within the city walls. In the strangely ambivalent inside/outside spaces of the novel, the romance plot, in which the mark of a woman's success is, as Maggie Tulliver realizes, attracting a man and, ultimately, having a child (the outward mark of 'winning the man') is transformed in *Romola* into an emphasis on stepmothers, adopted children and all-female households.

Thus, both the home and Florence itself—an increasingly domesticated space—are places where Romola renegotiates the role of the mother, the term which defines 'successful womanhood' in Romola. To explore this movement further, I trace the progression from physical space to a more metaphorical idea of inside and outside, showing how Romola herself transforms and complicates both the space around her and her own work as an educated, intellectual woman. Walking, wandering, breaking through or opening up the walls shapes a process by which Romola makes foreign, outside spaces her own, in a sense domesticating them. But after doing so, she needs new 'outsides' to walk through and know, name, map.

This sense of vagrancy, then, can be seen as a different model for knowledge from that of the men in the novel, who shudder at the 'wandering' of the feminine mind. So perhaps the image suggested by Romola as she moves from home to city to unmapped, unnamed village is one of a wandering, vagrant (and thus, as Bardo points out, 'feminine') mind, one able to do without maps, to disregard where it wanders but to do the best it can wherever it ends up. And perhaps what is really at stake here, in *Romola* as in George Eliot's other novels, is a model of knowledge not limited by walls— one that includes and indeed grows out of the struggles of women who are also intellectuals, and intellectuals who are also women.

Inside the library

To begin, I want to look at the ways in which Romola, this learned woman, this dutiful daughter of an educated man, finds herself mapped within physical space.[6] When she first appears she remains indoors, always enclosed; even her walks are within the loggia on top of her father's house, where she 'could at all times have a walk sheltered from observation' (179); the 'occasions on which she took the air elsewhere' are rare and 'much dwelt upon beforehand' (135). The enclosed spaces surround her like a womb, protecting her from, as her father describes it, 'the debasing influence of thy own sex', as well as the superstitions of religion and the temptations of the outer world (54). The library itself, where Romola spends most of her time, remains a place of order and stability; it is 'a long, spacious room, surrounded with shelves, on which books and antiquities were arranged in scrupulous order' (47). In it, Romola aids her father in his scholarly work; safe inside the library, Romola has learned the ways of the scholar, and longs to be 'as learned as Cassandra Fedele' so that her father will not be sorry that she is a daughter (54). So here, in this safe, womb-like place, Romola has ironically learned how not to be a woman; she is an intellectual, and wants no part of the world of women—or men—outside the walls. Enclosed in the male space of the library, Romola is as blind as her father to the outside world; her father's library, in effect, forms her entire world, so that she lives 'in a state of girlish simplicity and ignorance concerning the world outside her father's books' (57).

Bardo's desires to master knowledge remain, like Casaubon's in *Middlemarch*, frustrated to the end. And Romola, like Dorothea, desiring only to aid him in that work and perfectly capable of doing so, finds herself similarly frustrated. Her father confines her to the office of a clerk because she is merely a woman; after all, Bardo tells her with startling cruelty, 'the unbeaten paths of knowledge are still less reconcilable with the wandering, vagrant propensity of the feminine mind than with the feeble powers of the feminine body' (51). So we have from the beginning the idea of the feminine mind as wandering, with the library walls acting—unsuccessfully, according to Bardo's insinuation—to prevent Romola's mind (and body) from wandering.

But the protecting walls of Romola's intellectual cradle also form the 'grim' and formidable walls of a prison, hemming in a world of frustrated desires. Into this world the sun can barely struggle through 'the narrow windows' set infrequently in the 'large sombre masses of stone' (47). Thus, we see Romola looking around the library with 'a sad dreariness in her young face', and the objects ranged alongside the books appear violently mutilated in their lifelessness, not only dead but broken: a 'headless statue with an uplifted muscular arm wielding a bladeless sword' and 'rounded, dimpled, infantine limbs severed from the trunk' (47). Bardo's great work, to which Romola has dedicated her life so far, like Casaubon's, is already dead: 'that great work in which I had desired to gather as into a firm web, all the threads that my research had laboriously disentangled, and which would have been the vintage of my life' (51).

Into this protecting, suffocating prison walks Tito, straight from the fresh air of the outside world—not just the air of Florence, but of Greece and all Europe. Tito from the start feels threatened by Romola's presence in the male space of the library. He declares that he would like to see her outside, under a southern sun, 'lying among the flowers, subdued into mere enjoyment' (184); yet Romola trembles when he suggests leaving Florence, saying, 'Surely you do not think I could leave it—at least, not yet—not for a long while' (287). She stands here in stark contrast to Tessa, whom at this stage in the book we see only outside, caught in the crowds or under a plane tree outside the city gate, while Romola remains in the house, down a side-street, inside the walls.[7]

Tessa's relationship to space can be read on several levels. She is always outside because inside means inside the library, where women can show themselves intelligent and educated. In addition, class distinctions place her, as a peasant, squarely outside. But finally, and most importantly, her placement in the space of the novel revolves around male power; Tessa does eventually end up inside, but not in any space like that of the library. We see her inside only in the house Tito buys for her, only in the space he controls.

Similarly, after Tito's marriage to Romola, his attempts to control Romola herself revolve around controlling the space in which she lives and moves. Tito's redecoration of Bardo's house after the old man dies culminates in the selling of the library; he deliberately frustrates Bardo's greatest wish at least in part to expel Romola from the traditionally male bastion of her father's library and to force her to sit in airily painted chambers with roses and birds on the walls—a fake outside—instead of amongst her father's perfectly ordered books and shelves of antiques. Romola's move from the male space of the library to an 'outside' which is nevertheless contained and private, and which has none of the dangers of the real or public outside, echoes a movement occurring throughout Victorian society in England: 'Middle-class women were in the nineteenth century encouraged to withdraw more and more from the public to the private sphere, and the planning of dwellings that would increase the possibilities and stress the appropriateness of modest female withdrawal was in keeping with the new ideology'.[8] In middle-class English homes, the dining-room, the smoking-room and most importantly the library belonged to the men, while the women were increasingly barricaded into their elegant boudoirs and drawing-rooms.

This movement, of course, fits Tito's view of Romola; Tito from the very first wants her for his 'beautiful and loving' wife, not for the educated and intelligent woman that she is (120). After he sells her father's library, he longs that 'she should be reduced to passiveness' (291). However, even displaced from the library into the feminine 'saloon surrounded with the dancing nymphs and fauns', Romola can never love Tito as Tessa can, with 'that sweet clinging instinct, stronger than all judgments, which, he began to see now, made the great charm of a wife' (322). Even the description of Tessa's love involves space; 'clinging' implies a closeness that is both childlike and sexual. Tito begins to realize he cannot control Romola even by manoeuvring her into spaces he has created, as he has manoeuvred Tessa; at the same time, he finds his own life 'out of doors' growing 'more and more interesting to him' as he becomes caught up in the political intrigues of Florence (316). Thus the lines are drawn: the woman is relegated (perhaps unsuccessfully) to the private, protected spaces her husband controls—that is, spaces other than the library yet not outside—while her husband belongs to the public sphere.

But the commonplace Victorian divisions of male and female, public and private, do not suffice to describe the more complex spatial negotiations and renegotiations occurring throughout *Romola*. There is more at stake here: the roots of masculine power. Tito does not merely want his wives inside; he wants absolute control over their respective spaces. Thus, while he relegates Romola to painted chambers, he also forces Tessa indoors and she never goes out without his permission. Ironically, however, it is the forced expulsion from the library which propels Romola into the real outside world of the city—Florence itself—for good.

Inside the city walls

The city can frighten those not used to it. Eliot repeatedly describes its streets as labyrinthine and narrow (6, 9), and the town itself as a 'community shut in close by the hills and by walls of six miles' circuit' (6), even as a 'tomb' girdled by 'stone towers' (320). For Baldassarre, 'the narrow passes of the streets, with their strip of sky above, and the unknown labyrinth around them, seemed to intensify his sense of loneliness and feeble memory' (295). But the space within the walls can also protect. Tito, for instance, couches his reasons for not searching for his father in terms of the city; he wants to save himself 'from the necessity of quitting Florence' (117).

For Romola, the streets and piazzas of Florence create a space of both growing freedom and deadly imprisonment, as did the walls of her father's library. When she first ventures out of the close confines of her house, she feels liberated. Her brother's death brings her into the streets; although she remains thickly veiled, we are told that once in the streets 'the fresh sense of space revived her' (163). It is in this newly discovered space that Romola begins to think for herself. Her moments of recognition of Tito's true character come markedly after or during her walks outside, in the streets. For example, Romola—whom we have seen outside so rarely that it is still a shock to picture her anywhere but in her house—passes through crowds of French soldiers and Florentines 'on her way to the house of Piero di Cosimo, in the Via Gualfonda'; there, she sees the portrait of Tito and Baldassarre and realizes Tito is not the angel he appears on the outside (258). Later, Romola goes 'out without saying anything more' to Tito, and admits for the first time during her walk 'not only that Tito had changed, but that he had changed towards her' (279).

In the act of walking, Romola embodies her father's fear of the wandering female mind. So is Bardo right? No, the novel suggests that Bardo's flaw is that he himself *never* wanders—the light outside blinds him after the 'cool gloom' of his house. His refusal to wander is responsible for Bardo's own Casaubon-like staleness (60). Romola's walking outside into the city can thus be seen, especially at first reading, as a move into greater freedom.

Yet this space within the walls of Florence remains deeply ambiguous; it is a place where identities shift in and out of focus as private and public spaces run into one another. Within the city walls, Romola has many selves. She is, as we have seen, the isolated, dutiful daughter of a blind old man; she is also the public, duty-driven Madonna created by Savonarola; she at one time envisions for herself a life as another Cassandra Fedele, an 'instructed woman' supporting herself in a 'lonely life' (327); she is a usually quiet, docile wife who feels guilty after confronting Tito in Nello's shop, not for mistrusting Tito in the first place, but for 'the access of distrust and imagination which had impelled her to address her husband publicly on a matter that she knew he wished to be private' (415).

Romola is not the only character in the novel to experience a shifting sense of identity. Tito moves from the innocent youth in love with Romola, to the many-faced spy, to Tessa's gentle lover, to the hardened egoist who tries to control Romola by appealing to his role as husband and master. Savonarola, too, is torn between contrasts; he embodies the passionate and the rational, the pious and the worldly.[9] And so, for that matter, does Baldassarre, a 'man with a double identity' who is both a brilliant scholar and an old madman (340).

These divisions occur along the fault-lines of public versus private identity—how others see us lined up against how we 'really' are—but curiously, they take shape against the background of a persistent confusion of public and private spaces. The barber's shop, to begin with, contains a latticed screen which 'divided the shop from a room of about equal size, opening into a still smaller walled enclosure, where a few bays and laurels surrounded a stone Hermes' (32). In addition, Nello's business frequently spills out into the Piazza when it is too hot indoors, and he shaves his customers in full view of passers-by. The Piazza del Duomo itself becomes at festivals a space neither inside nor outside. The huge open courtyard is covered with a canopy, a great blue tent stretching 'from the octagonal baptistery in the centre to the facade of the cathedral and the walls of the houses on the other sides of the quadrangle' (84). The false sky is painted with 'yellow lilies and the familiar coats of arms, while sheaves of many-coloured banners drooped at fit angles under this superincumbent blue' (84). At festival times, too, the 'towers' that demarcate clearly the boundary of the city, as so carefully described in the Proem, are brought inside this canopied space in the form of the giant wax tapers of the procession (88).[10] And, of course, there are the loggias, those galleries which bring the outside in and the inside out. The narrator describes Romola's in detail: 'on the side towards the street the roof was supported by columns; but on the remaining sides, by a wall pierced with arched openings, so that at the back [it looked] over a crowd of irregular, poorly-built dwellings towards the hill of Bogoli' (179).

These ambiguous spaces, neither inside nor outside, can imprison as well as free, protect as well as endanger, as we have seen. The seemingly free spaces of the city can be as claustrophobic and suffocating as those of, say, Bardo's library. In addition, in such places, a breakdown of signification accompanies the confusion of outside and inside space, almost as if the confusion of identity finds itself echoed in the spatial ambiguity of the city. Disguises abound in the spaces of Florence; shadows flash, and symbols or outward appearances reveal themselves to be empty, meaningless—or meaning something other than the usual. Thus, meaning itself—and who controls it—becomes a theme in Romola.

Savonarola's youths, for instance, are required to 'drop their personalities, and walk as symbols of a common vow' (380). To Baldassarre in his misery, Greek letters look 'like mocking symbols of his utter helplessness'; they no longer speak to him of heroes and myths, as the 'magic signs that conjure up a world' (315, 339). When Baldassarre achieves his short-lived coherence, he is described as 'once more a man who knew cities [...] who felt the keen delight of holding all things in the grasp of language. Names! Images!' (339). Knowing the meaning of symbols, being able to read, connects him once again not only to books and jewels but to cities and the ways of men. He thus links the space of cities with the knowledge of names and images, with the work of scholars. He understands what Romola is yet to learn: that inside the walls of the city, meaning is imposed on letters, symbols, names, even work, by men in power—Savonarola, her father and husband—and by their cloistered, guarded knowledge.

Just as Tito tries to use his power to force his wives into a space of his choosing, the father-figures in Romola's life exert their power over meaning, symbols and reading, to force her into work which does not challenge their power over interpretation. Romola's work has until now rested with these symbols: reading, translating, transcribing, interpreting the texts for her father's fossil of a great work; reading her father's every whim; interpreting her husband's every action and inflection. She knows, for instance, that when Tito does not 'throw himself a little backward, and look up at her' as he usually does when she places her hand on his head, that something has gone vitally, irrevocably wrong in their marriage (279).

Inside the walls of the city, as inside the walls of Bardo's library, interpretation is imposed on Romola so that it seems she cannot interpret meaning for herself. We are told early on that 'every revelation, whether by visions, dreams, portents, or the written word, has many meanings, which it is given to the illuminated only to unfold' (18-19). Only the 'illuminated' have the power to interpret correctly; only those in power are believed; the proliferation of visions and revelations, and the certainty of those who like Savonarola, Dino and Camilla Rucellai interpret these dreams, terrifies Romola. The scene where the assigning of meaning occurs, as Baldassarre recognizes, is the city, and it is this walled, imprisoning space that Romola finally flees when the open spaces of the city rebel, the crowd turns bloodthirsty, and her godfather is executed in the court of the Bargello while her husband and her priest stand by. At this point, the city she tried to leave years before can no longer contain her: 'all clinging was at an end for her: all her strength now should be given to escape from a grasp under which she shuddered' (506). She exclaims her desire to escape Savonarola and the bloodshed with a spatial metaphor—a longing to be outside—as she tells her priest, 'God's Kingdom is something wider [than you describe]—else, let me stand outside it with the beings that I love' (499).

So the city that once meant freedom has become, just like Bardo's library, a sort of prison for Romola. But this occurs only after she has 'mapped it out', got to know it, and transformed it by her wanderings into a domestic space in which she can work. Thus, although Romola in the city moves outside the walls of her home, she somehow remains homebound; her home itself has expanded. This process of domesticating the space she finds herself in allows her to work, as we shall see, at the 'mothering' which becomes her passion.

Before we can understand her wandering outside the space inscribed by the city walls, we must first examine Romola's sense of work, and particularly its dependence on her transformations of the space within those walls.

Adoptions, stepmothers and a confusion of space

Women's work has always occurred within a domestic setting, so in this sense Romola must transform her city into a domestic space before she can work within it. She does this by walking, wandering, making the streets her own.

At the opening of Book Three, we see how much the space around her has been changed and redefined by Romola's wandering. She now works on the streets, walking amongst and bringing help to the needy—'in her place', as the chapter heading tells us—so that 'the idea of home' has become identified 'less with the house in the Via de'Bardi, where she sat in frequent loneliness, than with the towered circuit of Florence' (377). In other words, the streets are her home; in them she is more free than in the walls of her house. Rather than forming a prison, the walls of the city seem to form the stage for her work.

What is this work? Nursing the sick and poor. Here, in streets so crowded with the sick and poor that Romola has even opened up her own courtyard as a makeshift hospital, in a city whose walls bristle with strength yet open in welcome before a foreign king and his army, in a place neither fully inside nor out in the open, Romola works to provide the mothering she herself never received. The link between nursing the sick and mothering is made explicit by Romola's new title: she is the 'blessed mother' gracing the streets of Florence.

Of course, mothering is 'women's work'. It is not 'intellectual work' of the kind that so threatened Tito. In fact, Romola's detailed mapping of the city, her domestication of its space, lets her work without being too challenging to the men who have controlled her—her husband, Tito and the new, ultimate father-figure in her life, Savonarola. As a 'blessed mother' in the domesticated sphere of the city which is now her home, Romola does not present the danger of a Cassandra Fedele; in doing this kind of work, Romola is not the intellectual that Tito so feared in her father's library.

Romola, of course, is not a mother, nor does she ever become one; she never has children. Tessa, on the other hand, although always described as 'child-like' herself, is now a mother and proudly shows her 'bambino' to Baldassarre (303). There is, in fact, only one 'child' ever described as belonging to Romola: her love for Tito, which is soon as dead and mutilated as the infants' limbs in Bardo's library. When she realizes the truth about Tito, we are told that Romola mourns as a mother does whose baby has died: 'the woman's lovingness felt something akin to what the bereaved mother feels when the tiny fingers seem to lie warm on her bosom, and yet are marble to her lips as she bends over the silent bed' (323). Nevertheless, back in Florence after her first attempt to escape, helping the poor and sick, Romola metamorphoses into 'Madonna Romola', the mother of all (379). In fact, the narrator even tells us that it is Romola's 'ready maternal instinct' which causes her to stop in one of her walks ('along by the walls on her way from San Marco') and rescue a lost little boy, who of course turns out to be Lillo, the son of Tessa and Tito (465). The streets of the city themselves now welcome her in this role. Romola never comes to 'a turn of the streets' where she is not greeted 'with looks of appeal or of friendliness' (379). She repeatedly turns to her work of mothering to find peace from her private life with Tito.

I have up to this point been positing a reading in which Romola's adventures out of doors (not only her aborted escape but also her walks and work in the streets) appear as a sign of revolt against Tito and her role as dutiful wife. She brings what he would keep locked away into the public realm, at one point even demanding Tito's assurance about Savonarola's safety in the very public space of Nello's barber shop, and eliciting in Tito a feeling of 'near hatred' as a result (414). But even outside, Romola still does not do her own work; just as she struggled in the library for Bardo, she now struggles in the streets to fulfil the vision of another father, Savonarola. The Frate further complicates the question of Romola's relation to mothering, because he—the ultimate father-figure—has already taken on the role of the spiritual mother of Florence, telling his audience, 'Listen, O people, over whom my heart yearns, as the heart of a mother over the children she has travailed for!' (231). Now he takes the place of both mother and father for Romola, and tells her exactly what to do, while she too becomes a 'mother'.

Thus, it will not be until she physically escapes the walls of Florence that Romola can free herself not only from Savonarola's influence, but also from the power of all the men in her life: husband, father, godfather, priest. Having domesticated the space within the city walls, she must wander once again to find a new, unmapped space, one this time which we as faithful readers hope will not set limits on her interpretation of signs or wonders, or even work.

When Romola flees Florence the second time, it is not to seek Cassandra Fedele to find out how to live as an independent woman of learning. Romola now seeks only death. Almost wrapping herself in the close-fitting shape of a small boat—a shroud? a womb?—Romola pushes off to drift to her death like the Lady of Shallott. But the death she finds differs greatly from the one she was expecting. It is in effect a new life.

Only when Romola finally does leave the city and gives herself up to the waves does she escape the system of patriarchal control over meaning, over symbols, which Baldassarre rejoices at belonging to again. I agree here with Deirdre David, when she argues that Romola's escape from the enclosed space of Florence is an escape from all names, all labels, from the 'imposition of all badges' and duties.[11] And only outside Florence, in the strange, blank village, can Romola find the space to find a different vision, a sense of purpose, of work, within herself—not one ordained by her father, or by her husband, or by Savonarola, or by any man.

The boat which was to be her coffin becomes instead a womb, 'the gently lulling cradle of a new life', as it puts her gently ashore (559). The plague-stricken village she finds remains unnamed and undescribed, in stark contrast to the carefully named and mapped details which always surround the descriptions of Florence. The village thus appears more like a blank space in a dream than anything else. Only there does Romola find the public vocation previously denied her by her roles as dutiful daughter and wife and piagnone; there, she 'simply lives', 'with so energetic an impulse to share the life around her, to answer the call of need and do the work which cried aloud to be done, that the reasons for living, enduring, labouring, never took the form of argument' (567).

The key term here reveals itself to be 'work'. Fully outside the city for the first time, in a space unrecognized and unmapped by the men who previously had power over her, Romola finds worthy work independent of all men and gives up caring that the 'symbolic writing of heaven' holds no message of love, that symbols have no meaning, that the people she knows have no single identity (511). She chooses her own work. She rescues a Jewish baby, then the rest of the village. The few villagers left alive when she first appears take her to be the 'Holy Mother with the Babe' (563). Perhaps more importantly, after Romola has proven herself as a stepmother to all and taken care of the villagers, she is then in her turn mothered by the village: 'here on a thick heap of clean straw-a delicious bed for those who do not dream of down-she felt glad to lie still through most of the daylight hours, taken care of along with the little Benedetto by a woman whom the pestilence had widowed' (566). In her bed, Romola is visited by all the villagers, who bring her food and take care of her and call her 'blessed Lady' (566). At last, this woman who has had no nurturing or mothering her entire life, finds what she needs—not in the romance plot (Tito, obviously, fails miserably at being a nurturer), but as a result of her own work, and in the nameless, unmapped space of a village wiped clean by death.

So, the plague-village appears to be blank territory, waiting to be inscribed in interesting new ways, surely beneficial to our accomplished heroine; however, after Romola's recovery, in her mind lies always the vision of Florence, those 'piercing domes and towers and walls, parted by a river and enclosed by the green hills' (559). And so she returns to that proscribed space, as we always knew she would.

But Florence has changed since we first saw it through Romola's eyes. Father, brother, husband, godfather, priest are all dead; no traditional patriarchal authority is left in her life. She finds her aunt, Monna Brigida, then Tessa and Tessa's children, and brings them together under one roof where she cares for them all. Romola thus continues her work as a mother to all in need but, as in the village, she is a stepmother who does not need authority from anyone other than her self. The space where we see her working is, perhaps not surprisingly, a loggia which 'at its right-hand corner, looked all along the Borgo Pinti, and over the city gate towards Fiesole, and the solemn heights beyond it' (585). She is back in a space both inside and outside, but this time she has the power.

We are left with a vision of a matriarchy ruling from a space neither inside nor outside, floating above the roofs of the city. There, Tessa and her daughter are making wreaths; Romola is tutoring Tessa's son Lillo, who calls her 'Mamma Romola', and to whom she describes her admiration for none other than the martyred Savonarola (586). This space of the loggia becomes Romola's fittest setting. It is not a true 'feminine' space in the sense that the prettily painted, fully enclosed saloon or boudoir is a 'feminine' space; but neither is it a 'masculine' space like the library or the wide open, public places of the town. In it, Romola can be a mother while she is not a mother; and we can judge her success in terms other than that of the romance, in terms that perhaps even Maggie Tulliver might concede. Romola does not win the man, she does not have children (the outward sign of winning the man), but she ends up all right anyway.

Yet I am not quite happy with this reading. Back in Florence, Romola's work strikes me as questionable. While Romola tutors her husband's son in the learning taught her by her father, Tessa's 'pretty' daughter sits weaving flowers; although she appears bright, at least in her mother's eyes, she does not receive Romola's instruction as her brother does. Nor does Romola suggest a life of scholarship to her as she does to Lillo. And Romola now worships Savonarola again—or at least the image of him she has placed on the altar in her home—as if his last refusal to speak, his silence at the stake, were his final triumph.

So: silence, silent acceptance of duty and work; children, and the perpetuation of a system in which boys learn while girls do not—these are the contradictory messages with which Romola closes. And I am left with more questions. Why, for instance, is Tessa, the truly stupid woman in the book, the only one with whom Tito feels comfortable, the only one to achieve that symbol of 'real womanhood' by having children?[12] Why does the marriage of Romola to a handsome, bright, sexy young man turn out to be as awful as the marriage of Dorothea to the dried-out, scholarly Casaubon? Any response suggests that George Eliot continued throughout her writing life to struggle with the rules by which we judge the success of intellectual women, just as Maggie Tulliver did in her reading of *Corinne*.[13] The category of 'woman' in *Romola* thus seems to rely on an essential notion of womanhood which shifts slightly as the spaces in the novel shift, as Romola frees herself from the traditional roles of wife and daughter and religious penitent in the ambiguous space of the city, but which nevertheless remains one in which the image of the intellectual woman is subordinated to that of the caring nurse, the Madonna, the mother, even if that mother is a stepmother and the children adopted.

George Eliot's *Middlemarch* begins and ends with the plaintive observation that for women who desire to do great deeds there are no outlets, and suggests that many of them, unable to do some great thing, do nothing. Perhaps on this level, if anywhere, the idea of work in Romola brings into play a less uncomfortable message: if Romola cannot be Machiavelli or Cassandra Fedele, then at least she can do something, even if it is some form of mothering, even if it involves a return to the spaces we thought she had escaped. And we should not forget the subversiveness of the ending here. After all of Romola's wanderings, after all her attempts to push out the borders of the space allowed her, she does return home; yet it is a home where three women have set up house together.

And, as I take a step back out of the ambiguous space of the novel which bears Romola's name, my thoughts turn again in admiration to the author of *Romola*, who struggled to write this book in the severely limited space allowed an intellectual woman of her time: a book written, as she said, 'with my best blood'.

Notes

1. 'As soon as I came to the blond-haired young lady reading in the park, I shut it up and determined to read no further. I foresaw that that light-complexioned girl would win away all the love from Corinne and make her miserable. I'm determined to read no more books where the blond-haired women carry away all the happiness'. George Eliot, *The Mill on the Floss* (London: Dent, 1976), p. 312.
2. Toril Moi, *Simone de Beauvoir: The Making of an Intellectual Woman* (Oxford: Blackwell, 1994), p. 255.
3. Deirdre David points out Romola's resemblance to the Pre-Raphaelite ideal of beauty in *Intellectual Women and Victorian Patriarchy* (Ithaca, NY: Cornell University Press, 1987), p. 192.
4. Moi, p. 256.
5. Andrew Brown gives a brief biography of Cassandra Fedele in his notes to *Romola* (613, n. 54), as does Andrew Sanders in his edition: 'Born in Venice *c.* 1465, Cassandra was renowned throughout Italy for her learning. She was employed by the Venetian state as its Latin orator, a rare honour for a woman'. Andrew Sanders, notes to *Romola* (Harmondsworth: Penguin Books, 1980), p. 699, n. 25.
6. I am, of course, alluding to both Simone de Beavoir (*Memoirs of a Dutiful Daughter*) and Virginia Woolf (*Three Guineas*).
7. For examples of Tessa outside, see, for instance, p. 23 (the marketplace), p. 103 (in San Martino), p. 108 (outside the gates, under the plane tree), p. 150 (at the peasants' fair), and p. 198 (in the Via de' Bardi).
8. Donald Olsen, *The City as a Work of Art* (New Haven: Yale University Press, 1986), p. 108.

9. See, for instance, p. 531: 'Savonarola's nature was one of those in which opposing tendencies coexist in almost equal strength: the passionate sensibility which, impatient of definite thought, floods every idea with emotion and tends towards contemplative ecstasy, alternated in him with a keen perception of outward facts and a vigorous practical judgment of men and things'.

10. The narrator of the Proem describes at length the 'seventy or more towers that once surmounted the walls, and encircled the city as with a regal diadem' (4).

11. David, p. 193.

12. Note that even Monna Brigida has had children, and holds herself apart from Romola because Romola has not: 'But you must give up to me a little, Romola, about their eating, and those things. For you have never had a baby, and I had twins, only they died as soon as they were born' (574).

13. Toril Moi makes a similar point: 'after imprisoning her most accomplished female intellectual, Romola, in a disastrous marriage, [Eliot] makes Dorothea Brooke in *Middlemarch* literally fall in love with Casaubon's mind, only to realize that it takes more than the love of pure minds to satisfy an intellectual woman. Moi, p. 256.

CHAPTER FOUR

'Telling the Whole': Trauma, Drifting and Reconciliation in *Romola*

JULIAN CORNER

George Eliot's letters and journals, written while *Romola* was in its germinal stages, present a picture of self-inflicted torment. The project stretched her to her fullest intellectual and emotional capacities. She recalls having taken '*unspeakable* pains in preparing to write *Romola*—neglecting nothing I could find that would help me to what I may call the "Idiom" of Florence, in the largest sense one could stretch the word to' (*Letters*, IV, 301). Even Lewes was astonished at her dedication: he describes her as 'buried in old quartos and vellum bound literature which I would rather *not* read' (*Letters*, III, 473). Her phrase '*unspeakable* pains' indicates that her research engaged with the most emotional and unconscious levels of her being. It took possession of her, and was evidently driven by energies which were more obsessive than pedantic. Her obsession is symptomatic of a desire to ingest her material, to fuse with it, to break down its resistances. This process was reciprocal. She speaks of writing *Romola* under a 'leaden weight' of illness (predominantly migraines), of it having 'ploughed into her',[1] and of having written it 'with my best blood' (*Letters*, VI, 336). The creative process is marked by a physical sense of violence and interpenetration. George Eliot comments more than once that she would take to scourging herself if it would help her to write it. It is as though fusion with the material requires physical breakdown, the individual being laid open by the disintegration of boundaries.

The exhaustive research for *Romola* was a punishing regime, scourging the conscious self, reaching beyond the speakable to the lifeblood. Of course this statement is at odds with what previous scholarship has understood of the positivistic discipline of George Eliot, with its rigorous attention to empirically demonstrable relation.[2] However, I will argue here that *Romola* is the product of George Eliot's need to move the idea of relation beyond the confines of the observing, calculating, analysing ego. It is true that she always believed the individual should behave with strict regard for the law of consequences. However, she seemed haunted by the possibility that this discipline, while a necessary restraint for the excesses of an egoistic nature, was also a means of stifling larger natures. *The Mill on the Floss* presented the tragic implications of the law of consequences for a nature which George Eliot could not condemn: the loving, passionate impulsiveness of Maggie Tulliver. Tom Tulliver, on the other hand, highlighted the absence of sympathy and the suppression of self which must accompany the exclusive adherence to rational prudence. In him, empirical discipline replaces romantic subjectivity at the expense of the relation of the individual consciousness with its environment. The division between Maggie and Tom suggests that human nature is felt, in *The Mill on the Floss*, to have lost its spontaneous unity both with its environment and within itself. I will suggest that the stalemate denouement of that novel caused George Eliot to abandon the conscious mind as the exclusive medium of her quest for coherence, and to explore the possibility of reconciliation in the unconscious. This departure is necessarily realized poetically in *Romola*. However, I will show that George Eliot's engagement with the processes of the unconscious is so intense that it lends itself directly to elucidation in terms of psychoanalytic theory.

The traumatic process which led to George Eliot's fusion with her material informs the story of its eponymous heroine. Romola's life is one of rupture, loss and disinheritance; however, she does eventually find reconciliation with her environment. Her story may be characterized, using George Eliot's description of her preparations for the novel, as a search for a 'backbone',[3] a means of holding the whole together. George Eliot's journal reveals that the backbone of *Romola* is continually sought in an idea, and that each fresh idea is invariably followed by renewed despondency. She does not record how she moved beyond this pattern and there is certainly no mention of an idea finally answering to the need for a backbone. Romola's experience, as we will see, is strikingly similar. Her search for an idea, by which she may 'thread' her life together (370), is a cycle of hope and despair. Her movement beyond this cycle is marked by the drifting away scene. This scene signals George Eliot's appreciation of the necessity of forging a backbone outside the conscious ego. The drifting boat visits the irrational level at which fusion with externality must occur. It is therefore symbolic of the process of George Eliot's own artistic beginning. In order to discuss *Romola*'s engagement with this irrational level, I will draw upon two writers, one twentieth-century, one nineteenth-century, who provide a vocabulary for the irrational: the child psychologist D. W. Winnicott and Søren Kierkegaard. Despite being near contemporaries, George Eliot knew nothing of Kierkegaard. Both Kierkegaard and Winnicott will therefore help to move the discussion of *Romola* beyond George Eliot's conscious frame of reference.

The need to discuss the impulse towards reconciliation in *Romola* is highlighted by the shortcomings of positivistic criticism. These readings, while suggestive, are ultimately limited by their need to view the novel as the exclusive product of conscious design. For instance, there is Peter Conrad's characterization of the Victorians (he takes *Romola* to be their quintessential novel) as tending 'to identify creativity with work, to equate understanding with mastery of details'.[4] Secondly, there is Felicia Bonaparte's hyperbolic assertion that *Romola* is 'a symbolic narrative in which every character, every event, every detail—every word, in fact—is an image in an intricate symbolic pattern'.[5] *Romola* is not only about mastering details and realizing their symbolic significance. It is concerned with why we care about details, and how we come to care about them. Conrad is far from the mark when he declares that 'the details [...] have staged a rebellion against the whole'.[6] A desire for unity is central to the novel. A unity, not only of parts (details), but also of levels. Bonaparte's magnificent attempt to unify the parts (down to the last word) rests on the assumption that 'Eliot's poetic imagination was [...] philosophic'.[7] Ironically, she can only establish unity by sealing out the full process of personality. *Romola*, as I will argue, is a reconciliation of philosophical, empirical and emotional authorities, and it is *about* their reconciliation.

This reconciliation of authorities is precisely what George Eliot's previous fiction cannot deliver. The promotion of organic continuity is always strained in these works, seeming synonymous with loyalty to anachronistic institutions. The four imperatives which make up the 'word' of those novels—Work, Order, Resignation, Duty—point to a dislocation of inclination from action. There appears to be no way of describing behaviour which does not suggest either a desperate clinging to the past or a betrayal of the past. The possibility of making a new beginning seems completely against the grain of George Eliot's art. Much of her fiction is at pains to stress the diffuse unhistoric nature of beginnings. Moreover, beginnings which attempt to make a clean break from the past are shown to be fraught with moral and psychological dangers. *Romola* sees a culmination of these concerns, but it goes on to reach an intimation of how beginning may also be a means of reconciliation with the past.

The increased focus on the possibility of new beginnings is signalled by the novel's return to an era when the seeds of modern Europe were being sown in individual souls. The dome of Florence, we are reminded, 'the greatest in the world', which eclipses the hills, 'had been only a daring thought in the mind of a small, quick-eyed man' (4). The year is 1492 and Columbus is 'still waiting for [his] three poor vessels' (4). This date points to the nineteenth-century's association of human possibility with the American continent. Marian Evans rhapsodizes in an earlier letter:

> Is it not cheering to think of the youthfulness of this little planet, and the immensely greater youthfulness of our race upon it?—to think that the higher moral tendencies of human nature are yet only in their germ? I feel

> this more thoroughly when I think of that great Western Continent, with its
> infant cities, its huge uncleared forests, and its unamalgamated races.
> (*Letters*, II, 85)

Her cheerful notion of humanity's youthfulness is unconvincing. The future
writer of *The Mill on the Floss* understands too well the tragedy already
inherent in the rigid structures of society. She shifts her argument, therefore,
to the safer ground of the colonized American continent. However, the
discovery of America is *not* equivalent to the youthfulness of humanity's
existence. It takes her most optimistic rhetoric to mask the rupture implicit in
the new beginning of 'infant cities'. Setting off for new horizons is an
admission of defeat in the territory which is left behind.

Walt Whitman registers this ambivalence:

> We are like the voyagers of a ship, casting off for new seas, distant shores.
> We would still dwell in the old suffocating and dead haunts, remembering
> and magnifying their pleasant experiences only, and more than once
> impell'd to jump ashore before it is too late, and stay where our fathers
> stay'd, and live as they lived.[8]

This experience emerges in Maggie Tulliver's return to St Ogg's in *The Mill
on the Floss* and again in Romola's return to Florence following her first bid
for freedom. Both heroines are impelled homewards by a sense of duty
operating as the enforcer of continuity. Their sustained self-sacrifice becomes
the means of concealing the cracks which are letting in light from an
alternative world. In *The Mill on the Floss* the narrator exclaims: 'heaven
knows where [our] striving might lead us, if our affections had not a trick of
twining round those old inferior things'.[9] In *Romola* George Eliot recognizes
that our affections can lose that trick. She confronts the problem of what
follows when things stand unrelieved, in all their oldness and inferiority. This
is why attempts, such as J. B. Bullen's, to read *Romola* as George Eliot's
positivist allegory are unconvincing.[10] According to his formulation, we are
shown through the novel's heroine the march of mind by which humanity will
shrug off superstition and metaphysics. But such an embodiment of social
theory in the novel's central character would seem to be a facile escape from
George Eliot's earlier preoccupation with the clash of individuality and
corporate consciousness. As we will see, any attempt to prophesy through the
novel must forge—rather than impose—their reconciliation.

This reconciliation has a practical, as well as a prophetic, dimension. If
rupture remains unhealed in the individual, she will be unable to sustain her
sacrificial role. This anxiety is swept away in the flood which ends *The Mill
on the Floss*. We never learn whether Maggie could have sustained her self-
denial. *Romola* explores how rupture can be healed within the individual and
thus how she can be reconciled emotionally with the old inferior things.

In order to heal someone, of course, you must have some conception of what constitutes a healthy individual. In *Romola* there are three main interpretations. Each attempts to determine which details are to be privileged as forming the whole. *Romola* enacts, and Romola internalizes, the struggle of these interpretations for authority. They are represented in Piero di Cosimo's sketch of a Stoic, a Bacchic and a Christian mask. Each claims its own coherence and yet expresses only one aspect of the heroine's nature. Inclined to believe in their coherence rather than her own, she finds herself fragmenting:

> What thought could reconcile that worn anguish in her brother's face—that straining after something invisible—with [Tito's] satisfied strength and beauty, and make it intelligible that they belonged to the same world? Or was there never any reconciling of them, but only a blind worship of clashing deities, first in mad joy and then in wailing? (182-3)

Again, when she makes the decision to leave Tito, Romola has the sense that 'she was somehow violently rending her life in two' (325). The vague 'somehow' points to an incipient consciousness that the Bacchic Tito constitutes an irreplaceable element of her sense of self, the rejection of which must split rather than unburden her.

Romola's life is ruled entirely by duty, the residue of lost belief. Time after time, she is called upon to remain loyal to an idea long after she has tired of it. It is not belief which draws her on to the next idea, only the search for something 'other'. This process reflects a quality which the narrator asserts is characteristic of the Florentines: '"new things" were the nectar of Florentines' (21). Novelty is what attracts Romola to Tito, who 'seemed like a wreath of spring, dropped suddenly in Romola's young but wintry life' (59); and to Christianity: 'her courage was high, like that of a seeker who has come on new signs of gold. She was going to thread life by a fresh clue' (370). Romola seeks a coherent code to impose upon her life, rather than coherence within herself. The masks of Piero's sketch foreshadow the superficiality of the poses she will successively adopt. She could have learnt from her brother Dino when he asks: 'What were the maxims of philosophy to me? They told me to be strong, when I felt myself weak' (158). Romola is convinced of humanity's obligation to overcome its weakness. However, she seems permanently divorced from any source of strength. Even the old Bardi pride which she is said to have inherited is quickly exposed as the Stoic mask. In fact, we learn that she 'had inherited nothing but memories—memories of a dead mother, of a lost brother, of a blind father's happier time' (59).

Romola's constitutional weakness (and perhaps her brother's) is seen to originate in and emanate from her memory of 'a dead mother'. This first rupture is compulsively repeated until she is cut adrift entirely: 'The bonds of all strong affection were snapped' (507). The phrase 'memories of a dead mother' rather than 'the death of her mother' or 'her dead mother' accentuates the impersonal distance and the finality of the discontinuity which it causes. 'A dead mother' functions as a blank wall, blocking further access of memory and damming the flow of experience from the earliest stage of her life to the rest. The metaphysical systems in which she hopes to find coherence are represented by the men she trusts after her mother's death. In fact, all coherence seems doomed to rely upon metaphysical support following the loss of physical continuity which she experienced in her mother. Each subsequent loss recalls that primal loss, hence the disproportionately alienating and disorientating impact these experiences have upon her. The final rupture is the 'snapping' of her affections for Florence, and this tearing up of roots re-enacts the maternal severance.

D. W. Winnicott's interpretations of the mother-child relationship can give us some purchase on the process of maternal severance and its implications. Using his ideas, I will sketch in a psychological history of Romola, a history that I will suggest is implicit in the later drifting scene. Thus what seems speculative in my discussion now will, I hope, be justified by the textual analysis that follows. Like most child psychologists, Winnicott starts from the assumption that the infant is unaware of the externality of *'Not-me'* objects. This illusion, he asserts, is maintained by the solicitude of a 'good-enough mother': 'The mother, at the beginning, by an almost 100 per cent adaptation affords the infant the opportunity for the illusion that her breast is part of the infant'.[11] Here we find, as we would expect, the tension between subjective authority and empirical discipline which arose during the qualification of romanticism by positivism during the nineteenth-century. As Winnicott expresses it: 'From birth [...] the human being is concerned with the problem of the relationship between what is objectively perceived and what is subjectively conceived of'.[12] The omnipotence of the infant's fantasy allows it to move seamlessly from the fantasized breast to the reality: 'A subjective phenomenon develops in the baby, which we call the mother's breast. The mother places the actual breast just there where the infant is ready to create, and at the right moment'.[13] In effect, the facilitating environment, which the mother creates, repeats the child's fantasy outside of itself, so continuing the untroubled wholeness of the womb. This wholeness, which we may term a sense of being, 'is something', says Winnicott, 'that antedates the idea of being-at-one-with, because there has not yet been anything else except identity'.[14] In order to progress beyond this stage, the mother has to 'disillusion' the infant, reducing her adaptation to its needs. This is done gradually, allowing the infant to displace its drives on to other objects. These objects, which Winnicott terms 'transitional', most obviously include, at first, toys, thumbs, dummies and blankets. As the child's experience widens, so will the scope of its transitional objects. They are a means of perpetuating the illusion of continuity between inner and outer reality. Thanks to good-enough management by the mother, we care about objects as replacement maternal environments; they complete our world: 'The transitional phenomena represent the early stages of the use of illusion, without which there is no meaning for the human being in the idea of a relationship with an object that is perceived by others as external to that being'.[15]

The fact that Romola cannot find meaning in her relationship with external objects is attributable to the discontinuity in her relationship with her mother. Should the mother-infant relationship be snapped before the infant has bonded with transitional objects, should the mother be absent long enough for the transitional objects to lose their power of substitutive illusion, then the infant will become traumatized. The implications of trauma are powerfully expressed by Winnicott:

> We must assume that the vast majority of babies never experience [too much deprivation]. This means that the majority of children do not carry around with them for life the knowledge from experience of having been mad. Madness here simply means a *break-up* of whatever may exist at the time of *a personal continuity of existence*. After recovery from [too much] deprivation a baby has to start again, permanently deprived of the root which could provide *continuity with the personal beginning*.[16]

The unusual idea that Romola has 'inherited nothing but memories' indicates that she is dispossessed, or disinherited, of the presence of her personal beginning. The significance of the timing of her loss is emphasized by the narrative: 'It is but once that we can know our worst sorrows, and Romola had known them while her life was new' (Epilogue, 586). Romola has to struggle against the tendency of this primal rupture to define the rest of her life. Her deprivation of personal continuity is the weakness that leads to, and then disables, her search for coherence. Romola does indeed carry around with her *only* memories of '*break up*'.[17]

The re-enactment of her trauma as she leaves Florence causes Romola to experience an existential despair bordering on madness: 'Why should she care about wearing one badge more than another, or about being called by her own name?' (507). This breakdown in her identity extends to her sense of vocation: 'The vision of any great purpose [...] was utterly eclipsed for her now by the sense of a confusion in human things which made all effort a mere dragging at tangled threads' (507). But why should Romola's efforts to find consolation and belief be so completely vain? Good-enough disillusioning by the mother allows the activity of the imagination to compensate gradually for the absence of the maternal presence. Romola's trauma, however, has disillusioned her absolutely, leaving her with no intermediate area of mystery. Winnicott asserts that 'the task of reality-acceptance is never completed' and that 'no human being is free from the strain of relating inner and outer reality'.

Relief from this strain, however, is 'provided by an intermediate area of experience which is not challenged (arts, religion, etc.)'.[18] The traumatized subject, who is deprived of this intermediate area, can only adhere to the *precepts* of religion without sharing other people's *belief*. As for Romola's appreciation of art we are told that 'memories of far-off light, love, and beauty [...] lay embedded in dark mines of books, and could hardly give out their brightness again until they were kindled *for* her by the torch of some *known* joy' (59, my italics). It seems that Romola is utterly destitute of inner resource.

Her drifting away expresses the aimlessness which results when one's environment ceases to maintain its hold. Without external things there can be no structured narrative, only drift. It is also a relinquishing of ego-structures: she wishes to 'be freed from the burden of choice when all motive was bruised' (510). The resurgence of Romola's primal moment of supreme despair instigates a revolution both of her sense of self, and of George Eliot's own sense of possibility. Romola attempts to reach beyond her orphanage, to return to the physical oneness she experienced before her trauma: 'She longed for that repose in mere sensation which she had sometimes dreamed of in the sultry afternoons of her early girlhood, when she had fancied herself floating naiad-like in the waters' (509). Water is a common feature of *in utero* fantasies. It signals what Freud calls 'a wishful phantasy of flight from the world'.[19] In George Eliot's earlier short story 'The Lifted Veil', the narrator Latimer follows Rousseau's habit of rowing his boat out into the middle of a lake and then lying down, letting it drift. He describes his 'least solitary moments' as those when 'the glowing mountain-tops, and the wide blue water, surrounded me with a cherishing love such as no human face had shed on me since my mother's love had vanished out of my life'.[20] In his *Confessions* Rousseau describes how he would cry out with emotion: 'O Nature! O my mother! I am here under your sole protection. Here there is no cunning and rascally man to thrust himself between us'.[21] While *Romola* sees a return of George Eliot's preoccupation with this scene, in both the primal and the literary sense, there is a new emphasis: rather than an escape fantasy, it is an attempt to start again, in Winnicott's sense. However, there is more optimism in *Romola* than Winnicottian theory is prepared to entertain. He asserts that the traumatized subject is 'permanently deprived of the root which could provide *continuity with the personal beginning*'. Romola's drifting suggests a surrender to the undifferentiated matrix of the unconscious and, as such, is an attempt to access the 'memories of far-off light, love and beauty' without external aid; to re-inherit herself. She is *re*-forging her continuity with her personal beginning.

It is no accident that Romola is the only eponymous heroine of George Eliot's novels. George Eliot fought shy of naming her second novel after its heroine, Maggie Tulliver. In Romola she seems to have to found a female character who can attain the characteristics of a real hero as they are set out in 'Janet's Repentance', her only other fiction which contains a female name in its title: 'The real heroes, of God's making [...] have their natural heritage of love and conscience which they drew in with their mother's milk'.[22] I say that Romola *attains* these characteristics because she clearly is not a heroine 'of God's making'. Romola is a self-made heroine. Her heritage has to be claimed *in the face* of 'natural' lineage which excludes her. This is the fate of woman, who, as Luce Irigaray points out, is faced with almost insurmountable difficulties in her efforts to 'reestablish continuity': 'No return to, toward, inside the place of origin is possible unless you have a penis. The girl will herself be the place where origin is repeated, re-produced and reproduced, though this does not mean that she thereby repeats "her" original topos, "her" origin. On the contrary, she must break any contact with it'. Because the little girl has nothing comparable as a substitute for her place of origin, the intensity and likelihood of her trauma is far greater than the little boy's: 'she cannot turn back toward her mother, or lay claim to seeing or knowing what is to be seen and known of that place of origin'. This must be so, says Irigaray, 'at least as things stand at present'.[23] The problem of discontinuity is *par excellence* female. It is clear that a female subject's return to the place of origin must take place outside current systems of representation, or rather through their dissolution.

In the jargon of popular psychology Romola is searching for the *child within*. This child is her personal beginning from which she is severed. The conclusion of her search is already predicted by Piero's sketch: the three masks 'rested obliquely on the lap of a little child, whose cherub features rose above them with something of the supernal promise in the gaze which painters had by that time learned to give to the Divine Infant' (33). The divine infant, of course, is the promise of reconciliation. It is symbolic of a new beginning which forges links with previous ages following dislocation and despair.

Romola's crisis is supremely representative of the Victorian period's disinheritance and its broken connections with the past. For all the novel's insistence on the value of organic process, George Eliot appreciates, at the most poetic level of her text, that continuity is not achieved by insisting on our roots in a past from which we feel alienated. The dissolving of boundaries through drifting contradicts the novel's outward message, which is framed in a very different water image: 'The great river-courses which have shaped the lives of men have hardly changed; and those other streams, the life-currents that ebb and flow in human hearts, pulsate to the same great needs, the same great loves and terrors' (3). This stress on the continuity of human nature overrides the irresolvable uncertainties of the individual life. The nature of fifteenth- or nineteenth-century man, according to this view, has not floated free of previous generations. It *cannot* be 'disinherited'. The optimism inherent in historical fiction is its assumption that we can still access and identify with the psychology of past generations. Bulwer Lytton, in his preface to *The Last Days of Pompeii*, declares that he aims for 'a just representation of the human passions and the human heart, whose elements in all ages are the same'. The word 'human' becomes the bedrock of continuity upon which the fiction is founded. Although this is a commonplace of historical fiction, it is not the assumption of every nineteenth-century historian. In his essay 'On History', for instance, Carlyle signals the possibility of dissent: 'The inward condition of Life, it may rather be affirmed, the conscious, or half-conscious aim of mankind, so far as men are not mere digesting-machines, is the same in no two ages'.[24] In its conception that we can access history through the continuity of feeling, which we unify in the term 'human nature', historical fiction resists the possibility of fracture between ages. Florence is chosen as an 'unviolated symbol', the narrator tells us, 'to remind us that we still resemble the men of the past more than we differ from them' (3). There is a degree of enforced consensus here, none of the novel's readers having first hand experience of fifteenth-century Florence. Moreover, the recognition among George Eliot's contemporaries of nineteenth-century England in *Romola* is as much a result of her broad *a priori* assumption of human continuity than of any specific resemblance between the two ages.

Other parts of *Romola* indicate that historical memory, on the contrary, can be an insurmountable obstacle to continuity. As Romola embarks on her journey she struggles to break through the blank wall of her trauma:

> Had she found anything like the dream of her girlhood? No. Memories hung upon her like the weight of broken wings that could never be lifted— memories of human sympathy which even in its pains leaves a thirst that the Great Mother has no milk to still. Romola felt orphaned in those wide spaces of sea and sky. (511)

Conscious memory only reiterates the sense of trauma, expressed here in remarkably Winnicottian terms. The whole world becomes a mother who cannot love her enough. The light of the stars becomes 'the hard light of eyes that looked at her without seeing her'. She then covers her eyes and wishes 'that she might be gliding into death'. This death is the dissolving of the conscious ego, allowing her to engage with the repressed contents of the unconscious: 'Presently [Romola] felt that she was in the grave, but not resting there: she was touching the hands of the beloved dead beside her, and trying to wake them' (511).

Before following Romola to the plague village we should note that this sequence is not continuous in the novel. There are six chapters between her falling asleep and waking up. Indeed, the original *Cornhill* readers were required to wait two months in order to learn her fate. She fell asleep in the twelfth instalment only to wake up in the fourteenth. Romola's journey frames, even *contains*, the climax of the Florentine story and Tito's demise. The reason for this seems obvious. Tito's death purges *Romola*—and Romola—of the negative connotations of making a new beginning.

Tito is described by Bernardo del Nero as 'one of the *demoni*, who are of no particular country [...] His mind is a little too nimble to be weighted with all the stuff we men carry about in our hearts' (195). Tito's adopted status seems to have left him with a sense of freedom from his duty and affiliation. So long as his self-interest is not served by any exclusive loyalty he endangers the coherence of community.

Despite their opposed natures, Tito and Romola pose a *joint* threat to the empirical basis of the novel; indeed, Tito is the amoral reflection of the moral ideal which Romola approaches. In the exchange between Savonarola and Romola in her first escape bid, her argument collapses because 'she was too much shaken by the suggestion in Savonarola's words of a possible affinity between her own conduct and Tito's' (362). They illustrate the paradox (just as the earlier orphans, Hetty Sorrel and Dinah Morris had done) that only amoral and morally impeccable natures can migrate on to foreign soil. In *Adam Bede* Dinah's decision to leave her family to go and live among the spiritually needy of the nearest manufacturing town causes her aunt to accuse her of a lack of feeling towards her family. Likewise, Romola's 'Drifting Away' is in danger of implying that she possesses a nature aloof from the rest of humanity.

As an orphan Tito is identified with Romola. However, rather than despairing at the arbitrariness this engenders in *his* life, he revels in his freedom: 'his acute mind, discerning the equal hollowness of all parties, took the only rational course in making them subservient to his own interest' (403). Tito embodies the values of the Bacchic mask, which is drunkenly oblivious to origin. His lack of rootedness allows him to generate a great deal of the novel's narrative energy. Unlike the earlier treatment of Hetty Sorrel, the references to Tito's beauty are not patronizing or trivializing. It is felt as a source of power, representing the allure (and so the danger) of his hedonistic philosophy. He is truly the anti-hero, as his predecessor Hetty never could be, supporting his selfish instinct with proto-utilitarian argument. As such, he asks the rebellious question which the novel is written to answer: 'What was the use of telling the whole?' (99).

Tito and Hetty illustrate that suppression is a prerequisite to freedom from commitment. Hetty causes the death of her child in the hope of releasing herself from her obligations. This is echoed in the scene at the Rucellai Gardens when Baldassarre appears: 'at that moment [Tito] would have been capable of treading the breath from a smiling child for the sake of his own safety' (355). The emergence of the child-image at this moment is significant.

Rather than seeking coherence from an inheritance of primal unity, Tito attempts to deny any bond which suggests dependence. According to the psychoanalysis of Melanie Klein, when the infant decides that the parental figure is no longer all-encompassing but is placing constraints on its appetites, it fantasizes the destruction of that figure. These fantasies lead, in turn, to fears of retribution and this fear is the foundation of the super-ego.[25] Baldassarre is the super-ego figure, avenging the destruction which Tito has achieved by stealing Baldassarre's memory, selling his jewels, and asserting his madness. Baldassarre's pursuit of Tito demonstrates that the latter cannot cut himself off from the legacy of infantile dependency, hence the link between Baldassarre's appearance and the image of Tito crushing a child. Furthermore, the child not only points to Tito's primal dependency but also to the sub-rational roots of his own desire. Baldassarre embodies the raging madness which the infant projects onto the superego. This madness is not merely a plot device. Psychologically, it is consistent with the period of Tito's life which he is attempting to suppress. Tito must be overtaken by what lies outside his conscious talent, by contingency and irrationality.

Baldassarre completes the destruction of Tito which the revolution had begun. The uncontrollable rage of the mob is what sends Tito diving over the Ponte Vecchio. This chain of events signals the self-destructive nature of revolution. Tito assumes that he can harness revolution for his own self-interest. His attempt to make a new beginning by purging himself of his past is amplified by the political manoeuvring in which he is implicated. As with the infant who attempts to destroy the constraints on its desire, Tito soon realizes that he cannot seal himself off from the violence which ensues from revolution. The furious mob demonstrates that the direction of violence cannot be calculated. This is paralleled in the rage of Baldassarre, whose unstable identity anticipates the fluctuations of the mob. Just as the collapse of identity which follows revolution's attempt to forget or destroy the past is marked by an increasing dependency of its own violent means, so Baldassarre can only collect his wits, in the face of amnesia, through his thirst for vengeance.

Tito's inability to control the violence of revolution is matched by the frustration of his calculations to shrug off the past. The uncanny frequency with which chance throws Baldassarre in Tito's path is suggestive of the return of the repressed. Even before Baldassarre's arrival Tito is dogged by chance allusions to the old man: 'Anybody might say the saints had sent *you* a dead body; but if you took the jewels I hope you buried him' (11); 'your Christian Greek is of so easy a conscience that he would make a stepping-stone of his father's corpse' (37); 'Five hundred ducats! Ah, more than a man's ransom!' (70). Baldassarre himself 'had chanced to meet the stranger who wore Tito's onyx ring' in Genoa (274). After the coincidence of

Baldassarre's arrival in Florence 'under incalculable circumstances' (483), which is marked by his chance collision with Tito, his discovery of Tito's past is a matter of contingency: he happens to take lodgings at Tessa's house; Romola happens to offer him food during the famine. Of course this coincidence is as much Romola's, and we should remember that *she* twice discovers Tessa by accident. This identity between these two characters, which is suggested by Romola's fascination with this stranger, and which is further emphasized by the rupture/discontinuity of Baldassarre's amnesia and his compulsive reclaiming of the past, leads to their ultimate unity in water.

Baldassarre, as the super-ego, embodies the necessity which the individual must accommodate. Bonaparte notes that 'it was Balthazer who brought the gift of myrrh, [...] the symbol of life's bitterness'.[26] He is the origin which Tito's hedonism had attempted to ignore. When Tito and Baldassarre's bodies are discovered the latter's grip is so tight that 'it was not possible to separate them'. Like Maggie and Tom, in *The Mill on the Floss*, they must be buried together: 'In death they were not divided'. Baldassarre's insistent presence points to a level at which life becomes complete. This is suggested most powerfully as he waits by the river for whatever chances to pass: 'he waited for something of which he had no distinct vision—something dim, formless— that startled him, and made strong pulsations within him, like that unknown thing which we look for when we start from sleep, though no voice or touch had waked us' (551). Again the narrative threads along the boundaries of sleep and dream. It is at this level that Tito will be destroyed and Romola will be healed.

Tito is so obviously the dangerously attractive flip side of the course which Romola takes that this alternative must be destroyed through him: hence the uncharacteristically stark comment in George Eliot's Journal: 'Finished Part XIII. Killed Tito in great excitement'.[27] Tito exhibits the amorality implicit in a new beginning: 'the old life was cast off, and was soon to be far behind him' (552). The existence of this trait in Romola is highlighted, as was noted earlier, by Savonarola. He castigates her for assuming the habit of a nun, and this disguise motif is echoed in Tito's plans for the future: 'Could he not strip himself of the past, as of rehearsal clothing, and throw away the old bundle, to robe himself for the real scene?' (484). The parallel is important because Romola's second disguised escape is ostensibly no different from the first. On that earlier occasion, however, she was heading for Venice to visit Cassandra Fedele, 'the most learned woman in the world', to discover 'how an instructed woman could support herself in a lonely life there' (327). The subtle difference between 'learned' and 'instructed' alerts us to the hollowness of Romola's quest: she will never be another Cassandra Fedele while she cannot *care* for knowledge.

This first journey fails because it attempts to effect a solution through the conscious ego, where there are no answers. The second journey takes the opposite direction, into the unconscious. While this *is* a rupture of consciousness, the water imagery stresses a more fertile level of continuity in Romola's psyche: 'Romola in her boat passed from dreaming into long deep sleep, and then again from deep sleep into busy dreaming' (557). The parallel between the two journeys signals a rejection of the capacities of a self-sufficient consciousness (that cornerstone of positivism), just as the example of Tito was a rejection of its morality.

This conclusion mirrors Søren Kierkegaard's exploration of the ways that faith transcends the ethical in *Fear and Trembling*. Kierkegaard presents an important challenge to Feuerbach's rationalization of faith. However, George Eliot was unfamiliar with Kierkegaard's ideas, and so her own working through of the inadequacies of ego-bound structures was not placed on a fully conscious footing. We may therefore discuss her fiction in Kierkegaardian terms without any concern that George Eliot was allegorizing a pre-existing formulation.

Faith is a word which points to the irrational level at which we care about anything. Kierkegaard reflects upon Abraham that 'he had faith by virtue of the absurd, for all human calculation ceased long ago'.[28] Calculation, as Tito makes obvious, can be intensely egoistic. Moreover, the potential of a person who only calculates is confined to the structures of the conscious ego. Only irrationality can move us beyond our restrictive ego-structures. 'Every movement of infinity', Kierkegaard asserts, 'is carried out through passion, and no reflection can produce a movement'.[29] Romola makes her movement of infinity by virtue of committing herself to the destiny of the sea: a supremely absurd means of self-discovery.

We have been prepared for this disintegration of her rational self by her first meeting with Savonarola. He succeeds in breaking her pride (a word synonymous with rigid ego-structures) when he impels her to kneel.

> 'Kneel my daughter', the penetrating voice said again, 'the pride of the body is a barrier against the gifts that purify the soul' [...] Slowly Romola fell on her knees, and in the very act a tremor came over her; in the renunciation of her proud erectness, her mental attitude seemed changed, and she found herself in a new state of passiveness. (161)

Only by the breaking down of physical boundaries and, by implication, conscious boundaries, can Romola surrender herself to the influence of her brother's vision. However, this scene is complicated by the sexual aggression we hear in Savonarola's penetrating voice and Romola's passiveness. He forces her to concede, in her 'renunciation of her proud erectness', that she lacks phallic authority. This reminds us of Irigaray's point that woman can only be the site of origin. Origins may be reclaimed through her but never by her. It is Romola's mistake to believe that her Bardi pride actually enables her to maintain connectedness with her roots. It derives only from her father, who holds her feminine abilities in contempt. Her Stoic mask is therefore a mimicry of phallic authority, while the Christian mask signals that the 'sorrowing' woman's body (it is the only female mask) must submit to man's search for origin. The lack of a mask which might represent woman's connection with origin suggests that such a thing is either unobtainable or, more likely, unrepresentable. The Christian mask does highlight the necessity of surrender;[30] however, faith can only be attained by the renunciation of pride rather than the suppression of individuality.

The subject who strives for faith Kierkegaard calls a 'knight' and his 'movement of infinity' describes Romola's drifting away. It is also resonant of the artist's struggle for belief in the products of her imagination. The parallel is more than merely suggestive, however; the drifting scene was George Eliot's artistic beginning. It belonged, she asserted, 'to my earliest vision of the story' (*Letters*, IV, 104). Moreover, Romola's search for an intermediate area of experience is, in effect, an initiation into the artistic world.

Kierkegaard comments:

> In the first place, the knight [must] have the power to concentrate the whole substance of his life and the meaning of actuality into one single desire. If a person lacks this concentration, this focus, his soul is dissipated in multiplicity from the beginning, and then he never manages to make the movement; he acts as shrewdly in life as the financiers who put their resources into widely diversified investments in order to gain on one if they lose on another—in short, he is not a knight. In the next place, the knight will have the power to concentrate the conclusion of all his thinking into one act of consciousness. If he lacks this focus, his soul is dissipated in multiplicity from the beginning, and he will never find the time to make the movement; he will continually be running errands in life and will never enter into eternity, for in the very moment he approaches it, he will suddenly discover that he has forgotten something and therefore must go back.[31]

The 'focus' of the knight points to the intense single-mindedness of Romola's new beginning and of artistic beginning. It is distinguished from egoism, however, because the subject moves towards infinity in the unconscious rather than attempting to encompass infinity at the level of consciousness. The analogy of the financiers highlights the idea that contingency can only be met morally at an irrational level. Romola's journey to Cassandra Fedele is her contingency plan from which she is called back; on this occasion she is not a knight. Tito is the supreme contingency planner, but even his dazzling capacities cannot escape the net of Florence. His coat of mail becomes a 'garment of fear' (239) rather than a knight's armour. Contingency translates into necessity, as Leibniz first demonstrated, only when it reaches to infinity.

It is only at infinity that the causal sequence ceases to float free. It is only through the irrational movement of infinity, therefore, that contingency can be encompassed.

Contingency results from attempts to limit experience within the bounds of one's conscious ego, as we have seen with the parallels with Kierkegaard. Egoism may thus be defined in two ways: as ignoring the claims of one's environment or as sealing out the claims of one's unconscious. The positivistic attempt to equate morality with the law of consequences is viewed as calculation and expediency. *Romola* seems to posit a moral sense beyond the conscious ego.

At the pre-disillusionment stage of an infant's life it has not yet experienced the contingency of the mother's presence. Indeed the infant has not yet realized the otherness of the mother; it knows only a sense of being. When Romola wakes in the boat it is this sense of being which she experiences:

> She lay motionless, hardly watching the scene: rather, feeling simply the presence of peace and beauty. While we are still in our youth there can always come, in our early waking, moments when mere passive existence is itself a Lethe, when the exquisiteness of subtle indefinite sensation creates a bliss which is without memory and without desire. (557)

It is hard to see how 'indefinite sensation' can be moral, especially as it recalls Tito's earlier wish that he and Romola lived in Southern Italy 'where thought is broken, not by weariness, but by delicious langours' (184). However, despite her reference to Lethe, George Eliot is careful to justify Romola's feeling as connecting her with the sensations of her youth. Romola retains indefinite memory-traces which she is endeavouring to recall. These are the memories of the pre-disillusionment sense of being. Her moment of passive forgetfulness is therefore a kind of remembering; it is what Freud would call a reliving of the experiences which lie behind the delusive screen-memories. We should recall that evocative passage again describing Romola before she falls asleep: 'Had she found anything like the dream of her girlhood? No. Memories hung upon her like the weight of broken wings that could never be lifted' (511). Only memory-traces in the unconscious retain their vitality and fertility; screen-memories, those which contribute to our ego-structure, are so much dead-weight, inhibiting our sense of being.

Remembering this sense of being requires only a transient rupturing of consciousness. We are soon told: 'Already oblivion was troubled: from behind the golden haze were piercing domes and towers and walls' and then 'across the stillness there came a piercing cry' (559). In answering this cry of distress and tending to the plague victims in the village, Romola demonstrates her moral continuity with her actions in Florence. She therefore resists the temptation to escape the realities of life: '*Could* she not rest here? No sound from Florence would reach her' (559). Kierkegaard explains that, in regaining consciousness, the knight who has made the movement of infinity is not alienated from external things (the central Victorian fear concerning introspection). He says:

> The knight, then, makes the movement, but which one? Will he forget it all, for this, too, constitutes a kind of concentration? No, for the knight does not contradict himself, and it is a contradiction to forget the whole substance of his life and yet remain the same [...] Only the lower natures forget themselves and never become anything other than what they were. The knight, then, will recollect everything, but this recollection is precisely the pain, and yet in infinite resignation he is reconciled with existence.[32]

This pain of recollection suggests the 'piercing' of Romola's dream world. Moreover, when she lands in the village, the threat of plague underlines the continuity of the real. However, she walks fearlessly among the plague victims, telling them: 'I am used to pestilence; I am not afraid'. In Florence, despite her disinclination, Romola had nursed the sick. It is through that moral conduct, therefore, that Romola becomes one of the first fictional characters, if not *the* first, to benefit (albeit retrospectively) from the dawning of germ theory and the practice of vaccination in the nineteenth-century. She renders herself physically immune to infection before the boat journey reaches to a level at which she becomes psychologically immune to contingency and moral infection. The physical history helps to underline the continuity of the psychological process.

Romola's movement is therefore distinct from the brand of conversion we witness in Dino, who is led to 'dastardly undutifulness'. Moreover, it is also beyond the transformation which Kierkegaard describes as belonging only to lower natures, and which Ovid understands as death in his Lucretian theory of metamorphosis:

> In all creation, be assured,
> There is no death—no death, but only change
> And innovation; what we men call birth
> Is but a different new beginning; death
> Is but to cease to be the same.[33]

The 'old' Romola does not die in the drifting sequence; it is simply the moral germ of what is to follow: 'Romola had had contact with no mind that could stir the larger possibilities of her nature; they lay folded and crushed like embryonic wings, making no element in her consciousness beyond an occasional vague uneasiness' (250).[34] This imagining of the unconscious as 'embryonic wings' indicates how George Eliot had come to place her faith in the hidden potential of the human psyche. The unconscious no longer threatens the death of sanity, it is humanity's hope for the future. It becomes another America, the continent which George Eliot refers to in a letter as 'that cradle of the future' (*Letters*, II, 85).[35] Her optimism, her hope that 'the higher moral tendencies of human nature are yet only in their germ', is invested in its possibilities.[36] In an echo of the earlier image, we are told of Romola's boat that 'instead of bringing her to death, it had been the gently lulling cradle of a new life' (559). The theory of metamorphosis overcomes the sense of rupture which, as noted earlier concerning the discovery of America, seemed inherent in new beginnings. Tito had taken metamorphosis to mean that he could transform himself for the next chapter in his life. Romola, however, partly shares the Proem's understanding of new beginnings: it lists as one of life's invariables 'the faces of the little children, making another sunlight amid the shadows of age' (9). In the village Romola's sympathy immediately draws her to the cry of an infant, just as the cry of Lillo takes her to the home of Tessa. In the image of the infant, continuity and new beginning are reconciled.

George Eliot and Kierkegaard are both absorbed with the imperative for reconciliation. The latter assures us that 'in infinite resignation [the knight] is reconciled with existence'. While resignation smacks of duty, infinite resignation is a state of complete reconciliation. It is the spontaneous acceptance of external things which emanates from a bond forged at a level much deeper than the metaphysical. Whereas Romola had obeyed a sense of duty in Florence, in the plague village she is drawn 'irresistibly' by her instincts. She has therefore regained her sense of unity in (and with) external life:

> Her experience since the moment of her waking in the boat had come to her with as strong an effect as that of the fresh seal on the dissolving wax. She had felt herself without bonds, without motive [...] but from the moment after her waking when the cry had drawn her, she had not even reflected, as she used to do in Florence, that she was glad to live because she could lighten sorrow—she had simply lived, with so energetic an impulse to share life around her, to answer the call of need and do the work which cried aloud to be done, that the reasons for living, enduring, labouring, never took the form of argument. (567)

Romola's new level of existence is non-intellectual, her actions emanate from instincts which, before now, have remained crushed. This appears to be a collapse of the rigorous attention to universal laws and relentless sequence otherwise expected of George Eliot's characters. It returns Romola to a Golden Age of spontaneity. This is curious since George Eliot insists time and again (even in *Romola*) that the earth might have been 'a paradise to us all, if eager thought, the strong angel with the implacable brow, had not long since closed the gates' (109). Romola, of course, does approach an ideal, but even at the novel's romantic extreme she always remains an exploration of human potential. While Romola does overcome 'eager thought' (or conscious ego-structures), and so opens the gates of paradise once more, there is no suggestion that paradise can be wholly regained. What George Eliot strives for is an intimation of our inheritance from that paradise, and its reconciliation with the present.

The perfection of Romola's life is inevitably broken in upon by the pain of recollection. Her newly-forged bond with life has to include the scenes of its rupture. It remains to be seen whether Romola can now care for the details of Florence:

> Florence, and all her life there, had come back to her like hunger; her feelings could not go wandering after the possible and the vague: their living fibre was fed with the memory of familiar things. And the thought that she had divided herself from them for ever became more and more importunate in these hours that were unfilled with action. What if [Savonarola] had been wrong? What if the life of Florence was a web of inconsistencies? Was she, then, something higher, that she could shake the dust from off her feet, and say, 'This world is not good enough for me'? (568)

Now that Romola has renounced her search for structural simplicity, she is able to accept inconsistency as a legitimate quality of life. In her notebook, George Eliot copied Horace's statement of reconciliation: '*Rerum concordia discors*' (the discordant harmony of things) (Epode, I, 12).[37] This conviction materializes in the inclusive Epilogue, in which we are shown how Romola's infinite resignation is spreading among the previously discrete elements of the novel. Lillo exclaims: 'How queer old Piero is! [...] He abuses you for dressing the altar, and thinking so much of [Savonarola], and yet he brings you the flowers'. This is a conclusion of mutual tolerance, in which the differences of others are accepted, even cherished, in community. Romola demonstrates an 'exalted' (572) capacity to foster (literally) relation where before there was only sequestration. The responsibility which she feels for her husband's children is the consummating act of reconciliation. While Tito's other family is further evidence of his duplicity, it also suggests that his nature was not unmixed with positive elements. By fostering his children, Romola overrides all previous alienation and makes good Tito's redeeming qualities.

Towards the end of her life George Eliot saw *Romola* as marking a pinnacle of her career and reading it, she said, made her 'sob with a sort of painful joy' (*Letters*, VI, 336). This painful joy is, quite literally, the 'pain of recollection', and the oxymoron of this complicated response underlines *Romola*'s claim to be George Eliot's supreme work of reconciliation. In it she achieves a kind of prophetic synthesis, not only of her theories and beliefs,[38] but of the different levels of the human psyche.

Reconciliation might lead us to expect a depletion of energies. Certainly George Eliot repeatedly asked herself, following the conclusion of *Romola*, whether she would write anything worthwhile again. A recognition of a loss of power seems to be indicated in her retrospective comment: 'I began it a young woman—I finished it an old woman'.[39] If her output had declined following *Romola* we would perhaps be justified in claiming that too much was resolved by its drifting scenes. Instead, we are able to say, with *Middlemarch*'s Finale, that 'Every limit is a beginning as well as an ending'. *Romola* is the last novel of her youthful struggle (we note that she does not allow herself a middle age), which I have characterized as driven by a struggle for origin. These novels give way to more poised narratives, which are more concerned with the multiplicity and the interplay of their different strands. The preoccupation with linear connectedness becomes counterbalanced by the connectedness of the web. *Romola*, therefore, tells us not only how George Eliot worked through the struggles of her youthful career but also how she achieved her artistic maturity.

Notes

1. J. W. Cross (ed.), *George Eliot's Life as Related in her Letters and Journals* (Edinburgh and London: Blackwood, 1885), p. 361.
2. Positivism will be understood throughout as 'scientism', as opposed to Auguste Comte's religion of Positivism.
3. Gordon Haight, *George Eliot: A Biography* (Oxford: Oxford University Press, 1968), p. 351.
4. Peter Conrad, *The Victorian Treasure-House* (London: Collins, 1973), p. 11.
5. Felicia Bonaparte, *The Triptych and the Cross* (Brighton: Harvester Press, 1979), p. 10.
6. Conrad, p. 132.
7. Bonaparte, p. 4.
8. J. D. Jump (ed.), *Tennyson: The Critical Heritage*, (London: Routledge & Kegan Paul, 1967), p. 350.
9. George Eliot, *The Mill on the Floss*, ed. Gordon S. Haight (Oxford: Clarendon, 1980), p. 133.
10. J. B. Bullen, 'George Eliot's *Romola* as Positivist Allegory', *Review of English Studies* **26** (1975), pp. 425-35. It will be necessary, for the purposes of this article, to view Romola in a manner diametrically opposed to Bullen's allegorical treatment. In other words, she will be treated as an autonomous entity whose psyche can be analysed using methodology which would have been, in part, alien to Victorian England.
11. D. W. Winnicott, 'Transitional Objects and Transitional Phenomena', in

Through Paediatrics to Psychoanalysis (London: Hogarth Press, 1975), p. 238.

12. Ibid., p. 239.
13. Ibid.
14. D. W. Winnicott, *Playing and Reality* (London: Tavistock Publications, 1971), p. 80.
15. Winnicott, *Through Paediatrics to Psychoanalysis*, p. 239.
16. Winnicott, *Playing and Reality*, p. 97.
17. Dianne F. Sadoff also discusses *Romola* in terms of trauma; however, her reading centres on how the traumatic memory of the primal scene of seduction operates in George Eliot's fiction. See *Monsters of Affection: Dickens, Eliot, and Bronte on Fatherhood* (Baltimore: Johns Hopkins University Press, 1982), pp. 88-99.
18. Winnicott, *Through Paediatrics to Psychoanalysis*, p. 240.
19. Sigmund Freud, *Case Histories II*, trans. James Strachey, ed. Angela Richards (Harmondsworth: Penguin, 1991), p. 340.
20. George Eliot, *The Lifted Veil,* in *Silas Marner, The Lifted Veil, Brother Jacob* (London, New York, Toronto: Oxford University Press, 1906), p. 205.
21. Jean-Jacques Rousseau, *The Confessions*, trans. J. M. Cohen (Harmondsworth: Penguin, 1953), p. 594.
22. George Eliot, 'Janet's Repentance', in *Scenes of Clerical Life*, ed. Thomas A. Noble (Oxford: Clarendon Press, 1985), p. 256.
23. Luce Irigaray, *Speculum of the Other Woman*, trans. Gillian C. Gill (Ithaca, NY: Cornell University Press, 1985), pp. 41-2.
24. Thomas Carlyle, 'Critical and Miscellaneous Essays II', *Centenary Edition of the Works of Thomas Carlyle*, 30 vols (London: Chapman and Hall, 1897-1902), vol. xxvii, p. 61.
25. See for example, Melanie Klein, *Love, Guilt and Reparation* (London: Virago Press, 1988), pp. 248-57.
26. Bonaparte, p.142.
27. Cross, p. 361.
28. Søren Kierkegaard, *Fear and Trembling; Repetition*, trans. Howard V. Hong and Edna H. Hong (Princeton: Princeton University Press, 1983), p. 36.
29. Ibid., p. 42.
30. It is George Eliot's conviction that life's lessons have by and large been learnt by Christianity, only misapplied.
31. Kierkegaard, pp. 42-3.
32. Ibid., p. 43.
33. Ovid, *Metamorphosis*, trans. A. D. Melville (Oxford: Oxford University

Press, 1987), p. 359.

34. It is worth noting Bessie Rayner Parkes's description of Marian Evans in a letter to Barbara Leigh Smith: 'There is as yet no high moral purpose in the impression she makes, and it is that alone which commands love. I think she will alter. Large angels take a long time unfolding their wings; but when they do, soar out of sight. Miss Evans either had no wings, or, which I think is the case, they are coming, budding' (*Letters*, II, 8). Whether or not George Eliot came to know of this comment, it seems that Parkes anticipated the incarnation of the artist George Eliot in remarkably similar terms to the psychical metamorphosis of Romola.

35. This connection is underlined by the fact that the Leweses read Anthony Trollope's *North America* in the early stages of *Romola*'s composition.

36. George Eliot's insistence on the germ of hidden potential resists the alternative germ of human disease. The difference lies between the unfolding of personal capacities and infection by impersonal elements. Infection is suggestive of revolutionary fervour. In *A Tale of Two Cities*, Charles Dickens draws an explicit parallel between 'the raging fever' of France and 'the fever of one patient'. *A Tale of Two Cities* (New York: F. P. Collier and Son, n. d.), p. 285 (Book 3, chapter 4). The germ of hidden potential also suggests the revolution of new beginnings, but it is always already located within the individual. Personal revolution entails the destruction of barriers, but these barriers are psychological rather than material.

37. *George Eliot: A Writer's Notebook 1854-1879*, ed. Joseph Wiesenfarth (Charlottesville: University Press of Virginia, 1981), Entry 114.

38. In this respect my claims for *Romola* agree with the thesis of Diana Postlethwaite's book, *Making it Whole: A Victorian Circle and the Shape of their World* (Columbus: Ohio State University Press, 1984), p. xvii. She asserts that 'the Victorian frame of mind [...] seeks a synthesis of the empirical and the intuitive, head and heart'. However, Postlethwaite approaches the issue from the opposite direction, concentrating on the philosophical/scientific theories of her chosen writers.

39. Cross, p. 361.

CHAPTER FIVE

From Romola to *Romola*:
The Complex Act of Naming

SUSAN M. BERNARDO

'The law was sacred. Yes, but rebellion might be sacred too'.

The political and private morasses of fifteenth-century Florence fail to defeat Eliot's quiet but determined heroine. Romola, by appropriating and transforming the patriarchal power of naming, re-creates herself and eventually confers that freedom of self-determination on others.

Naming, as the most pivotal use of language for Romola, works within a system of other manifestations of the power of language in *Romola*. Allusions to literary works from Homer to Boccaccio, episodes that highlight the force of written documents in the forms of contracts, letters and wills and instances of the persuasive strength of spoken language, such as the sermons of Savonarola, pervade the novel. In tracing Romola's eventual appropriation of naming, which brings with it the power to confer meaning, create new bonds and establish personal autonomy, the reader must also examine her progress through the patriarchal politics of language events.

Romola's initial place as scribe/servant to her father's scholarly enterprises places her figuratively and literally in the realm of language and patriarchy. Her struggle to maintain a place within the universe of her father's work and words leads her to enact a series of displacements as she looks from one male figure to another to infuse her experience with significance. As she struggles, the novel presents the reader with political events and relationships that at first appear to act as rivals to Romola for the focus of the narrative, but Florence's need for a firm leader and Romola's search for meaning gradually emerge as analogous—both seek order, autonomy and direction. Romola's solution to her quest, though, offers an alternative to the martial language, political conspiracy and public hypocrisy of Florence. Her journey towards self-definition and purpose, while it parallels Florence's struggle for order, focuses on the mutual creation of bonds between people rather than the imposition of hierarchy as a political tool. Romola does carry with her a structure that she gradually transforms, a structure that has been responsible for her travails, from her disastrous marriage to Tito to her disillusionment with Savonarola's religious fervour. To achieve transformation she must go through a suspension of struggle, shaping her own use of language to help re-create herself as she reinvests language's power with her own positive intensity, taking on her new role, and name, as Madonna or 'Blessed Lady'.

Fathers, gems and the marketplace of language

When the reader first sees Romola she appears within the limiting boundaries of the four walls of her blind father's library where she works at the edges of the manuscripts, writing only at his request. Her relationship to Bardo, as well as her role as mistress of marginalia, pushes her to the outer edges of any meaningful activity. For Bardo, whose son Dino has run off to become a monk, Romola cannot act as son-substitute. Her limitation, says her father, is her womanhood: 'I cannot boast that thou art entirely lifted out of that lower category to which Nature assigned thee' (54). Thus the marginal tasks that she undertakes in the study act as a reflection of her 'natural' inferiority. Because she cannot participate in the creation of scholarly language, or even take dictation of any of her father's important ideas, language signals her deprivation. To wield the pen, to usurp the power of the father, would be to gain her own creative power; but Romola's final route is one that goes beyond the fetters of pen and ink to the quintessentially fluid form of spoken language and the communication of command.

Initially, though, Romola engages in an attempt to satisfy the requirements of her father and patriarchal primacy by offering her husband as surrogate for her brother Dino. In marrying Tito she thinks she has solved the problem of providing help for her father by bartering herself. Her uncle refers to Romola as just such exchange material: 'Remember, Bardo, thou hast a rare gem of thy own; take care no man gets it who is not likely to pay a worthy price' (74). Gems, as Eliot knew[1] signify far more than simple bartering material. The gems in this novel always have a connection with tradition and family honour. Thus, Romola, as she becomes tied to the language of the marketplace by her uncle's statement, is also tied to the structure of the family that has its most tenacious representation in patriarchy and what Lacan calls the Name-of-the-Father—system of law, limitation and social order.[2]

This circulation in the male marketplace does not provide any immediate rewards to Romola for her willing role as commodity. Her love and respect for her father, in effect, freeze and free her simultaneously. As wife to Tito she separates herself from her father. The change in her name acts as a token of the separation and signal of a new alliance. But as a commodity Romola cannot control her destiny and remains powerless to influence Tito's actions. His ambitions do not include playing the role of devoted son-in-law that

Romola has expected. Yet Romola's expectations themselves, in the light of her subservient position as a daughter/marketable good, are at best illogical. As object in the transaction she cannot suddenly occupy the place of powerful subject. Tito, the power-hungry political interloper, who has usurped the power and gems of the Father without bothering with loyalty, maintains control, which essentially means the continued subservience of Romola to the letter—whether the letter of the scholar's thought or the words of the marriage contract.

Tito himself is not, however, detached from the law and letter of the father, though he pretends that he acts apart from any obligation. The obligation to the father reaches Tito literally in the form of the letter from Baldassarre via Fra Luca—Romola's brother, Dino. Tito chooses to set aside the will of the father and thus becomes the opposite of Romola, who honours her father. Tito's surname does not change in Florence, because he never bore the name of his adoptive father in the first place. Not tied by name, he feels no strong bond to Baldassarre and goes ahead with his plan to translate his father's ring into cash. In selling this tie to his father he has, in effect, mortgaged his own identity; however much he thinks he has succeeded in making a clean break with the past. Not only does he sell his own past, he also sells Romola's remembrance of her father: the Bardi library. Tito uses love and attachment as mediums of exchange as he plays his political games in Florence.

Romola, in a different sense, also becomes an agent of exchange. She exchanges one loyalty for another when each one proves empty, and in this way, she embarks on a search for significance. She first places her faith in her father, then Tito, then Savonarola and her uncle Bernardo del Nero. In shifting her faith from one man to another as they desert her or become unavailable to her through death and politics, Romola switches signifiers as she shifts loyalties, while the signified (a father figure) apparently remains the same. In other words, she tries to re-create these men as substitute fathers in order to maintain her own sense of context and meaning. What she cannot realize at this point is that there is no such possibility: one cannot change the label, name or identity in this novel without changing the essence. This series of displacements leads to a re-examination of her own sense of self, and therefore acts as the preparation for her later role as the 'Blessed Lady', a name which brings with it great significance for Romola.

Her escape from Florence, however, has its problems. Her first attempt fails not because she changes her mind about Tito's capacity for deception, but because Savonarola's words turn her back to the city. She can go no further than the margins of Florence, just as she could do no more than write in the margins of her father's books, for the voice of authority speaks:

> Of what wrongs will you complain, *my daughter,* when you yourself are committing one of the greatest wrongs a woman and a citizen can be

guilty of—withdrawing in secrecy and disguise from a pledge which you have given in the face of God and your fellowmen? Of what wrongs will you complain when you yourself are breaking the *simplest law that lies at the foundation of the trust which binds man to man—faithfulness to the spoken word?* (362, emphasis mine)

Savonarola significantly calls her 'daughter', for he has indeed usurped the power of Romola's absent father as he directs her towards the city. He elevates the spoken word here above other expressions of the marriage bond, licences or legal documents. In doing so he makes the spoken word a law—'the simplest law that lies at the foundation of the trust which binds man to man'—thus defining or limiting the word to act as the creator of ties. Romola is on her way out of the city to create, or try to create, new ties for herself. Her destination in leaving Florence would have been Venice where she would 'go to the most learned woman in the world, Cassandra Fedele [...] and ask her how an instructed woman could support herself' (327). Her disguise, that of a nun, though it does not fool Savonarola, has symbolic meaning—she will eventually be a sister who answers to a mother, rather than a daughter who heeds a father. This time, however, she does not actually leave Florence and her attire as Pinzochera—the word, though it is used as a name for an order of nuns, in its pejorative sense carries with it a notion of hypocrisy and bigotry[3]—has a double meaning which speaks of her confusion. Even the details of her garb are loaded with significance, for she carries a purse and a rosary. The purse gestures towards her past and Tito's selling her father's library, as well as her position as means of exchange, and it gestures to her future and the time she does leave Florence which necessitates her buying a boat. The rosary points towards her imminent meeting with Savonarola, her brother's much earlier decision to become a monk and her future role as a Madonna figure.

She leaves her father's house literally weighed down by her past, then, although she has written letters of farewell and removed her betrothal ring. Her writing, as an act of authorship, is ultimately ineffective, however, for with her physical return comes the destruction of these farewell letters. She destroys her own attempt at independence by returning to the city. Her letters, unlike the letter Baldassarre writes to advise Tito of his plight, or the bill of sale for her father's library, do not arrive at their destinations, for the sender gives up her own intended destination. Rather than exchange her loyalty once again and place faith in a woman, she continues with the displacement pattern of faith in father figures.

Eventually Romola realizes that her passive stance within patriarchy must change. She must go beyond the system of disillusionment in order to become an active force. The process of disillusionment that Romola undergoes involves a triangular structure of character relationship, one that is consistently resolved into a binary relationship. For example, we learn that the Bardi family really consists of Romola, Bardo and Dino, but that the brother is no longer able to assist the father and thus Romola and Bardo are left. The novel, in one sense, proceeds as the repetition of Romola's attempts to supply the missing family member. Initially Tito comes into the gap, but proves to be worse than useless to the family. When her father dies, Romola tries to replace him with Savonarola, who also acts as a father figure.

This displacement pattern acts as more than a simple repetition. Desire, according to René Girard, expresses itself in just such a series of substitutions. Each serves as a trial object of desire and this desire (straining towards an undefined/indefinite something) is fundamental to the human condition.[4] Romola, in a sense, has to realize that she herself is an agent of desire— searching for an object, rather than letting herself be an object of the desire of others. She, in other words, needs to recognize that she has an independent identity which she has helped to repress.

The fact that her husband tries to create a role for her succeeds in confusing her for a time. Tito tries to cast Romola in the role of Ariadne as he asks Piero di Cosimo to paint a triptych on a box with Tito as Bacchus and Romola as Ariadne, crowned with stars. Tito in reality miscasts himself, for he is truly Theseus the betrayer; the one who uses the woman and then abandons her.[5] Whichever role we ascribe to Tito, Romola's role as Ariadne provides an intriguing model: the deserted woman does not remain forlorn, for the myth provides Ariadne with a way off the barren island where Theseus has left her. Bacchus saves her. Romola, too, will have an unexpected new life as she eventually becomes her own Bacchus, while Tito will pay for his Theseus-like betrayal.

Tito's attempt at recreating Romola and himself through mythological allusion and his talent for rationalizing his betrayal of Baldassarre illustrate his misunderstanding of the power of language and symbols as creators and expressions of the tenacity of bonds of duty. When Baldassarre challenges Tito, the younger man engages in a game of language and naming that works only temporarily. Tito does not expect that a duel with Baldassarre will be one of words: after all, he wears chain mail because he expects the old man to attack him physically. But he rises to the occasion of a linguistic challenge while the old man cannot. Baldassarre has lost the ability to recognize written language, but he has moments of lucidity during which he poses the greatest threat to Tito. When Baldassarre addresses the company gathered at Rucellai's home, Tito tries to deny his father by renaming him: 'His name is Jacopo di Nola [...] without any reason, he has conceived a strange hatred towards me; and now I am convinced that he is labouring under a mania which causes him to mistake his identity' (355). Renaming in this setting engenders violent separation, for Baldassarre cannot be Tito's father and the betrayed benefactor if he is called Jacopo. Renaming here becomes a weapon in Tito's hands. It is worth noting that language and violence have the ability not only to negate the father, but also to create the individual as separate from the mother. The name as a separate label in language sets the child apart as subject while reminding him/her (in the surname) of the connection to the authority of the father. Tito's renaming of Baldassarre is his attempt to cover the forbidden name of the benefactor/father that would lead to the discovery of the unwanted connection between him and the old man. While those gathered know of Tito's loss of such a figure, Tito must ensure that they think the real Baldassarre is dead. He declares, 'It is certain that my father is dead' (356).

The confrontation finally comes to a test of words as Baldassarre, to prove he is not Jacopo, must find the passage in Homer engraved on one of the rings Tito sold to Rucellai. Baldassarre, because he has lost the ability to read, to make sense of pattern on a page, fails the test. Language here cannot take the place of the guarantor of truth, for we have what the narrator calls 'the apparent verification of his [Tito's] lie' (358). The oral test, though, not the text from Homer, is the device by which Baldassarre becomes Jacopo for those in the room. Tito uses the words of an ancient father of epic to undermine Baldassarre's paternal claim, thus playing a dangerous game with patriarchal authority. Tito here triumphs, but this encounter with his father begins a process which will end in the encounter that costs Tito his life. The ring as the link between father and son seems to have failed in the scene in Rucellai's house; but the ring will take other forms and will catch up with Tito. Indeed, it provides more than a casual link. Rings represent bonds that are supposed to be permanent and not even Tito's elaborate lie can destroy the bond. Tito himself wears the rings that make up his chain mail, or 'garment of fear', and Baldassarre will have his revenge by strangling or clasping his hands in an ever-tightening ring around Tito. The will of the father, represented by the ring in its capacity as symbol of a pledge, comes full circle in the novel. The circle brings change with it while enforcing the dominant claim. Destroying the bond really means destroying the self, as Tito finds out when Baldassarre enacts the suicide that Tito commits when he sells the rings and denies his father.

The link between Baldassarre and Tito, however, involves other people's stories as well.[6] Both Romola and Tessa meet Baldassarre, and Romola and Tessa know each other as well. Tessa, as Tito's mock wife, wears the necklace he gives her as though it had the same significance as a wedding ring and, indeed, it does for her. Just as words have specific meanings because we agree on those meanings, so the necklace as circular shape binds Tessa to Tito (he is 'Naldo' to her: in addition to renaming others, he renames himself). But the relationships in *Romola* are not as simple as Tito would like to make them; he cannot simply rename himself Naldo and live with Tessa as though they are both untouched by all that is happening around them in Florence. His fraudulent marriage to Tessa takes place before his legal marriage to Romola. In other words, the marriage that is not a marriage sets the conditions for the legal marriage that is, in another sense, not a marriage. Neither the spoken promise nor the written word means anything to Tito.

The spoken word in this novel has life and the power of command for Romola that the written word cannot have. Both fathers, Bardo and Baldassarre, centre their lives upon the written word. One is blind and the other, though he still sees, can no longer read. Without the ability to manipulate words, both become powerless. We know that Bardo never succeeds in bringing his work together and, furthermore, always refuses to let others use his manuscripts. The reason he refuses to share his manuscripts is that 'some other scholar's name would stand on the title-page of the edition— some scholar would have fed on my honey' (55). The perpetuation of his name as scholar concerns Bardo here. Obviously, Bardo could never have fame without being more public about his work; names that exist separate from a structure of society have little significance beyond the individual's notion of them. In addition, not only does Tito sell his library, but Bardo also loses any hope of the continuation of the family name, for his son is a monk and Romola's maiden name changes when she marries Tito. Patriarchal authority can deaden or give life depending on the subject's position in relation to it. Romola, who has paid homage to the father throughout, leaves the realm of the father as she leaves Florence; but unlike Tito, who tries to manipulate the law of the father in order to advance himself, she seeks, initially at least, only escape from grief.

From chaos to creation: the language of command

When Romola finally succeeds in escaping the confines of Florence she drifts away to an unknown destination. The formlessness of the sea on which her small boat glides becomes a picture of the situation of language: the signifier ('Romola' as title of the novel) over the fluid signified. The title or word, 'Romola', is constant while the meaning or ideas to which the term refers shift as the novel's focus changes. Romola herself participates in this fluidity, for her identity is in question. With the sale of her father's library Romola's past has been dismembered, for her past is intricately tied to the word of the father as it appears on the written page. The narrator describes her state by using such terms as 'slipped away', 'utterly eclipsed', 'confusion' and 'a mere dragging at tangled threads'. Romola realizes, too, that Savonarola's 'striving after the renovation of the Church and the world was a striving after a mere

name which told no more than the *title of a book*' (508, emphasis mine). Titles
or names do not always directly indicate content; language and words as
signifiers fail through inaccuracy, incompleteness, or indecipherability. And
thus we come to reflect on the title of the novel itself. Romola, in many ways,
has not always been the driving force of *Romola*. Her story becomes
complexly linked to men, politics and power plays that she never completely
understands. Carol Martin's claim that Romola becomes a secondary
character in a book that bears her name[7] has validity in the early pages of the
novel, but Romola's success in creating a new identity for herself helps
reassert her claim to centrality in the narrative.

  If the rift between name and content were to remain in place for the rest of
the novel, Romola's taking on a new identity would tell the reader very little
at best; however, her renaming proves to have significance. In her drifting
state she sees the possibility and even the instance of the abuse of the power
of language. As she thinks of Savonarola the narrative reports, 'she saw all the
repulsive and inconsistent details in his teaching with a painful lucidity which
exaggerated their proportion' (508). The abuse, however, does not negate the
underlying force of words and names. The inaccuracy or slippage of language,
paralleling the gap in the unconscious, as Lacan says, proves to be the very
'place of discovery' in a text.[8] In other words, discrepancy or lack signals to
the astute interpreter that meaning exists and can be discovered at this point.
Though this seems ironic, or at least strange, the events of the novel support
the notion that failure leads to the formation of success. The tension caused by
the discrepancy proves to be the beginning of action and even creation of self
and/or narrative.

  Romola seems almost to have swallowed up Romola, but here she floats off
into another story. She has come to a still point in the novel that proves
pivotal. We finally get a narrative with Romola as the obvious centre and
master. This is not simply a story within a story or case of embedded
narrative, rather it is totally separate from the fictional world the novel
presents to this point. Romola's reference here to Boccaccio and the Gostanza
story signals the departure. All the tales we have heard before this one that
figure as important parts of the narrative come from antiquity—the Ariadne
myth and the ring's reference to Homer, for example—but here we find a
narrative written in Italian. Use of the modern language separates Romola's
reading from the reading of her father in his scholarly pursuits. 'In her longing
to glide over the waters that were getting golden with the level sun-rays, she
thought of a story which had been one of the things she had loved to dwell on
in Boccaccio, when her father fell asleep and she glided from her stool to sit
on the floor and read the *Decamerone*' (509). Just as she used to 'glide' away
from her appointed place on the stool when her father's attention lapsed in
order to read for her own enjoyment, so she longs to 'glide over the waters'

after she has escaped the city and all its 'fathers'. Reading Boccaccio for her was a means of escape when she served her father, thus the memory of this text at this point is truly appropriate. The link to water also ties her present longing to the story from Boccaccio and implies that one watery text helps supply some material for another one. The reference to the outside text also focuses our attention on Romola as part of a story, on her departure as the start of her role in creating her own story.

Romola does not take over the task of narration—we retain the same narrator that we have had throughout the novel. But that narrator almost slips into the text. That is, within this chapter called 'Drifting Away', it becomes difficult to separate the narrator's thoughts from Romola's. Romola herself would like to become part of the water as she remembers her childhood: 'She longed for that repose in mere sensation which she had sometimes dreamed of in the sultry afternoons of her early girlhood, when she fancied herself floating naiad-like in the waters. The clear waves seemed to invite her: she wished she could lie down to sleep on them and pass from sleep into death' (509). This passage describes a state which Lacan would call 'pre-language' or pre-separation from outside elements. Mingling with water would at once diffuse the individual and reconstitute the person in a larger, freer, fluid medium. To mingle with the water would obviously also suggest the idea of reentering the waters of birth. As Eugen Bär points out in a 1974 article on Lacan, the original split between unconscious and conscious paradoxically creates and frustrates the subject who always desires the recovery of pre-conscious wholeness.[9] Just as the entry into consciousness creates frustration and desire for lost wholeness, so the lack or gap becomes the place of potential significance and motivation. Stasis or death would be the ultimate consequence of a 'whole' subject and language in all its complexity and potential inaccuracy would not exist. But even the supposedly less problematic and imperative patriarchal language can no longer control Romola as she refuses to allow names to have meaning. We hear her through the narrator: 'Why should she care about wearing one badge more than another, or about being called by her own name?' (507). Just as these distinctions of language cease to matter for this brief time in which the larger plot of the narrative stands suspended, so the distinction between the narrator's voice and character's thoughts begin to blur.

All that keeps that mingling of narrator and character from continuing is the appearance of a truly minor character: a man who sells Romola a boat. With the brief summary of the Boccaccio story a turning point occurs as the narrator reports that Romola sees a figure. Before the sighting of the man, the narrator is in Romola's mind and alternates between narrative observation and statements and questions that only Romola would ask. The narrator then enters the mind of the fisherman in the same way and is thus saved from floating off with Romola. Thus both the shift from Romola's mind to another's and the mention of the Gostanza story help separate the narrator from her character here.

Eliot's narrator can and does enter the character's mind, but in doing so must be careful not to 'fall into the text', a phrase Neil Hertz uses as he discusses the speaker in Wordsworth's *Prelude*:

> The encounter with the beggar triangulates the poet's self in relation to his double, who is represented, for a moment, as an emblem of minimal difference fixed in relation to itself. The power of the emblem is that it reestablishes boundaries between representor and represented and, while minimizing the differences between them, keeps the poet-impresario from tumbling into his text.[10]

If we remember the timely appearance of the fisherman here in *Romola*, who becomes the 'emblem' in Eliot, the danger and its avoidance become clearer. In other words, the narrator can never be more than a character who observes others: Eliot's narrator cannot act. Sublime moments, moments that help confound boundaries and suspend will, however, allow established distinctions to fade. Romola, at this stage of nascent identity, arrives at just such a potentially fluid moment which becomes more distinct in its departure from her previous experience through the narrator's sympathy with her. The narrator shifts from 'she' to 'we' in describing Romola's state: 'With the sinking of high human trust, the dignity of life sinks too; we cease to believe in our own better self, since that is also a part of the common nature which is degraded in our thought; and all the finer impulses of the soul are dulled' (508). The narrator's voice in this chapter then, is dual: the distanced narrator's voice that can make detached comments and put Romola's disturbed thoughts in perspective, and the sympathetic voice that shares Romola's misery. The narrator reinstates the separation between herself and Romola just before Romola buys the boat and drifts away; thus the narrator is not, strictly speaking, in the boat with Romola, but outside the situation describing it once again.

The fact that the Gostanza story that Romola remembers in this scene does not exactly fit her own situation reminds us of the distinction between the two voices; for just as Romola cannot be Gostanza, so the narrator cannot become Romola. In other words, the Gostanza story acts as the necessary third term of mediation between Romola and the narrator, and the narrator acts as the mediating entity between George Eliot and her narrative.

Interestingly, in Boccaccio Emilia tells the story of Gostanza at the request of the Queen who has chosen the topic: reward for constancy. Those in control of the narrative, both in Eliot and Boccaccio, are women. But Emilia tells a fairy-tale of reunited lovers, while Eliot's narrator shows us Romola not as a contented lover, but as a powerful, authoritative matriarch. In other words, Romola is like the Queen who can command that a narrative be set in motion. Romola has achieved this status through resignation and the willingness to give up the proper name, the name conferred by the father, the name that signals bonds and connection to the structure of law and language. Her initial inaction becomes the ultimate appropriation of strength. Unlike Tito, she avoids confronting the Name-of-the-Father and instead creates herself anew after her separation from Florence. What follows is a new narrative, neither the Gostanza story, nor another displacement exercise. Romola's mental act of speaking in a way that puts her into a new story mimics the writer's task in creating fiction.

Romola, unlike the characters in the frame narrative of Boccaccio's *Decameron*, manages to arrive at a plague-stricken place instead of fleeing from one. The difference here becomes Romola's position in relation to this small society of the village. Her appearance seems miraculous to those whom she helps and she does nothing to persuade them that she is anyone less than the 'Blessed Lady'. Her mode of speech as she commands the priest to carry out his duty in helping the sick sets her above the male order of the church and the realm of fathers. Her words, furthermore, do not meet with much resistance as the priest carries out her bidding. She says 'Come down [...] Do not fear. Fear rather to deny food to the hungry when they ask you' (647). She also fetches water for those in need, thus bringing their rebirth with her. Her role as saviour and benevolent ruler manifests itself in another way: she claims the power of naming as she bestows a Christian name on the child that she finds clinging to his dead mother. The figure of the dead mother here also acts as a reminder that Romola herself has undergone death and rebirth in her journey on the small boat, for like Romola, these people have come to the village by traveling over the water. They, like her, have occupied the place of the marginalized:

> The strongly marked type of race in their features, and their peculiar garb, made her conjecture that they were Spanish or Portuguese Jews, who had perhaps been put ashore and abandoned there by rapacious sailors, to whom their property remained as prey. Such things were happening continually to Jews compelled to abandon their homes by the Inquisition. (560)

Romola's capacity for imagining narrative comes into play in this passage as she thinks about this dead woman's life as outcast. In addition the maternal figure acts as an immediate instruction to Romola: this clinging, crying, live child needs a mother, needs a protector and a saviour who can provide him with identity as well as care. Romola becomes Bacchus/Blessed Lady/Creator of Story all at the same time. The usually patriarchal weapon of the name that succeeds in leading to the destruction of Tito, becomes part of a blessing in Romola's new matriarchy. The name she gives the child, 'Benedetto', of course literally means 'blessing'; but even beyond this obvious signal is the fact that she does not confer a patronymic on the child, instead he has a first name, that which implies familiarity rather than formality and avoids attaching him to any father.

Like the power of naming Benedetto, Romola's power in the village is directly related to her powers of speech.[11] In her new role Romola finds what she hoped she might find instead of death: a new duty of her own choice. Her awakening at the shore of the village, like Baldassarre's regaining his ability to read Greek, is both old and new. When he expects to see incomprehensible print, he is able to read, and Romola, who expects death, awakens into life. Baldassarre's relationship to Romola as her double finds another point of correspondence in Romola's wandering. Baldassarre moves from place to place before he finally comes to Florence and Romola drifts until her tiny boat lands. The difference, of course, is that Romola has no stated goal, while Baldassarre is bent on revenge. She has chosen not to choose, to suspend choice at this point in the novel where action itself is suspended.

Throughout the novel Romola, though an apparently passive character— with the exception of this one still point in her life when she sets herself afloat—mediates between characters and assists in a variety of situations. She acts as a buffer between Tessa and the overzealous crowd who are eager to relieve the young woman of her necklace because they see it as one of the vanities. Romola takes command as she orders the followers of Savonarola to leave Tessa alone. In another instance she intervenes and brings Tessa's little boy back to her after the child has run off. For Tessa, Romola and Tito are as gods who descend to help her in time of need. Tessa sees Romola as a 'heavenly lady'. By the time Romola intervenes on Tessa's behalf for a third time she knows of Tito and Tessa's relationship, but her concern is for Tessa. This time Romola brings the news that Tito has been murdered. Romola here replaces Tito as provider for Tessa and her children. Romola becomes the new head of the family. The triangle that has existed between Tito, Romola and Tessa, then, does not become reduced to a binary relationship if we see Romola in two roles here: protector (and thus substitute for Tito) and widow.

Romola has experience in the role of protector since she has aided the plague victims of Florence while she was under the auspices of Savonarola. This assistance, with Romola as nurse, acts as preparation for her later leadership in the village she 'escapes to'. In this novel, however, repetition gives us far more than simply more of the same situation. In each second case we see the change that has taken place. Romola in both final instances (final for the novel itself in the case of Romola's headship of the family) moves from passive to active. She moves beyond the margins of Florence as well as beyond the confines of the library, and almost moves beyond the limits of the novel's events when the narrator and she all but blend. She never participates in the realm of the written word that seems reserved for the male world. She will not be limited and deadened by that fixing of language and people, rather her power remains the power of the spoken word.

If the written word deadens within the world of the characters, then we must explore the possibility that the written word that makes up the novel itself could be an act of freezing meaning. In Eliot's case, and especially in *Romola*, however, the written word becomes the conveyor of the power of language and of the power of the spoken word. Thus, the pen itself does not constitute the problem or the means of limitation, but the wielder of the pen, the subject in question, does. In other words, just as Romola's letters do not arrive at their destinations because she, as sender or creator, destroys them, so the intentions of the creator of any message help determine the outcome of the effort. But Romola, through the spoken word, through creating her own narrative, goes from being the object of exchange to the subject in control. For Lacan, the letter takes on an independent existence and demands to be read, the word demands an answer, as he says in *Speech and Language in Psychoanalysis*.[12] Lacan privileges the system behind language and patriarchy, effectively ignoring the power of individual will, but Eliot acknowledges and celebrates the individual. At the same time, though, in Eliot's Florence the will of the father as part of the existing structure of the city, proves tenacious.

Romola, in order to act without that will of the father, must literally flee the physical environment which functions as home to male order. Rather than being 'hopelessly trapped',[13] Romola creates a household of meaning and takes control of her situation at the end of the novel.[14] Both Eliot and Lacan see that characters are indeed created by language and create themselves though language,[15] but Eliot shows herself far more willing to allow that subject formed by language a voice that, while it must work through language—the very medium that often has strong ties with oppression—can be part of a transformation that involves both speech and personal will.

Notes

1. See *George Eliot, A Writer's Notebook. 1854-1879*, ed. Joseph Wiesenfarth (Charlottesville: University Press of Virginia for the Bibliographical Society, 1981), pp. 75-82. Entries numbered 169 through 184 contain Eliot's notes on gems, signets and scarabs. Her notes provide a history of the development of the signet which, she points out, often bore the likeness of its owner. Thus, the signet, which replaced the seal as an identifying mark, is self-referential.

2. Jacques Lacan, *Écrits: A Selection*, trans. Alan Sheridan (New York and London: W. W. Norton and Company, 1977), p. 199.
3. Thanks are due to Elizabeth H. D. Mazzocco, Assistant Professor of Italian at the University of Massachusetts, for this point.
4. René Girard, *Deceit, Desire, and the Novel: Self and Other in Literary Structure*, trans. Yvonne Freccero (Baltimore: Johns Hopkins University Press, 1965).
5. Sandra M. Gilbert and Susan Gubar, *The Madwoman in the Attic: The Woman Writer and the Nineteenth Century Literary Imagination* (New Haven: Yale University Press, 1979), p. 527.
6. J. Hillis Miller, 'Ariadne's Thread', *Critical Inquiry* (Autumn 1976), p. 74.
7. Carol Martin, *George Eliot's Serial Fiction* (Columbus: Ohio State University Press, 1994), p. 152.
8. Jacques Lacan, *The Four Fundamental Concepts of Psycho-Analysis*, ed. Jacques-Alain Miller, trans. Alan Sheridan (New York and London: W.W. Norton and Company, 1981), p. 25.
9. Eugen S. Bär, 'Understanding Lacan', in eds Leo Goldberger and Victor H. Rosen, *Psychoanalysis and Contemporary Science: An Annual of Integrative and Interdisciplinary Studies*, vol. 3 (New York: International Universities Press, 1974), pp. 473-544.
10. Neil Hertz, 'The Notion of Blockage in the Literature of the Sublime', in *The End of the Line: Essays on Psychoanalysis and the Sublime* (New York: Columbia University Press, 1985), p. 60.
11. Curiously, Margaret Homans claims 'that it is primarily as an object of vision that Romola becomes the Holy Mother for the villagers'. See her *Bearing the Word: Language and Female Experience in Nineteenth-Century Women's Writing* (Chicago and London: University of Chicago Press, 1986), p. 206.
12. Jacques Lacan, *Speech and Language in Psychoanalysis*, trans. Anthony Wilden (Baltimore: Johns Hopkins University Press, 1968), p. 9.
13. Laurie Langbauer, *Women and Romance: The Consolations of Gender in the English Novel* (Ithaca and London: Cornell University Press, 1990), p. 191.
14. Alison Booth, *Greatness Engendered: George Eliot and Virginia Woolf*, (Ithaca and London: Cornell University Press, 1992), p. 191.
15. Lacan, *Écrits*, p. 362.

PART THREE
Rethinking Authority

CHAPTER SIX

George Eliot Martyrologist:
The Case of Savonarola

DAVID CARROLL

I

George Eliot frequently expressed a fear, at times amounting to horror, that the living spirit of historical development would become entrapped, permanently confined in the prison of past forms, institutions and conventions. True progress was a life or death struggle:

> Our civilization, and, yet more, our religion, are an anomalous blending of lifeless barbarisms, which have descended to us like so many petrifactions from distant ages, with living ideas, the offspring of a true process of development. We are in bondage to terms and conceptions which, having had their root in conditions of thought no longer existing, have ceased to possess any vitality, and are for us as spells which have lost their virtue.[1]

This is the reason why terms and conceptions upon which we still rely have to be continually redefined to embody the living ideas by which we live. In no area was this task more pressing than in that of religious belief, and one way of reading George Eliot's *oeuvre* is to see it as a sustained attempt to recast the lexicon of Christianity in terms applicable to an age about to embrace the religion of humanity. This redefinition, begun in *Scenes of Clerical Life* with terms such as faith, incarnation, redemption, providence, life after death, judgement and justification, is continued throughout her career.

Romola is George Eliot's radical attempt to redefine for her Victorian readers the idea of martyrdom, through the life and death of Savonarola. This was to prove difficult terrain for the novelist as she explored the complex and contradictory motives of the Dominican priest expressed in the contemporaneous records and their multiple interpretations. It is a difficulty re-created in the novel as Romola agonizes over Savonarola's confessions and retractions. One might add that even an official martyr's freely chosen death provides a 'witness' which is not without its ambiguities and uncertainties. As the Catholic theologian, Karl Rahner, explains:

> For it might be asked whether the death of a martyr is in fact exempt
> from the general law that every moral decision remains ultimately
> enigmatic, for oneself and certainly for others? [...] Even in the case of a
> martyr's death, does not the radical problem still remain unanswered
> whether an act which is good in itself is necessarily good in execution,
> and whether anything that we see happening will remain valid when it is
> weighed upon God's scale.[2]

The orthodox answer he provides to these questions is that the Church
bestows the divine validation: 'Church and martyrdom bear witness to one
another'.[3] But what if, as with Savonarola, the so-called martyr is the
Church's victim? What validation is available to the heretic and schismatic?
This is the challenge George Eliot faces in *Romola* as she continues her
programme of the humanistic redefinition of Christian concepts and ideas in a
fictional world emptied of divine sanction.

There were also more specific reasons why her interest focused on this
enigmatic historical figure. The most immediate was that the Florence of
1860, in which George Henry Lewes suggested to the novelist that the
Dominican priest might be a good subject for a novel, was a hotbed of
speculation over the significance of his life. Could his ideas about the
reformation of Florence and Italy provide inspiration and guidance to the
rising excitement of the Risorgimento? For the New Piagnoni historians,
named after Savonarola's original followers, they certainly could, and the
Convent of San Marco became the meeting-place where they began to collect
and edit his sermons, letters and treatises. The reconstruction of his life at
which they aimed was accomplished by the Neapolitan professor, Pasquale
Villari, who had fled to Florence from Bourbon persecution in 1848. His fine
biography, *La storia di Girolamo Savonarola e de' suoi tempi*, appeared in
two volumes, in 1859 and 1861, and it may well have been the first volume of
this work that Lewes was reading when he suggested to the novelist that
Savonarola's 'life and times [would] afford fine material for an historical
romance' (*Letters*, III, 295).

Secondly, there was the appeal for George Eliot of the place and
significance of Savonarola in the Positivist pantheon. As J. B. Bullen
indicates, 'In Comte's chronology, Savonarola comes at perhaps the most
crucial moment in the moral history of the West. He was situated at that point
where the final stage of the Theological era—Monotheism—has begun to
decay and the revolutionary Metaphysical period has been initiated'.[4] His
pivotal position in several synthetic philosophies and histories of this kind
helps to account for the many conflicting interpretations of his life in
mid-nineteenth century Europe.[5] Villari, for example, presents Savonarola as
the champion of Florentine liberty against the tyranny of the Medicis. He
maintains that the Dominican, combining the best qualities of the Middle

Ages and the Renaissance, sought, like Columbus, to create new worlds: 'theirs is the prophetic mind, the hero's heart, the martyr's fate'.[6] Here were values to inspire the Risorgimento. But there were other, more sceptical views. Jacob Burckhardt in *The Civilization of the Renaissance in Italy* (1860) made a clear and influential demarcation between the Middle Ages and the Renaissance, and depicted Savonarola as a monk unable to come to terms with the modern world taking shape around him: 'He was at bottom the most unsuitable man who could be found for such a work [.] He stood in no more relation to mundane affairs and their actual conditions than any other inhabitant of a monastery'.[7]

How does one interpret the evidence of a life lived, as Savonarola's was, at the cusp of European historical change in the fifteenth century and now again in retrospect, in the nineteenth? The closest George Eliot had come to the topic in her previous fiction was in the provincial life and death of the Revd Edgar Tryan, the public reformer of small-town Milby in 'Janet's Repentance'. The Evangelicalism he brought 'was good, though it had that mixture of folly and evil which often makes what is good an offence to feeble and fastidious minds, who want human actions and characters riddled through the sieve of their own ideas, before they can afford their sympathy or admiration'.[8] Tryan can easily be labelled—'One of the Evangelical clergy, a disciple of Venn'—but this obscures any genuine understanding. In *Romola*, as in this early fiction, '[T]he mysteries of human character have seldom been presented in a way more fitted to check the judgments of facile knowingness than in Girolamo Savonarola' (238). The 'bird's-eye glance' of the critic or historian with their 'analysis of schools and sects'[9] must be replaced by the rather different forensic skills of the novelist. A historical romance might provide some answers.

Finally, the life and death of Savonarola provided the novelist with an opportunity to re-examine not simply the conventions of the Victorian historical novel but, more especially, those of its once popular sub-genre: the novel of martyrdom. This had achieved a new level of popularity as a result of the 'No Popery' agitation following the restoration of the Roman Catholic hierarchy in England in 1850.[10] Charles Kingsley's novel of Christian martyrdom, *Hypatia: or, New Foes with an Old Face* (1853), came out of that agitation. Though set in Alexandria early in the fifth century, its aim was to attack the 'new foes' of Tractarianism and Catholicism through the life and death of the heroine, the beautiful Neoplatonist lecturer in pagan philosophy, murdered by the mob, which included rioting monks, on the high altar as she was about to be converted to Christianity. The response of Cardinal Wiseman, the recently created Archbishop of Westminster, was to initiate 'The Catholic Popular Library' whose aim was to present a true picture of the Church through the ages; its launch provides a fascinating insight into the role of fiction in mid-Victorian England. He himself quickly produced the first novel for the Library, *Fabiola: or, The Church of the Catacombs* (1854). Again, a haughty Roman heiress, living in Rome during the last of the Imperial persecutions under Diocletian, is gradually converted to Christianity through contact with a series of Christians, several of whom are martyred in very specifically unpleasant ways. Newman was then prevailed upon to complete the twelfth volume in the series, *Callista: a Sketch of the Third Century* (1856), a novel which carried its pedagogy more lightly than Wiseman's but otherwise followed the same plan: the heroine is a beautiful Greek sculptor living in North Africa who, through contact with Christians at the time of a fresh outburst of persecutions, is slowly and painfully converted to Christianity just before she dies brutally tortured for refusing to sacrifice to the Emperor. On the rack she makes her final witness in language typical of the genre: 'For Thee, my Lord and Love, for Thee! ... Accept me, O my Love, upon this bed of pain! ... And come to me, O my Love, make haste and come!'[11]

Though written by men, these novels contain features similar to the fictions George Eliot had labelled 'the modern-antique species' in her satirical taxonomy of 'Silly Novels by Lady Novelists' (1856) written at this time. These 'unfold to us the domestic life of Jannes and Jambres, the private love affairs of Sennacherib, or the mental struggles and ultimate conversion of Demetrius the silversmith'. Her critical comments are two-pronged. On the one hand she ridicules these novels which, possessing 'a ponderous, a leaden kind of fatuity, under which we groan', contain characters 'converted to Christianity after the shortest and easiest method approved by the "Society for Promoting the Conversion of the Jews"', and who use such racy, idiomatic phrases as 'the expiring scion of a lofty stem'—'the virtuous partner of his couch'—'ah, by Vestal!'—and 'I tell thee, Roman'. But, on the other hand, she uses the opportunity to define the true nature of the historical imagination. It is a power, she writes, which will always be 'among the very rarest, because it demands as much accurate and minute knowledge as creative vigour', but it 'can sometimes, by the force of its sympathetic divination, restore the missing notes in the "music of humanity", and reconstruct the fragments into a whole which will really bring the remote past nearer to us, and interpret it to our duller apprehension'.[12] Written a few days before she began her first short story, this essay, we now realize, is both a critical and an aesthetic manifesto, similar in many ways to Jane Austen's and Thackeray's early parodies. Just as her ironic comments on 'the white neck-cloth species' of fiction prompted a definition of 'the real drama of Evangelicalism',[13] which in turn led shortly after to 'Janet's Repentance', so the critique of the 'modern-antique species' prepared the way for *Romola*.

There are, of course, significant differences between the sub-genre described so far and George Eliot's novel. One of the most obvious is that the former fictions are usually located in the early Christian centuries during periods of persecution when pagan and Christian forces were in violent conflict. But it is clearly possible to see George Eliot's Renaissance Florence as a reprise of that conflict. Just as the conversion of the Emperor Constantine in 312 is anticipated as the origin of the universal church in those novels, so the events in Florence in the 1490s are presented as the birth of modern European civilization. A second major difference is that the role of the martyred saint is in *Romola* shared between the martyred Savonarola and the saintly Romola. As we shall see, the latter's chief task—after playing the part of the Madonna, 'the sweet and sainted Lady' (566), in the plague-stricken village—is to interpret the life and death of the former to the world, having lived through his agonized conflicts in her domestic life.

Despite these differences, it remains striking how many of the elements in Newman's *Callista*, which is typical of the species, recur, suitably transformed, in *Romola*. The patrician and high-minded heroine belongs, like Romola, to hagiography rather than to realistic fiction. Callista, too, undergoes a gradual conversion through contact with a series of male protagonists, each of whom represents a strand of belief from pagan or Christian antiquity. Her final spiritual experience is in the form of a dream: 'She slept sound; she dreamed. She thought she was no longer in Africa, but in her own Greece, more sunny and bright than before; but the inhabitants were gone';[14] in this heavenly landscape there appears her Christian slave-girl, who is first transformed into the Madonna, then into the resurrected Christ before a sudden cry alerts her to the reality of her imminent capture and trial. Then, there is the careful recording and cautious assessment of Callista's trial documents which have come down to us, to the second of which, comments the narrator, 'we attach no such special value [...] since it comes to us through heathen notaries, who may not have been accurate reporters'.[15] Finally, there is the worship of the martyr's sacred relics and the subsequent healing miracles which correspond to Savonarola's shrine and his afterlife of sacred memory celebrated on 23 May, the birthday—the *dies natalis*—of his martyrdom, in the Epilogue to *Romola*.

Behind such similarities of detail there are the more profound similarities which originate in the traditional patterns of the lives of saints and martyrs. These go back to the *Acts of the Martyrs* in the first Christian centuries, and are repeated in various forms through the Middle Ages, the Reformation and counter-Reformation, especially the latter as recorded in Foxe's *Acts and Monuments*.[16] We will look at the type of the female saint's life later when we examine Romola's role in Savonarola's martyrdom, but his life and death follow the pattern established originally by Stephen, the first Christian martyr, in the Acts of the Apostles: his witness, persecution, arrest, trial, condemnation, execution, canonization. All the novelists writing in this sub-genre deploy this dramatic sequence in some form or other. How does George Eliot use it and other features of the genre in the re-creation of Savonarola in her own novel of martyrdom?

II

There are essentially four phases in Savonarola's public career in *Romola,* extending from the arrival of Charles VIII in Florence in 1494 to the excommunicated priest's trial and death in 1498. It is a clearly defined sequence of increasing complexity and ambiguity as events exert a steady pressure upon his religious beliefs. The first phase of this developing martyrdom is the most orthodox. On 17 November 1494 the French army enters Florence—the day on which Savonarola is preaching his Advent sermon in the Duomo, the climax of his warnings to the city. In the style of a Hebrew prophet he warns the Florentines that the Bible 'showed that when the wickedness of the chosen people, type of the Christian Church, had become crying, the judgments of God had descended on them' (211). His lengthy sermon in chapter 24 is an elaborate typological interpretation of current events: the French army is the 'new deluge which was to purify the earth from iniquity' (213); the French king is the new Cyrus, God's chosen instrument; Italy is the promised land; and Florence its sanctuary.

The sermon begins by exposing the pollution of the city, the sanctuary from which God's presence has departed. Savonarola attacks Florentine corruption with such vehemence because God 'has made his purpose present to my soul in the living word of the Scriptures; and in the deeds of his providence; and by the ministry of angels he has revealed it to me in visions'. This opening condemnation ends with the warning: 'Behold! the ministers of his wrath are upon thee—they are at thy very doors!' (229). Like so many other characters in Romola—like Dino, Tito, Bardo, Baldassarre—he imposes his own vision upon the turbulent city. Look! See! It is all so clear. But there is a pause, he believes, before judgement, a time for repentance with the sword of vengeance hanging over the city. The tyrants and the unbelieving priests will be punished under the old covenant, but the new covenant offers hope and forgiveness: 'But thou, O Florence, take the offered mercy. See! the Cross is held out to you: come and be healed' (231). But everything hostile to true religion must be destroyed. And then, after the admonitions and promises, the sermon modulates into entreaty as Savonarola offers himself ('Take me, stretch me on thy cross') as a sacrifice for the city: 'let my witness be remembered among men, that iniquity shall not prosper for ever' (232). This should be the martyr-witness's crowning moment as he proclaims the true faith in the face of danger and imminent death: 'A loud responding sob rose at once from the wide multitude, while Savonarola had fallen on his knees and buried his face in his mantle. He felt in that moment the rapture and glory of martyrdom without its agony' (232). This, however, is the closest he is to come to the genuine martyrdom of the saints; the agony will come later but without either the rapture or the glory.

In general, one may say that the dilemmas, defeats and deaths in *Romola* occur when the intense Renaissance mythic visions, Christian or pagan, become entangled in the gritty realities of Florentine life. This is the case with Savonarola. The threat to his dramatic and clear-cut typology is already implicit in its power: 'one secret of the massive influence lay in the highly mixed character of his preaching' (237), which appeals to a 'heterogeneous' audience whose loyalty he will need to sustain by a variety of means. At the time of the Advent sermon this has not yet become apparent. Only later will his mixed personality and the mixed audience seek increasingly desperate accommodation, 'And up to this period, when his more direct action on political affairs had only just begun, it is probable that his imperious need of ascendancy had burned undiscernibly in the strong flame of his zeal for God and man' (238). The 'probably' announces, even at this stage of Savonarola's career, George Eliot's scepticism about the unified, unwavering faith of the martyr celebrated in the novels of Kingsley, Wiseman and Newman and their early Christian models.

By the time of Savonarola's Lenten sermons in 1495, the second phase of his public career, complications are apparent. With excommunication imminent, the attempt to balance the roles of priest and politician is becoming increasingly precarious. This-worldly and other-worldly imperatives alternate without reconciliation: 'As to his own destiny, he seemed to have a double and alternating prevision: sometimes he saw himself taking a glorious part in that revolt [against the Church] [...] sometimes he saw no prospect for himself but persecution and martyrdom:—this life for him was only a vigil, and only after death would come the dawn' (444-5). This oscillation becomes apparent to his audience when self-vindication and personal exasperation begin to mingle with his religious zeal. For the novelist there is an inevitability in this process: 'In the career of a great public orator who yields himself to the inspiration of the moment, that conflict of selfish and unselfish emotion which in most men is hidden in the chamber of the soul, is brought into terrible evidence: the language of the inner voices is written out in letters of fire' (446). In other words, doubleness becomes the key to the way in which George Eliot's martyr sees and is seen; it is in the chamber of the soul that Savonarola's canonization will be determined. Tito (and his friend Machiavelli) are sympathetic to the selfish motives, Romola to the idealism; both sides are baffled by anything which conflicts with these.

From an early age George Eliot had shown herself to be fascinated by the intricate and shifting relationship between the self and the not-self, self-assertion and self-denial, especially in the lives of public figures. In a letter to her teacher, Maria Lewis, in 1842, she refers apologetically to her own egoism and then comments:

> But where is not this same ego? The martyr at the stake seeks its gratification as much as the court sycophant, the difference lying in the comparative dignity and beauty of the two egos. People absurdly talk of self-denial—why there is none in Virtue to a being of moral excellence—the greatest torture to such a soul would be to run counter to the dictates of conscience, to wallow in the slough of meanness, deception, revenge or sensuality. (*Letters*, I, 27)[17]

The same hermeneutic of suspicion is applied to Mr Tryan 15 years later in *Scenes of Clerical Life*. Surely, says the narrator, the clergyman's reforms, however difficult, were simply 'carrying out objects which were identified not only with his theory, which is but a kind of secondary egoism, but also with the primary egoism of his feelings'. In such a situation, persecution may even become desirable: 'a self-obtrusive, over-hasty reformer complacently disclaiming all merit, while his friends call him a martyr, has not in reality a career the most arduous to the fleshly mind'. But Tryan is redeemed from this charge; he is 'not cast in the mould of the gratuitous martyr'[18] since his keen sensitivity and dependence on people's sympathy make him wince in private at the hatred and ridicule he provokes. It is here in the private conflict between high ideals and inner doubts that the martyr's true witness is to be found.

The third phase of Savonarola's martyrdom occurs in February 1497 with his rejection of the Pope's authority, his subsequent excommunication, and the botched trial by fire. Now the scrutiny of his motives becomes even more intense as he is deprived of any external authority for his attempts to reform Florence. Official martyrdom is out of the question; this is when he becomes what George Eliot names 'a sacred rebel' (533), the next step towards his final secular martyrdom. As Romola also learns, 'The law was sacred. Yes, but rebellion might be sacred too [...] To her, as to him, there had come one of those moments in life when the soul must dare to act on its own warrant' (474). But how to act when the self must authenticate itself, especially when the Florentines are demanding a miraculous sign—preferably a trial by fire— as the price of their allegiance. Again, the typological vision is being forcibly dragged into the marketplace, and now it is not only the political conflict of law and rebellion which makes clear decision impossible but also Savonarola's inability to reconcile the two sides of his nature. He believes in miracles but he is also vividly aware of the realities of the fiery trial:

> Savonarola's nature was one of those in which opposing tendencies co-
> exist in almost equal strength: the passionate sensibility which, impatient
> of definite thought, floods every idea with emotion and tends towards
> contemplative ecstasy, alternated in him with a keen perception of
> outward facts and a vigorous practical judgment of men and things.
> (531)

These are the contrary states that George Eliot is balancing so meticulously in
order to create her own definition of the martyred conscience, a kind of
perpetual oscillation: 'The conflict was one that could not end' (533).

As the trial by fire approaches, the conflict within Savonarola of outward
confidence and inward doubt is sharpened excruciatingly: 'the doubleness
which is the pressing temptation in every public career, whether of priest,
orator or statesman, was more strongly defined in Savonarola's consciousness
as the acting of a part, than at any other period in his life. He was struggling
not against impending martyrdom, but against impending ruin' (539). And
when the trial becomes a fiasco, a parody of the martyr's final act of witness,
the discrepancy in his behaviour becomes publicly apparent. He had said he
was prepared to die for the sake of Florence: 'But to die in dishonour—held
up to scorn as a hypocrite and a false prophet? "O God! *that* is not
martyrdom! It is the blotting out of a life that has been a protest against
wrong"' (543). And yet, for George Eliot, this is a necessary purging in a
world where 'the complications of life make self inseparable from a purpose
which is not selfish' (539). Her kind of martyr must not be allowed to enjoy
the satisfactions of either primary or secondary egoism. This is confirmed
when the Frate is arrested by the guards of the Signoria and dragged along to
prison: 'the worst drop of bitterness can never be wrung on to our lips from
without: the lowest depths of resignation is not to be found in martyrdom; it is
only to be found when we have covered our heads in silence and felt, "I am
not worthy to be a martyr: the Truth shall prosper, but not by me"' (546).

The final phase of Savonarola's career is an agonized recapitulation of its
previous three phases in the confessions extracted by interrogation and
torture. His supporters and opponents interpret these in contradictory ways
according to their own needs. It is left to Romola to provide greater insight.
The confession, she realizes, is a reliving by the priest of the three phases we
have already examined. First, there is the self-confidence of the reformer,
'[t]hat blending of ambition with belief in the supremacy of goodness', with
George Eliot's characteristically cautious rider: 'In moments of ecstatic
contemplation, doubtless, the sense of self melted in the sense of the
Unspeakable' (579). The confession then acknowledges, secondly, the
duplicity into which Savonarola was forced and which the novelist is quick to
exonerate: 'And perhaps this confession, even when it described doubleness
that was conscious and deliberate, really implied no more than that wavering

of belief concerning his own impressions and motives which most human beings who have not a stupid inflexibility of self-confidence must be liable to under a marked change of external conditions' (579). The martyr is like the rest of us; inflexibility would have been stupid. Then the third phase of the priest's career is recalled and repeated in his prison writings after the torturers have finished their work, after the claims, the retractions and the retractions of the retractions. Self-vindication and self-assertion are now replaced by self-abasement. The voice of Sadness tells him: 'thou, by thy pride and vainglory, hast scandalized all the world'; while Hope can only reassure him that 'Thou art not forsaken, else why is thy heart bowed in penitence?' (580-81).

This is George Eliot's redefinition of Christian martyrdom: the final realization and acceptance by Savonarola must be that he is not fit to be a martyr. Under interrogation he is forced to relive his public career confessionally with its three phases—the self-confident vision, the vacillating doubleness, the self-abasement—so as to be left in no doubt. And here the comments of Romola modulate into those of the novelist: 'There is no jot of worthy evidence that from the time of his imprisonment to the supreme moment, Savonarola thought or spoke of himself as a martyr' (581). There is to be no triumphalism, not even the comfort of the last words asserting his faith for which Romola waits in vain at his execution. This was too much for some contemporary critics who complained that George Eliot, too, was tampering with the record for her own prejudiced purposes. Richard Holt Hutton, for example, despite his admiration for the novel, reminds his readers of Savonarola's final bold response to his excommunication, as given in Villari: 'No, not from the Church triumphant, they cannot shut me out from that', and feels consequently that 'George Eliot's conception of the great Reformer probably lost power in consequence of her own deep distrust of religious faith and her reluctance to conceive of it except as a kind of noble self-deception'.[19]

In addition, of course, there is to be no promise of life after death towards which the Christian martyrs hasten in confidence. 'The idea of martyrdom had been to him a passion dividing the dream of the future with the triumph of beholding his work achieved'. The moral reform of Florence and Italy was the only future allowed in his idea of martyrdom and with its failure has come 'resignation which he called by no glorifying name'. This stoical endurance of failure provides the final italicized imprimatur: *'But therefore he may the more fitly be called a martyr by his fellow-men to all time'*. His greatness consisted of his attempt to make the world noble and it was this which destroyed him: 'And through that greatness of his he endured a double agony'—torture and death as well as 'the agony of sinking from the vision of glorious achievement into that deep shadow where he could only say, "I count as nothing: darkness encompasses me: yet the light I saw was the true light"'

(581). At the beginning of his reforms, as we saw, Savonarola acted out the glory and rapture of martyrdom without its agony; now only the agony remains. This 'double agony',[20] private and public, his Gethsemane and Crucifixion, is the end of the process which has removed every trace of egoism and duplicity from his ambitions in Florence. The early Christians also saw martyrdom as a means of purification—but in their case it was a second baptism which initiated a new life; this, however, is reserved for the heroine. Savonarola's martyrdom has removed any belief or faith in a spiritual power to which the martyred self might make its final witness.

III

In this redefinition of martyrdom it is the saintly Romola, not the Church, who carries out the final reassessment and canonization of Savonarola. Her status has been established by the repeated comparisons to Saint Catherine of Egypt, to the Madonna, to the Holy Mother, the Blessed Lady and, finally, to the 'sweet and sainted Lady' (526) from over the sea. As Gillian Beer has observed, 'It is as though the only discourse which George Eliot can trust when she seeks to express the vision of woman coming to authority is that of the saint's legend'.[21] Equally important is the trajectory of her career in the novel which is similar in many ways to the heroines of the novels of martyrdom mentioned earlier. Just as they encounter a series of informants, opponents, and guides who lead them gradually but inevitably towards Christian conversion, so Romola's intense relationships with her father, brother, husband, godfather and priest define the course of her reformation. This is a type of narrative which has a long history, as Thomas J. Heffernan points out in *Sacred Biography*, his study of saints and their biographers in the Middle Ages. Renunciation of the world is a lengthy process:

> It can only be accomplished by a series of struggles with male protagonists [...] Typically, her first dispute is with her father; the next, being with someone who is also a suitor, is fraught with sexual overtones; and the last, when she is fully matured in her belief, is political, being with the representative of the state. In all three of these contests, the saints' lives exemplify the maid's intelligence (she defeats all comers in offering a rationale for her newfound religion), her irresistible beauty (all of her interlocutors, including the parent, are physically attracted to her), and her insistence on principle (she is killed for her belief).[22]

Or sometimes she survives, like Wiseman's Fabiola, who becomes the witness to the martyrdom of Saint Sebastian.

Romola's education, which is a similar series of struggles and renunciations, enables her to come to an eventual understanding of Savonarola's martyrdom and its implications for the future of humanity. She is, after all, the daughter of a classical scholar, the wife of a pagan god and the catechumen of a Christian prophet. But, more significantly, she sees through and rejects, as Felicia Bonaparte has shown in convincing detail, a variety of world views which represent the history of European civilization as it is epitomized in Renaissance Florence. In each case, Romola is appropriated by these powerful male visions until she comes to discern, in turn, their inner contradictions. The appropriations usually begin with an annunciation. Dino tells her that his dying vision 'is a revelation meant for thee [...] it calls upon thee to dedicate thyself' (162); Tito appears as an image of 'bright youthfulness, as of a sun-god' holding out a dream of pastoral bliss; while Savonarola offers the Cross: 'Conform your life to that image' (364).

Romola seeks to live according to these prescriptions until she discerns in each case the conflict between their grand designs and natural human affections. In a complex series of permutations she is first appropriated, then resists and finally rebels, using the rationale of their world views against the mentors who are promoting them. Their views are both subsumed and superseded in her expanding vision of human possibilities as she relives the main epochs of European history, experiencing a series of personal renaissances. The most significant and agonizing of these rebellions is against Savonarola himself, who has taught her the meaning of sacred rebellion which she now asserts in defence of her godfather: 'Father, you yourself declare that there comes a moment when the soul must have no guide but the voice within, to tell whether the consecrated thing has sacred virtue. And therefore I must speak' (497). The weaknesses and self-contradictions of the various Florentine world views become apparent as their proponents seek to systematize and institutionalize their insights under the pressure of local, political and social realities. Romola then becomes their assessor and judge. The saint remains outside culture. Though apparently appropriated, she always remains semi-detached from complete discipleship. Her response to her father's Stoical maxims, for example, is that '[she] had endured and forborne because she loved [...] She had appropriated no theories: she had simply felt strong in the strength of affection' (325-6). Each restrictive world view, philosophy, theory or religion is tested to destruction and rejected.

This is the point in the life of the orthodox saint when she would be baptized into the Christian faith and martyred like Hypatia or Callista. For Romola the sequence is secularized. With all her options closed, she drifts away in her boat and finally 'dies' to the world: 'Presently she felt that she was in the grave, but not resting there: she was touching the hands of the beloved dead beside her, and trying to wake them' (511). But she wakes in 'a village of the unburied dead' (561) with its call to action and duty, an answer to her earlier troubled question: 'What force was there to create for her that supremely hallowed motive which men call duty, but which can have no inward constraining existence save through some form of believing love?' (507). It is the experience in the plague-stricken village which answers this question with 'a new baptism' (567) after all else has failed. For George Eliot, this is the saint's sanctification—'she had simply lived, with so energetic an impulse to share the life around her, to answer the call of need and do the work which cried aloud to be done, that the reasons for living, enduring, labouring, never took the form of argument' (567). Here is the novelist's essentialism: 'she had simply lived'. The saint finally frees herself from all the debris of history and civilization, declares her faith in unmediated 'life', and becomes, at the end of a sequence of annunciations, 'the Holy Mother with the Babe' (563). These culminating events, the novelist acknowledged, 'were by deliberate forecast adopted as romantic and symbolical elements' beyond the confines of realist fiction (*Letters*, IV, 104).

When Romola returns to Florence she is given the task of interpreting Savonarola's confession in order to make an estimate of his life. She is qualified to do this because she understands the reason for his various confessions and retractions. As George Eliot comments in one of her own intimidating generalizations: 'All minds, except such as are delivered from doubt by dulness of sensibility, must be subject to this recurring conflict where the many-twisted conditions of life have forbidden the fulfilment of a bond' (568). Romola has herself experienced a similar series of apostasies in freeing herself from her mentors and knows from this experience that all systems of belief are in the last resort untenable, a fact which ultimately destroys Savonarola's mission in the world as the doubleness of his life oscillates out of control. She recognizes in the three distinct phases of his career this inevitable dismantling process; for him, however, there is no escape out of history into symbol and romance. In his own final rejection of the title of martyr he comes to share in this recognition; only his purity of motive redeems him. In George Eliot's scheme of things there are no spiritual authorities, no principles of belief—her dreaded theories, maxims, doctrines—for which the self is worth sacrificing. And finally, Romola understands him uniquely because she has been empowered by his (holy) spirit to experience the new baptism of her life in the village. She now comes to see her rejection of Savonarola, 'the man who had been for her an incarnation of the highest motives' (577), as her dark night of the soul which had 'produced a reaction which is known to many as a sort of faith that has sprung up to them out of the very depths of their despair' (538). In other words, the rejection of her final mentor indicates that, while his beliefs have been superseded, the essential purity of his motives has been subsumed in her instinctive actions: 'Impossible that it had not been a living spirit, and no hollow pretence, which had once breathed in the Frate's words, and kindled a new life in her' (578). To return to our opening quotation, this is the life-or-death struggle through which the living spirit frees itself from the 'barbarisms' and the 'petrifactions from distant ages'. And it is the gift of this spirit which now enables Romola to approach the documents of the priest's confession with insight and sympathy—and to declare with the narrator that he is a martyr in a new sense of that term. He is a martyr because he rejected the title of martyr.

Underpinning the lives of both martyr and saint is the basic pattern of life itself, as George Eliot expresses it in various ways in her writings, and it is in this context that Savonarola and Romola can finally be understood. This pattern is envisaged as a disruptive rhythm in which a theory of life is first formed, then subjected to the rigours of experience, after which it inevitably collapses into meaninglessness. 'None of our theories are quite large enough for all the disclosures of time', says the narrator in *Felix Holt*.[23] But the process continues: a new coherence and wholeness is discovered in the fragments of the old and the rhythm repeats itself endlessly. One of the most personal and vivid descriptions of this process appears in the well-known letter of 1848 which dramatizes 'the fate of poor mortals' waking up to find that their 'poetry or religion' has been replaced by the 'naked prose' of the world. 'It is so in all the stages of life [...] and at last the very poetry of duty forsakes us for a season and we see ourselves and all about us as nothing more than miserable agglomerations of atoms'. But this 'state of prostration— the self-abnegation through which the soul must go' is essential if life is to retain its vitality and meaning (*Letters*, I, 264). This is the experimental or hypothetical model of life which proceeds by repeated falsifications. And what is true for the individual is true for society and civilization as one myth or religion succeeds another.

The difference between the martyr and the saint in George Eliot's scheme of things is that the former dies acquiring this knowledge, the latter lives by it. Savonarola is trapped within his own epoch, not realizing that his religious beliefs are a mythical hypothesis which will inevitably be superseded. If this is the case, then specific beliefs become secondary to the kind of humanitarianism they engender. Richard Simpson saw this clearly in his review of George Eliot's career, published in October 1863, two months after the final part of Romola appeared in the *Cornhill Magazine*. His liberal Catholic reaction to the novel helps us to place George Eliot's redefinition of martyrdom in a clear Victorian perspective. The novelist, he writes, accepts Savonarola's dubious methods because 'by such means he strove "to turn beliefs into energies" for the very highest end'. This confirms Simpson in his critique of the Religion of Humanity as he applies his own hermeneutic of suspicion to the novel:

Now here is a dishonesty inseparable from positivist religion, in which religious belief does not correspond to objective truth, but is only an impression on the imagination, useful to excite, direct, and give energy to the feelings. It is necessarily transient and unstable; here to-day, gone to-morrow. Yet the religious teacher of men must pretend that his own faith is firm, or he will not confirm that of his hearers. 'It is the lot of every man who has to speak for the satisfaction of the crowd, that he must speak in virtue of yesterday's faith, hoping it will come back to-morrow' (chap. lxii); just as George Eliot preaches yesterday's Christianity, but without the corresponding hope. It is the misery of religion, she says, that it should have so much of superstition and conscious imposture at its roots (chap. lii); that it should be at once necessary, and founded upon falsehood. And this, we may add, is the condemnation of positivist religion, that it justifies falsehood and imposture, by making them the necessary roots of religious energy, which, again, is necessary for the moral advancement of mankind. It founds morality on falsehood, and roots up honour from the religious mind.[24]

Whereas the traditional martyr dies for his religious beliefs, Savonarola becomes a martyr by witnessing agonizingly their inevitable destruction, only holding on desperately to the purity of motive which energized them in the first place: 'the light I saw was the true light'. Only by disclaiming the title of public martyr can he safeguard his pure humanitarianism from the taint of religious belief.

On the other hand, the saint in this scheme of things passes through the apparent cul-de-sac of unyielding beliefs and doctrines time after time in her apostasies, to the death of a new baptism, and finally to 'life' itself. Having experienced the positivist truth that all religions are, in fact, myths, she herself becomes a myth to the villagers. But it is the blood of the martyr Savonarola which is the seed of the modern world Romola comes to represent, the Renaissance breakthrough into a new reality where the terms martyr and saint become thoroughly secularized and domesticated. In provincial Middlemarch, for example, 'a world with no coherent social faith or order',[25] there is a sense in which everyone is a martyr as their reality never measures up to their ideals. And this is supremely the case with the saintly Dorothea who was 'likely to seek martyrdom, to make retractations, and then to incur martyrdom after all in a quarter where she had not sought it'.[26] She is like 'the boy in the legend', Ladislaw suggests, the ninth-century Scandinavian missionary whose martyrdom was not to be the martyr he had spent his life anticipating.[27] Martyrdom ultimately becomes another term for the human condition in the sombre world of George Eliot's fiction and it is in Romola that the implications of this redefinition are most fully revealed: 'if the glory of the cross is an illusion, the sorrow is only the truer' (567).

Notes

1. 'The Progress of the Intellect', in *George Eliot: Selected Critical Writings,* ed. Rosemary Ashton (Oxford: Oxford University Press, 1992), pp. 18-19.
2. Karl Rahner, 'On Martyrdom', in *On the Theology of Death* (New York: Herder and Herder, 1961), p. 99.
3. Ibid., p. 104.
4. J. B. Bullen, *The Myth of the Renaissance in Nineteenth-Century Writing* (Oxford: Clarendon Press, 1994), p. 222.
5. One of the best accounts of these conflicting views is to be found in Donald Weinstein, *Savonarola and Florence: Prophecy and Patriotism in the Renaissance* (Princeton: Princeton University Press, 1970).
6. Pasquale Villari, *Life and Times of Girolamo Savonarola*, trans. Linda Villari (London: Fisher Unwin, 1896), p. 771.
7. Jacob Burckhardt, *The Civilization of the Renaissance in Italy*, trans. S. G. C. Middlemore (London: Harrap, 1929), p. 460.
8. George Eliot, *Scenes of Clerical Life,* ed. Thomas A. Noble (Oxford: Clarendon Press, 1985), p. 256.
9. Ibid., p. 257.
10. See Robert Lee Wolf, *Gains and Losses: Novels of Faith and Doubt in Victorian England* (New York and London: Garland, 1977), especially chapters 1 and 4.
11. John Henry Newman, *Callista: a Sketch of the Third Century* (London: Burns and Lambert, 1856), p. 286.
12. 'Silly Novels by Lady Novelists', in *George Eliot: Selected Critical Writings*, ed. Rosemary Ashton (Oxford: Oxford University Press, 1992), pp. 316-17.
13. Ibid., pp. 313, 315.
14. Newman, pp. 275-76.
15. Ibid., p. 279.
16. See, for example, John R. Knott, *Discourses of Martyrdom* in *English Literature, 1563-1694* (Cambridge: Cambridge University Press, 1993).
17. Quoted by Felicia Bonaparte in her invaluable study of *Romola, The Triptych and the Cross: The Central Myths of George Eliot's Poetic Imagination* (New York: New York University Press, 1979), p. 215.
18. Eliot, *Scenes of Clerical Life*, p. 246.
19. Richard Holt Hutton, *Essays on Some of the Modern Guides to English Thought in Matters of Faith* (London: Macmillan, 1888), pp. 207-8.
20. John Henry Newman reappropriates this phrase for his own Christian purposes in *The Dream of Gerontius* (1865) where it is used twice, most

famously in the hymn 'Praise to the Holiest in the height': 'The double agony in man/For man should undergo'. That Newman was familiar with *Romola* is clear from his 'Memorandum on Charles Newman', written in May 1874, in which he compares his wastrel brother 'in his deficient command of his own faculties [to] the old man introduced into Romola, whose memory and mind gave way suddenly whenever he had come to the point of reaching some decisive act', *The Letters and Diaries of John Henry Newman*, eds Ian Ker and Thomas Gornall (Oxford: Clarendon Press, 1978), vol. 1, p. 182.

21. Gillian Beer, *George Eliot* (Brighton: Harvester Press, 1986), p. 123.
22. Thomas J. Heffernan, *Sacred Biography: Saints and their Biographers in the Middle Ages* (Oxford: Oxford University Press, 1988), p. 269.
23. George Eliot, *Felix Holt,* ed. Fred C. Thomson (Oxford: Clarendon Press, 1980), p. 77.
24. *George Eliot: The Critical Heritage,* ed. David Carroll (London: Routledge and Kegan Paul, 1971), p. 231.
25. George Eliot, *Middlemarch,* ed. David Carroll (Oxford: Clarendon Press, 1986), p. 3.
26. Ibid., p. 8.
27. Ibid., p. 215. For this identification, see Gillian Beer, '*Middlemarch* and *The Lifted Veil*', in *This Particular Web: Essays on 'Middlemarch'*, ed. Ian Adam (Toronto: University of Toronto Press, 1975), p. 106.

CHAPTER SEVEN

Power and Persuasion:
Voices of Influence in *Romola*

BERYL GRAY

The sound-track of *Romola is* a very insistent one. Constant demands are
made on our auditory attention by, for example, the great city bells, which
compete with, or dominate, drums and trumpets, street-market cacophany,
raucous revelry and pious chanting. But the variety of domestic or rural,
everyday sounds that English ears would find evocative, and that quicken life
and make experience immediate throughout George Eliot's fiction before and
after *Romola,* are almost entirely absent from this novel. In my view, this
absence goes some way towards accounting for the relative unpopularity of
the work.

The constraints George Eliot imposed on herself by undertaking to
re-create late fifteenth-century Florence meant that she strove, rather than
flourished, in an environment with which she could not be intimate, despite
her impressions of the city, and encyclopaedic knowledge of its history and
topography. Like many of the novel's contemporary reviewers, we admire,
and are instructed—even overwhelmed—by the formidable complexity of the
cultural representation (or re-presentation), but although George Eliot 'took
unspeakable pains' to find the 'Idiom' of Florence (*Letters*, IV, 301), the
experience of reading *Romola is* pervaded neither by a sense of shared
personal heritage, nor by a conjured familiarity with scene, object, natural
sound—or mode of speech. George Eliot's expressed fear that she would not
be able to 'work freely and fully enough in the medium' she had chosen, was
well founded (*Letters*, III, 417).[1]

In his excellent introduction to the Penguin English Library edition of the
novel, Andrew Sanders observes that 'we miss the inflexions of a Mrs Poyser
or a Dodson aunt in the speech of the lower and middle classes'.[2] To this truth
I would add that we miss the idiosyncrasies, the rhythms, hesitations and
emphases of George Eliot's English gentry and nobility. We miss, too, the
subtly individualizing, stylistic distinctions between social equals and
relations; between, say, Arthur Donnithorne and Mr Irwine in *Adam Bede,* or
Maggie and Tom in *The Mill on the Floss*, or Dorothea and Mr Brooke or
Celia in *Middlemarch.*

On the other hand, what is not absent from *Romola* is narrative force (even if this is periodically in abeyance), or psychological penetration and analysis. The realization of Tito Melema is one of George Eliot's greatest achievements. As Andrew Sanders says, Tito is the most vivid character in the book; but the bright smile that captivates most of the Florentines fails to captivate the reader, who is fascinated instead by George Eliot's monitoring of accreted ambition and motive, by her investigation of the process of self-corruption and by her charting of the murderous reach of the tentacles of betrayal.

But if Tito is *Romola*'s most vivid character, there is another whose impact on the novel's heroine, and on the reader, is perhaps more commanding, and whose influence is appropriately more permeating. That character is, of course, Girolamo Savonarola, whose 'career and martyrdom' were integral to what George Eliot called her 'historical romance' from its inception (*Letters*, III, 339).

In her portrayal of Savonarola, George Eliot can be said to emulate the historian Jacopo Nardi (1476-1563), who makes a brief, beneficent appearance in the last numbered chapter of *Romola*. Nardi, says the narrator, 'deserve[s] honour as one of the very few who [...] have written about [Savonarola] with the simple desire to be veracious' (583-4). But although the virtually obsessive focus and copiousness of George Eliot's Savonarola-related reading testify to her own quest for true enlightenment, her aim was manifestly not simple: to give us the Savonarola of *Romola,* she had to know what it was to *be* him.

The brief moment of Florentine history with which *Romola* is concerned is dominated by Savonarola, whose subtle and mysterious, movingly powerful personality is distilled as the influence of a voice—a voice that, in the course of the novel, penetrates, swells, fades and is eternally silenced. The effect of this voice and its message is essentially transmitted through its effect on Romola herself, who shares with Maggie Tulliver both an ardent nature, and its corollary in George Eliot: a profound susceptibility to sound. It is therefore both intrinsic to the dramatic shaping of Savonarola's career, and fitting to the presentation of Romola's character, that—before she is able even to see his face—she is caused by his assured, yet benignly rich voice, to vibrate. She is in the chapter-house in the outer cloister of San Marco, where her brother lies on his truckle-bed, delivering his dying message in a feeble, struggling voice. The strong quiet tone of the prior heightens and transforms the closeted tension between Romola's conflicting emotions, and her brother's 'low passionless' (158) religious tyranny.

Although Savonarola speaks gently to her, the inherent authority that characterizes this phase of his career symbolically forces Romola to renounce her own 'proud erectness', and fall to her knees 'in a new state of passiveness'

(161). Until this moment, Romola had felt only 'incurious, indignant contempt' (157) for the Church; an 'unconquerable repulsion' (155) for monkishness; and so her submission now to the force of Savonarola's personality is indicative of the influence he is gaining over her fellow citizens, and will gain over her. But while it is his denunciatory fanaticism that rivets the multitude, it is his 'very voice' that, as she later confesses to Tito, seems to penetrate the as yet unmarried Romola 'with a sense that there is some truth in what moves [the Dominicans]' (181). Significantly, that crucial perception is not independently explored after marriage, but is suppressed 'by that subjection to her husband's mind which is felt by every wife who loves her husband with passionate devotedness and full reliance' (251).

After 18 months of married life, however, Romola has grown vaguely uneasy, and is battling with a sense of disappointment. That which Savonarola had stirred in her reasserts itself as a spiritual need, and she goes to the Duomo to hear his Advent sermon hoping to be moved again—even though her conscious motive is only to gauge his political influence. Initially, she is distanced and unshaken, and remains so until the moment when Savonarola invokes martyrdom. Then, in unwitting unison with the monomaniacally vengeful Baldassarre, who is also 'possessed' (234) by Savonarola's voice, 'she sobbed with the rest' (251). Again,

> she felt herself penetrated with a new sensation—a strange sympathy with something apart from all the definable interests of her life. It was not altogether unlike the thrill which had accompanied certain rare heroic touches in history and poetry; but the resemblance was as that between the memory of music, and the sense of being possessed by actual vibrating harmonies. (251)

In the early stages of her labour to produce *Romola*, George Eliot told John Blackwood that she heard her characters talking, and that there was 'a weight upon her mind as if Savonarola and friends ought to be speaking Italian instead of English' (*Letters*, III, 427).[3] Whether or not that weight was ever lifted from the author's mind, much of the novel's dialogue surely remains idiomatically hobbled by, for example, exclamatory Italianisms ('Fediddio!' 'Santiddio!'), and English archaisms masquerading as Italianisms, such as Dolfo Spini's 'Malediction!' (523). Ironically (in the light of her confession to Blackwood), the one character for whom she arguably found an entirely persuasive language and mode is, in fact, Savonarola—except, that is, when he addresses Tito. Because his instinctively biblical magniloquence is drawn from George Eliot's own liberating familiarity with the King James Bible, the need for him to speak his native Italian is obviated. George Eliot might have taken an inspired risk in offering what she acknowledged to be a 'free representation'[4] of Savonarola's sermon, but the achievement is extraordinary. The inflexions and cadences of his voice bring conviction to his utterances.

The Old Testament thunder is solemnized by the force of his passion, which is transmitted and controlled as though it were, indeed, music—the spell of his voice sustained by the spell of his silence. Accordingly, even Baldassarre vibrates in response like a musical instrument, though a mutilated one: 'a harp of which all the strings had been wrenched away except one' (232).

George Eliot's command of her Savonarola—her reinvention of his genius, of his power to sway—is most masterly at the moment of transition in the sermon, when the 'incisive tone of authority' (231) melts into yearning entreaty; an entreaty that is surely inspired by the Song of Solomon:[5]

> Listen, O people, over whom my heart yearns, as the heart over the children she has travailed for! God is my witness that but for your sakes I would willingly live as a turtle in the depths of the forest, singing low to my Beloved, who is mine and I am His. For you I toil, for you I languish, for you my nights are spent in watching, and my soul melteth away for very heaviness. (231)

The sermon concludes:

> For it is thy will, O God, that the earth shall be converted unto thy law: it is thy will that wickedness shall cease and love shall reign. Come, O blessed promise! and behold, I am willing—lay me on the altar: let my blood flow and the fire consume me; but let my witness be remembered among men, that iniquity shall not prosper for ever. (231-2)

In comparison, the rhetoric of the version exemplified in the following extract—taken from Margaret Oliphant's review of Leonard Homer's translation (published while *Romola* was still being serialized in the *Cornhill*) of an important source-book for George Eliot, Pasquale Villari's *La storia di Fra Girolamo Savonarola e de' suoi tempi* (1859-61)—seems mechanical and inert, despite Mrs Oliphant's interpolation:

> 'Behold, the sword has descended, the scourges have commenced, the prophecies are being fulfilled ...' cried the great orator, abandoning himself, like an Italian and a poet, to the passionate anxiety and earnestness which *would* not fail. 'O, Florence, the time for music and dancing is at an end! now is the time for pouring out rivers of tears over your sins. Thy crimes, O Florence; thy crimes, O Rome; thy crimes, O Italy; are the cause of these chastisements. Repent, then; give alms, offer up prayers, be an united people'.[6]

As presented by George Eliot, Savonarola's melting entreaty and appeal for martyrdom culminate in the sob to which the congregation emotionally responds—'carried along by the great wave of feeling which gathered its force from sympathies that lay deeper than all theory' (232). It is true that his gratification is immense, for we are told with sympathetic irony that '[h]e felt in that moment the rapture and glory of martyrdom without its agony' (232).

Yet his egoism still gives no taint to his integrity. His desire for the people of Florence—his longing to 'hear their voices rise in concord as the voices of the angels' (231)—is his soul's desire and longing, and Romola's sense of being possessed by vibrating harmonies is sanctioned by her author.

This response prepares the way for Romola's later submission to the 'Arresting Voice', which gives Chapter 40 its title—the voice which orders her back to Florence after her attempted escape from the city, and from Tito. However, her obedience is not the consequence of mere spiritual fatigue or susceptibility, but a positive submission to the energy of Savonarola's beliefs, and to his inherent authority. And so his effect on her in the Duomo both signals her future discipleship, and establishes the preacher's influence as a counter-force to Tito's. As Romola says to Lillo, Tito's son, in the last words of the novel, she perhaps learned to love Fra Girolamo because he helped her when she was in great need. Born of Tito's betrayal of his own adoptive father, and of his burgeoning betrayal of Romola's (now dead) father, the seed of that great need is already sown when she makes that first excursion to hear Savonarola preach.

Following the earlier episode in the chapter-house, Romola is haunted by the disturbing memory of her wasted brother's fixated yearning after the crucifix; of his 'straining after something invisible' (182). She is unable to reconcile the effect of what she has witnessed with the pagan exultation that seems to radiate from Tito's Apollo-like 'satisfied strength and beauty' (182), and she wonders whether there is 'only a blind worship of clashing deities, first in mad joy and then in wailing' (183).

Mad, pagan—Bacchic—joy and religious wailing are indeed to conflict in Florence as, increasingly entangled in his own duplicity, Tito advances in spiritual opposition to Savonarola—and, of course, to Romola. Initially, this is merely the opposition of the Care-dispelling pagan to the exhortations of the Christian, but it is to clarify as the opposition of baseness to integrity. And, just as Savonarola's voice is charged with the authority, conviction and energy that express the true essence of the man, so is Tito Melema's voice of honey—an endorsement of his name—both his self-advocate, and his own intimate betrayer.

Expressly 'singular' (24) (for, of course, Tito comes as a stranger to Florence, owing it no allegiance), his voice is liquid, melting, viscous, gentle, beseeching—utterly un-Tuscan, and therefore (as far as the peddler Bratti is concerned)—significantly unintelligible to 'a Christian and a Florentine' (11). Like Tito himself, who wishes always to be welcome, it is essentially pleasing, and George Eliot uses it to convey his moral fluidity without impeaching Romola's judgement. To Tessa, it is like 'a soft breeze that fanned her gently when she was needing it' (148), while its youthful tones beguile and misguide the blind Bardo, suggesting to him that the young Greek can supply the scholar's needs in place of his son.

Tito's qualities of voice are strongly and repeatedly stressed, and their influence established, before Savonarola's potency is demonstrated. It is a voice that, in contrast to the full, clear, resonant purity of Romola's, insinuates rather than proclaims itself, so that the reader is prevented from entirely succumbing to the seductive charm that persuades so many of his indispensability: indeed, its very softness and liquidity are the characteristics that most repel Romola once she has grasped the fact that her husband has betrayed her father's memory by selling his books and his antiquities. Then it makes her shudder 'as if it had been a narrow cold stream coursing over a hot cheek' (293)—a revulsion that is transmitted to the reader when Tito softly repeats to the father he has forsaken, robbed and denied, his very words of parting on the shores of Greece: '*Padre mio!*' (313).

Tito's coaxing tones are enhanced by his persuasive touch on the lute, to which he sings as enchantingly as the magical lyrist, Orpheus, whose identity Nello the barber bestows on him (132). This identification relates to another, that of the sun-god—and god of the intellect and of music—Apollo (variously Orpheus' father, patron, or inspiration), who, according to legend, presented Orpheus with his lyre: conjured image, divine gift and beguiling influence are harmonious. But Tito perceives himself as Bacchus, a personification that had already suggested itself to Nello, who had nevertheless rejected it in favour of (Phoebus) Apollo, taking Tito's beauty, warmth and brightness at his face's apparent value.[7] It is as Bacchus, crowning Romola as Ariadne, that Tito commissions Piero di Cosimo to portray him on the little wooden tabernacle in which Romola's brother's crucifix is both ceremoniously buried and, ironically, preserved.

Tito's self-identification with Bacchus is corroborated both by his intoxicating, amorously ecstatic evocations to Romola of the south, and by his delight in noisy, feast-day confusion. He even finds a sort of opiate in the 'hooting and elbowing' (139) of the peasants' fair. But if the Orphean[8] and the Bacchic (or Dionysian) coexist within him, fidelity to the novel's predominant mythical strand requires that the possessor of powers to charm and to tame must fall victim to the forces of frenzy. Appropriately, the required resolution is fully dramatized after the satirically-ritualized, gourmet feasting in the Rucellai Gardens, when Tito, at the high point of a career built on deceit, is elated by his political success—a success crowned by Lorenzo Tornabuoni's exaggeratedly flattering suggestion that he could be a cardinal some day.

In acknowledgement of the god of wine, new flasks of Montepulciano have been ordered after the supper when Tito, as chief minstrel of the occasion, is asked to lead the Bacchanalian chorus from Poliziano's *Orfeo*,[9] for which he has 'found such an excellent measure' (354). (It is a nice touch that the necessary wine comes from Poliziano's birthplace.) As Tito strokes the lute 'in a preluding way' (354), the vengeful figure of Baldassarre makes its appearance, unobserved by his adopted son.

> [T]here was a confusion of speech and musical humming all round the table. Bernardo Rucellai had said 'Wait a moment, Melema', but the words had been unheard by Tito, who was leaning towards Pucci, and singing low to him the phrases of the Maenad-chorus. He noticed nothing until the buzz round the table suddenly ceased, and the notes of his own voice, with its soft low-toned triumph, 'Evoe, evoe!' fell in startling isolation. (354)

It is an exactly judged moment of dramatic truth. In characteristically insinuating tones, Tito is celebrating his own triumph as well as that of the Maenads, while the deceptively muted chorus is actually a riotous pledge to the god—Bacchus—who, in his youthful form, is Tito's chosen self-representation. No longer united to Romola, his already self-discrowned Ariadne, the immortal youth portrayed on the little tabernacle has metamorphosed, or corrupted, into the abandoned votary, the destroyer of the bard it was given him to be; for the victim of the triumphant Maenads is, of course, Orpheus. Empowered to restore his frenzied father's faculties, Tito 'pinche[s] the neck of the lute' (354) he has laid aside as he instead consigns Baldassarre to hate-propelled, Bacchic madness.[10]

That isolated voice softly proclaiming its own cruelty is the climax of the whole scene. Tito's course is now determined. Plasticity is transformed into ruthlessness, and with his traduced father led sacrificially off to prison, he once more leads the Maenad-chorus with which Poliziano's entertainment ends—this time, not in a soft, preluding sort of way, but—as in the play—emphatically and conclusively:

> He was in a state of excitement in which oppressive sensations, and the wretched consciousness of something hateful but irrevocable, were mingled with a feeling of triumph which seemed to assert itself as the feeling that would subsist and be master of the morrow.
>
> And it *was* master. For on the morrow [...] he had the air of a man well satisfied with the world. (359)

With the beneficent Orpheus within him now morally slain, the narrative impetus carries him with fateful inevitability towards the lethal reprise of the Bacchic ritual that occurs in Chapter 67, when, in order to escape the orgiastic rending of the Florentine Furies—or Maenads—he leaps into the Arno, only to be delivered to Baldassarre's throttling fingers, the instruments of the destiny that Tito's own symbolic destruction of Orpheus (and his lyre) has already prefigured. Lost to the mob though he is, even his image as he is carried by the river's current conjures that of the murdered but, conversely, magically unextinguished Orpheus, whose severed head, flung into the Hebrus by the Maenads, floated—still singing, it is said—to the island of Lesbos.[11] Tito's visually disembodied head is distinguishable to no one but the reader, who is made to scrutinize

> a pale olive face [...] looking white above the dark water: a face not easy even for the indifferent to forget, with its square forehead, the long low arch of the eyebrows, and the long lustrous agate-like eyes. Onward the face went on the dark current, with inflated quivering nostrils, with the blue veins distended on the temples. (553)

The chapter in which Tito determines his own moral destiny, and establishes his course as irreversible, is followed immediately by 'An Arresting Voice', the chapter in which Romola draws from Savonarola the strength to renounce her resolve to leave Tito; to retrace her steps and resume her place. This virtually coincidental decision to reverse *her* own course and return to Florence throws into perspective both the opposition of her nature to her husband's, and the oppositeness of their separate journeys. As she develops into the visible Madonna who is invigorated by Savonarola's influence, so Tito's enmity to her beliefs, to her allegiances, and to her great guide, gathers threatening momentum. But the juxtaposition of these two chapters also heightens the contrast between the pitiless self-devotion of Tito, and the austerely beneficial will of Savonarola. No longer struggling 'to subdue her nature to her husband's' (251), Romola yields instead to the authority and—crucially—the defined humanity of the Frate: it is significant that, although it is his voice that arrests her attention and her purpose, it is the sacramental silence of his blessing that intensifies the feeling that flows through his utterances to confirm her new spiritual condition.

Savonarola's influence over Romola's life replaces Tito's: not to re-subdue her, but effectively to infuse her innate religiousness and emerging authority with his own, until her spiritual emancipation is achieved. Until that moment, Romola's development depends on her degree of faith in him, and in his sense of divine purpose. But his intense purity of conviction itself becomes politically compromised. The 'mighty music' that had stirred Romola in the Duomo becomes jarred by 'self-vindication' and 'a tone of defiant confidence' (445) as Florence is scourged by famine and disease, until he succeeds in quelling his own 'inner voices' (494) in order to reconcile party politics with his vision of a regenerate Florence. Once those all-important inner voices are quelled, Savonarola's pitilessness in refusing to speak to save Romola's Medicean godfather from execution, recalls Tito's towards his own father. Romola is no longer able to hear the 'real voice' (498) of Savonarola's judgement. Now is the time for her voice to dominate and, full of contempt, she warns him: 'Take care [...] lest your enemies have some reason when they say, that in your visions of what will further God's Kingdom you see only what will strengthen your own party' (499). Now Romola's voice seems to

Savonarola 'the voice of his enemies' (499).

But Romola cannot be his enemy for long, for it remains true that, as we are told, his 'voice had waked in her mind a reason for living, apart from personal enjoyment and personal affection' (389). So when, after her own great crisis, she returns from the green valley by the Mediterranean as the religiously humanistic Madonna, there is complete concord between her creed and her sympathy for the now fallen, tortured Savonarola, and her belief in his essential integrity is restored. One passage in particular from his printed confession epitomizes for her—and for George Eliot—the whole man, who 'shone forth', says the narrator, 'as a man who sought his own glory indeed, but sought it by labouring for the very highest end—the moral welfare of men' (578). The passage concludes:

> 'It was not much in my thoughts to get myself made a Cardinal or Pope; for when I should have achieved the workI had in view, I should, without being Pope, have been the first man in the world in the authority I should have possessed, and the reverence that would have been paid me. If I had been made Pope, I would not have refused the office: but it seemed to me that to be the head of that work was a greater thing than to be Pope, but *such a work as I contemplated demanded a man of excellent virtues'*.
>
> That blending of ambition with belief in the supremacy of goodness made no new tone to Romola, who had been used to hear it in the voice that rang through the Duomo. (578-9, italics in original)

And so the voice that had penetrated her and shaken her before her own inner voice—her own authority—had asserted itself, echoes in her memory as the echo of his spirit. His anguish, too, though she does not witness it, is—like that conveyed in Stephen Guest's letter to Maggie Tulliver—a *heard* anguish:

> Romola had seemed to hear, as if they had been a cry, the words repeated to her by many lips—the words uttered by Savonarola when he took leave of those Brethren of San Marco who had come to witness his signature of the Confession: 'Pray for me, for God has withdrawn from me the spirit of prophecy'. (582)

In that George Eliot intended Savonarola's voice to convey the essence of the man, the triumph of his persecutors lies in the stifling of that voice—which yet casts its spell on 27 February 1498, the last day of the Carnival, even though he has been excommunicated, and even though the crowd is determined to resist him:

> But then came the voice, clear and low at first, uttering the words of absolution—'*Misereatur vestri*'—and more fell on their knees; and as it rose higher and yet clearer, the erect heads became fewer and fewer, till, at the words '*Benedicat vos omnipotens Deus*', it rose to a masculine

cry, as if protesting its power to bless under the clutch of a demon that
wanted to stifle it: it rang like a trumpet to the extremities of the Piazza,
and under it every head was bowed. (515)

Romola returns to Florence just six weeks before Savonarola's execution,
which, filled with the consciousness of his anguish, she feels compelled to
attend. She hopes that he will speak 'a last decisive word', but 'expectation
died, and she only saw what he was seeing—torches waving to kindle the fuel
beneath his dead body, faces glaring with a yet worse light; she only heard
what *he* was hearing—gross jests, taunts and curses' (584). But the moment
passes. Romola covers her face in order not to see his death-throes, and 'she
only knew that Savonarola's voice had passed into eternal silence' (584).

Savonarola's downfall is expressed, then, as a fall from an authori-
tativeness made preternatural by the powers of his voice, to the ignominy of
becoming the discredited, captive audience of a mob he had once subdued
into silence. His dispatch is entirely integrated with his being; and, except for
the Epilogue (which belongs to an idealized Romola and to moral fiction), it is
powerfully with this awful 'Last Silence'—the title of the last chapter—that
George Eliot appropriately concludes her partial revival of Savonarola's
Florence.

Notes

1. She felt at this point that she might have to give up her Italian project.
2. Andrew Sanders, Introduction to *Romola* (Harmondsworth: Penguin,
    1980), p. 18.
3. John Blackwood to Mrs John Blackwood.
4. A note at the end of the first volume of the Cabinet Edition of *Romola*
    states that the sermon 'is not a translation, but a free representation of Fra
    Girolaramo's preaching in its more impassioned moments'. George Eliot,
    Romola (Edinburgh and London: William Blackwood and Sons, 1878), p.
    446.
5. Compare Savonarola's appeal with the following, for example: 'My
    beloved spake, and said unto me, Rise up, my fair one, and come away/
    [...] [T]he time of the singing of birds is come, and the voice of the turtle
    is heard in our land/[...] My beloved is mine, and I am his'. The Song of
    Solomon 2:10-16.
6. 'Girolamo Savonarola', *Blackwood's Magazine* (June 1863), p. 702.
    There are several inaccuracies in Mrs Oliphant's transcription, which, in
    fairness to Homer, I have corrected from his translation (*The History of
    Girolamo Savonarola and his Times* [London: Longman, Green,

Longman, Roberts and Green, 1863], vol. 1, p. 201). Although Mrs. Oliphant concedes that, while marred, *Romola* presents a 'vivid and living' (ibid., 695) picture of the time, it is noteworthy that neither this article nor her subsequent book, *The Makers of Florence: Dante, Giotto, Savonarola, and their City* (London: Macmillan, 1876), which devotes five chapters to Savonarola, has anything to say about George Eliot's portrayal of him.

7. In *The Triptych and the Cross: The Central Myths of George Eliot's Poetic Imagination* (New York: New York University Press, 1979), Felicia Bonaparte deals comprehensively and illuminatingly with Tito's identification with Bacchus. However, her association of the charms of Tito's voice with the voice of that god (p. 222) is difficult to accept, as is her assertion that Tito 'plays the lute, as Bacchus plays the lyre' (p. 143). Bacchus is normally shown in possession of symbolic objects of a quite different nature, while the music accompanying his orgiastic festivals is produced by tympana, pipes, and cymbals. It is with Apollo and, essentially, the supreme musician, Orpheus, that the lyre is readily associated.

8. I have used this term rather than 'Orphic' in order to preserve a distinction between the characteristics abidingly associated with Orpheus himself, and Orphic mythology comprehensively.

9. According to Poliziano's translator, Louis E. Lord, the play was first presented in 1494. It was written at the request of Cardinal Francesco Gonzaga of Mantua, and 'given at Mantua on the 18th, 20th, and 22nd of July, 1471, on the occasion of the visit of Duke Galeazzo Maria Sforza' (*A Translation of the* Orpheus *of Angelo Politian and the* Aminta *of Torquato Tasso* [London: Oxford University Press, 1931], p. 70).

10. In a persuasive discussion of the relationship between the Eucharist and the 'Bacchic' ritual in the Rucellai Gardens, Felicia Bonaparte attributes the role of Maenad to Baldassarre, pointing to the fact that, 'before his arrival, Baldassarre had been stirred to memory and, awakened as though to life again, had felt like a "Maenad in the glorious amaze of her morning waking on the mountain top"', and suggesting that it is 'hatred, awake like a Maenad on the mountain, that brings Baldassarre now to the Rucellai Gardens', though he appears at 'the Last Supper [...] as a Bacchic perversion of Christ' (Bonaparte, pp. 171-3). Consumed as Baldassarre has become (and is again to become) with passionate vengefulness, he clearly does have a Bacchic role in Tito's fate. It is significant, however, that the amnesia which Felicia Bonaparte herself says is 'one of the most common characteristics of the Bacchic *ekstasis*' (ibid., p. 158) has fallen from him. Though he indeed shakes with passion

as he denounces Tito, his lucidity and cogency are quite un-Bacchic. His role of Maenad is in abeyance, for Tito can still make a moral choice. It is only when Tito's decision to commit the 'act of murderous cruelty' (*Romola*, 355) has in effect committed him to the god whose rites he had before been merely 'preluding', that Baldassarre, stupefied with horror by Tito's calumnies, becomes 'Lost, lost!' (357)—a pitiful victim in the ritual, whose intellect will be consumed by his passion. (For an additional discussion of Tito and Baldassarre in relation to Greek myth, see Lesley Gordon, 'Tito, Dionysus and Apollo', *The George Eliot Review* **25** [1994], pp. 34-8.)

11. Poliziano's play ends with the Maenads' triumphant revelling and drinking after their dismemberment of Orpheus, but, as W. K. C. Guthrie says in his authoritative *Orpheus and Greek Religion* (London: Methuen, 1935), Orpheus' oracular, singing head lives on in the version of his fate that 'was the most widely spread in antiquity' (p. 35). Descriptions of Orpheus' death are discussed by Ivan Mortimer Linforth, *The Arts of Orpheus* (Berkeley and Los Angeles: University of California Press, 1941), pp. 9-16.

CHAPTER EIGHT

The Prophetic Fallacy:
Realism, Foreshadowing and Narrative
Knowledge in *Romola*

CAROLINE LEVINE

In the critical world, we have heard a great deal about the failures of realism. The category of the 'real' has been shown to be empty of content; and realism, its faithful champion, has been revealed, in turn, as naive and impossible, historically contingent and unwittingly ideological. For two decades, most critics have simply begun with the contention that representation is always partial, mired in dominant ideology and conventional form. They denounce realism as a fallacy, or as an aesthetic implicitly colluding with a conservative politics.[1] And it has become a critical commonplace that realist art takes on its convincing verisimilitude only in the eye of the contingent beholder, caught in a particular cultural context: 'those qualities we would currently associate with the effect of realism are products of our own historical situatedness and subject to modification by later, necessarily partial because historically conditioned, observers'.[2]

But if we suspend our sophisticated preconceptions, realism—on its own terms—can look rather more unruly, more recalcitrant, more *interesting*, than it might at first seem. Its first curious dilemma is its patent superfluity. Why, after all, should one seek to *duplicate* reality? What is the point of having copies? More profoundly, what and where is the 'reality' to be copied? How do we know the 'real'? And given the infinite number of possible realities, which criteria should guide the realist artist in selecting a subject? How does value enter into images of truth? The nineteenth century, famously the 'age of realism', took these questions seriously indeed. Victorian writers posed questions about the ontology of the 'real' and our capacity to gain access to it, and asked *why* it was worth representing; they probed sceptically into the limitations of representation and both articulated and appreciated constructivist arguments. If they differed at all from their Modernist successors, it was that they refused to abandon the problem of mimesis, however fraught and troubled it revealed itself to be.

To give an influential example, John Ruskin's *Modern Painters* is a sceptical and radical aesthetic project. Ruskin begins by urging his readers to refuse authority—both the authority of artistic tradition and the dogmatic opinions of contemporary critics. Truth, he claims, requires no special talents to discern, and thus it forms the most impartial and egalitarian basis for the evaluation of painting. He supplants the reliance on experts with the celebration of the ordinary eye, insisting that we are all capable of judging the truth-value of art. But the truths of the world are themselves unconventional, according to Ruskin, since we find, when we look closely, that the natural world is infinitely various, irreducible to the conventional rules of painting. This means that painters must learn to resist conventional modes of representation, which reduce images of the real to established and repetitive patterns. In this context, Ruskin invites his readers to become thoroughgoing sceptics, capable of recognizing the failures of Old Master paintings to represent the 'real'.

The method by which we arrive at sound conclusions in *Modern Painters* is an empirical one: in order to judge the truth-value of representations, we must go out into nature and match these pictures against the realities they seek to portray. After this dose of experience, we return to representations with a new, tested understanding of their honesty or duplicity. First doubt, then the process of testing, and finally the certainty of knowledge. *Modern Painters* begins to look like the novel of suspense. Indeed, it is my contention that the sceptical testing of Ruskin's empirical realism is perfectly suited to the pattern of *plotted narrative*. Empirical science and narrative suspense rely on a comparable formal structure: both call for a lag or interval between initial surmise and later knowledge, between dawning suspicions and decisive conclusions. Both involve a delay between tantalizing mysteries and the ensuing satisfactions of certainty. Thus the proleptic narrative moment—the 'snare' or enigma of the plotted text[3]—becomes the perfect vehicle for a *sceptical epistemology*, which involves a temporal gap between deceptive appearances and the tested truths of later understanding. Plotted suspense serves the ends of sceptical, empirical realism. We will return to this marriage of plot and realism later. For now, it is important to recognize that Ruskin sets up a series of small plots in *Modern Painters*, directing us to become wary of representation, trusting only to the evidence of our own experience and desiring nothing but the tested truth that our visual experiments promise to yield. With *Modern Painters* as our guide, we become sceptical subjects with a confidence in our own—ordinary—experience.

It is my eccentric conviction that *Romola*, brimming as it does with symbolic images and prophetic voices, is none the less a realist text in the mould of *Modern Painters*. The ending of *Romola* brings its heroine to recognize, in good Ruskinian fashion, that she must obey the tutelage of her own lived experience, casting off all orthodoxies and authorities that do not accord with her own hard-won understanding of the realities of the world. She throws off the established systems of her contemporaries, just as Ruskin rejects the Old Masters, because they do not match the 'real'. In her most subversive moment, the protagonist comes to the anti-conventional conclusion that 'The law was sacred [...] but the rebellion might be sacred too' (552).

As her narrative progresses, Romola is increasingly prepared to create her own unconventional models. By the time we reach the Epilogue, she has radically revised conventional relations between wife and mistress, having adopted her husband's lover as her own partner. Affirming a startling independence, the women run the household together, free from the demands of men. Thus Romola creates an entirely new model of the family, ending her story by rejecting orthodox patterns of living and understanding.

Romola's education, too, can be described as an empirical, Ruskinian process. She comes to realize that all of the authorities—her father, husband, brother and spiritual father—misrepresent and misread the reality of her experience. After trying to live by their authoritative paradigms, she finds, one by one, that these are either internally contradictory or fail to fit her world. Little by little, she comes to be sceptical of authority itself. The form of Romola's *Bildung* is therefore familiar enough: like Ruskin's visual experiments, it follows the pattern of empirical science, the testing of provisional hypotheses against the evidence of experience. Finally, after disappointments in all of the models she tests, she is ready to come to her own conclusion—and it is a conclusion that fits her experience. To live in accordance with the realities of her life, she concludes, is to live by the guidance of universal sympathy:

> [T]he simpler relations of the human being to his fellow-men had been complicated for her with all the special ties of marriage, the State, and religious discipleship, and when these had disappointed her trust, the shock seemed to have shaken her aloof from life and stunned her sympathy. But now she said, 'It was mere baseness in me to desire death. If everything else is doubtful, this suffering that I can help is certain'. (567)

Romola has tested the complicated paradigms of loyalty to marriage, state and religion, and her dutiful attempts to honour these 'special ties' give way to a new understanding of the problem of duty—the 'simpler relations' among human beings, free of complex institutional bonds. And importantly, once she has cast off the conflicting obligations of her Florentine 'ties', she no longer needs to test the validity of her hypotheses:

> she had not even reflected, as she used to do [...] she had simply lived, with so energetic an impulse to share the life around her, to answer the call of need and do the work which cried aloud to be done, that the reasons for living, enduring, labouring, never took the form of argument. (567)

Here, Romola's ethical conclusion is an ideal point of closure: to live freely by the law of universal sympathy involves no sacrifice, self-discipline or betrayal; no deliberation, rebellion or consent; it is an impulsive, involuntary, indisputable paradigm. Without internal resistance or contradiction, there is no further need for 'argument'—and no further need for plot. In the end, Romola learns how to live happily ever after, having tested conventions against experience, and refusing all authority but her own.

I will argue, below, that the reader of *Romola*, like its heroine, is also brought to settled, knowing closure through a process of empirical testing. The text proposes intriguing hypotheses for us, and prompts us to wait to see whether these 'fit' the narrative. Eventually, the 'experience' of the narrative either validates or disproves these hypotheses. This model, then, brings us through doubts and experiments to satisfying closure. Our own empirical education relies on the workings of plotted suspense.

Of course, despite the novel's emphasis on the empirical method, we and Romola are no ordinary scientists: it is the *moral* world that we test as if it were an object of empirical knowledge, verifiable by lived experience. But the novel implicitly brings ethics and empirical science together, arguing that the testing of hypotheses against experience teaches us how to live ethically, or, conversely, that the right way of living grows out of a verifiable, empirical understanding of the ways of the world. The text's moralizing conclusion reinforces the idea that Eliot's novel unites an empirical, narrative epistemology with an ethics. And it is my contention that this union of epistemology and ethics—of knowledge and value—is a hallmark of Victorian realism. Nineteenth-century writers sought to represent reality accurately not simply for the sake of mimetic perfection, but because a secure knowledge of the real *mattered*. Realists wanted their readers to know the way the world worked so that they would understand how to act in that world.

If my own hypothesis is true, then what we and Romola learn about the world from the experience of the text should make us better ethical agents. What, then, is the content of that knowledge? I want to suggest that both characters and readers, in this novel, learn the 'fact' of moral responsibility. In support of classic bourgeois values, both we and Romola come to know that human choices carry real and significant consequences. And this moral lesson brings with it an emphasis on the time-bound connections between cause and effect—thereby uniting not only knowledge and ethics, but knowledge and *narrative*. Indeed, the future-oriented desire for knowledge, the doubts and tests of sceptical empiricism and the value of real experience in time join to bring us the important truths of the world. Plot and scepticism unite to reveal tested, anti-conventional reality. *Romola* is therefore the realist novel *par excellence*. Eliot even makes the value of narrative abundantly clear in the novel's epilogue, where the moral tale Romola tells her adopted son is a clear indication that her own knowledge can be transmitted narratively.[4] Storytelling would seem to yield the ethical and epistemological benefits of experience.

If the text affirms the power of stories, it dismisses paintings, visual appearances and prophecies as misleading—as inimical to a genuine and useful knowledge of the real. The visual, as we will see further below, fails to tell the truth and, by its very failure, prompts us to want the knowledge that only narrative time can provide. Similarly, the supernatural provokes our interest, only to fail and give place to the firm facts of the empirical. If the text urges to put our faith in plotted narrative, it instructs us, equally, to refuse the power of visions and painted images.

Yet, it is in Romola's attempt to dismiss the visions of painting and the voices of prophecy that this text begins to show the hidden tensions of the realist narrative. Prophecy and narrative knowledge are not as dissimilar as the novel would have us believe. Prophecy, unlike the other paradigms that fall by the novelistic wayside, is rejected but never—like the others—disproved or shaken by experience. And this is because the prophetic model is effectively the *same* as plotted narrative. Narrative and prophetic meanings alike take shape only when we look back from the perspective of the future to read significance in the past. These formal similarities between narrative knowledge and prophetic persuasion mean that when the novel tries to discredit prophecy it also calls its own methods of persuasion into radical question. With *Romola*, that is, Ruskinian realism reaches its limits.

Treacherous vision, or learning to be sceptical

The truth in *Romola* is not immediately manifest. Appearance does not correspond to essence, exteriors can be misleading and vision is epistemologically problematic from the outset. We learn in the first few pages of the novel that the young Greek stranger, Tito Melema, is impossible to decipher on the basis of visual clues alone. For Bratti Ferravecchi, he is literally illegible: 'I picked up a stranger this morning as I was coming in from Rovezzano, and I can spell him out no better than the letters on that scarf I bought from the French cavalier' (22). And, of course, Tito will succeed as a traitor because he remains thoroughly indecipherable to most of Florence. Even the visionary Dino, who sees Tito as the 'Great Tempter' in a dream, cannot make out his features: 'And at the *leggio* stood a man whose face I could not see—I looked, and looked, and it was a blank to me, even as a painting effaced' (161). Tito's 'blank' face becomes the ideal vehicle for an exploration of the epistemological failures of the visual.

Immediately after we readers first learn that Tito is hiding a guilty secret, the narrator offers us a description of his face:

> there was no brand of duplicity on his brow; neither was there any stamp of candour: it was simply a finely formed, square, smooth young brow. And the slow absent glance he cast round at the upper windows of the houses had neither more dissimulation in it, nor more ingenuousness, than belongs to a youthful well-opened eyelid with its unwearied breadth of gaze [...] Was it that Tito's face attracted or repelled according to the mental attitude of the observer? Was it a cipher with more than one key? (102)

For those who rely on visual clues alone, Tito's face lacks both legible signs of honesty and obvious marks of guile: the narrator's description shows that the face reveals only shape and colour, youth and beauty, and his expression, the narrator claims, is 'a negative one' (102). Only blankness results from vision.

Consequently, all those who try to make sense of Tito on the basis of sight alone simply generate their own prejudices and preconceptions, the untested assumptions of conventional wisdom. Romola trusts him to be compassionate and generous like herself, and she universalizes her confidence in him, claiming that pleasing exteriors are always evidence of trustworthy interiors: 'It seems to me beauty is part of the finished language by which goodness speaks' (195). Here, the protagonist generates an example of what Roland Barthes calls the 'implicit proverbs' of the cultural code.[5] Her truth-statement draws links between text and world, since Romola clearly includes the reader's reality, too, in her sweeping maxim. Her statement is not bounded by perspective, circumstance, or context—it claims universal application.

This incorporation of the universalizing maxim hints at the social role of the realist text. The 'implicit proverb' suggests that general statements about the world of the reader fall within the novel's evaluative scope, and that the events represented by the text can either validate or invalidate a generalized statement about the 'real'. That is, when the text comes to prove Romola wrong—as it will—it also discredits a conventional way of seeing the world. In this case, we learn that external beauty does not necessarily signal internal goodness. Thus Romola initially suggests a way of reading the world based on visual appearance, but her model will fail, giving way to other interpretative paradigms. And we readers learn from this, presumably, to be suspicious about the correlation between appearance and essence. We learn to be sceptical readers of the real. Here, then, is a generalizable pattern for the realist *Bildungsroman*: the novel proposes a hermeneutic model, which encompasses the reader's world as well as the world of the text, rejects it and replaces it with a new way of seeing. In this case, we learn to be wary of the conventional wisdom that the truth of character can be deduced from visual features alone.[6]

Early in the novel when we, like Florence, know very little about the anonymous stranger, Nello, the barber, and Piero di Cosimo, the painter, argue about the relationship between Tito's face and his character. After laying eyes on him for the first time, the painter asks Tito to pose as a model for the traitor, Sinon. Nello immediately objects: 'What trick wilt thou play with the fine visage of this young scholar to make it suit thy traitor?' (42). The barber trusts the young Greek on the evidence of his appearance, and, like Romola, universalizes this response: 'I shall never look at such an outside as that without taking it as a sign of a loveable nature' (44). Here is Romola's cultural code, again, in paraphrase: beautiful faces signify lovable natures.

Responding to Nello, the painter argues that it is precisely the beauty of Tito's face that would allow the Greek to act the traitor successfully:

'[T]hou has just shown the reason why the face of Messere will suit my traitor. A perfect traitor should have a face which vice can write no marks on—lips that will lie with a dimpled smile—eyes of such agate-like brightness and depth that no infamy can dull them—cheeks that will rise from a murder and not look haggard. I say not this young man is a traitor: I mean, he has a face that would make him the more perfect traitor if he had the heart of one, which is saying neither more nor less than that he has a beautiful face'. (42)

Piero, here, insists on potential rather than actual characteristics: Tito may in fact be entirely honourable, but he could also become an effective double-crosser. Tito's unmarked visage—his very blankness—will allow him to escape being read: and it is the absence of visual clues that might also allow him untold freedom of action, whether or not he is willing to take advantage of it. In fact, the visual image is illegible, and tells us nothing about character. But because it tells us nothing, it cannot be a reliable index of goodness, and might as well be the face of a traitor as the image of a saint.

Of course, Piero's interpretation of Tito as Sinon also suggests a generalization about visual clues, as Romola and Nello have done—but his is a different cultural code. For Piero, a successful deceiver is one who appears unmarked by deception and can therefore dupe his audiences. But this statement will only hold true for a credulous audience. In other words, it is only in a society that believes in the correlation of beauty and goodness that beautiful faces can, quite literally, get away with murder. If that same society comes to recognize, like Piero, that appearance is not a reliable index of character, then beautiful traitors will no longer be trusted. To put it simply: if we learn to be sceptical, we will not be betrayed.

None the less, Piero's model clearly suggests that vision contributes nothing *in the present* to the viewer who seeks knowledge of character. Confronted with an unmarked visage, we can say nothing about the person who owns it, since, if we are to believe the painter, it is impossible ever to draw strict links between external appearance and internal reality. Our knowledge of character must come from other sources. In short, if appearances can be misleading, it is impossible to bear irrefutable marks of character on the face. Yet, Piero's words prompt the reader to be alert to the *possibility* that Tito is treacherous, and when the text later validates this hypothesis, we may well be persuaded to have our own suspicions about beautiful faces in the world.

Foreshadowing and narrative knowledge

Piero and Nello return to their dispute over Tito's face a number of chapters later, and by this time the reader knows that Piero is right—the beautiful stranger has begun to act the traitor. Tito, again in the barber shop, is suddenly distracted by fears that his guilty secrets will be publicly disclosed. Nello feels sure, however, that Tito is 'absorbed in anxiety about Romola' and throws 'a challenging look at Piero di Cosimo, whom he had never forgiven for his refusal to see any prognostics of character in his favourite's handsome face' (169). Conspicuously, Nello misreads Tito's face for the second time, and the text, in noting this misinterpretation, reminds us of the earlier dispute. This time, however, we know of Tito's emergent duplicity, and recognize that Piero's analysis of treachery has been validated by the events of the text, while Nello's proverb has been soundly disproved. The signifying code that Romola and Nello produce is quite simply mistaken: beautiful faces can indeed mask treacherous natures.

The first debate about Tito's face offers us the sense that there is an unknown meaning in the debate, a mystery to be solved, and then, when it is mentioned for the second time, we re-read it from the perspective of the more knowing present. We return to the ignorant past with our new knowledge, and have no trouble deciding which of the two—Piero or Nello—was right. We have been educated. And we have been educated in two ways: on the one hand, we have learned that appearances are deceptive in the world, and it is thus wise to be sceptically wary; and on the other, we have learned that narrative time brings a knowledge that visual appearance cannot offer.

The first prescient moment in the barber shop, when Piero first reads Tito as a traitor, is an example of foreshadowing, or prolepsis—a moment that gestures towards a future revelation. The painter's interpretation of Tito's face functions as a clue, a hint, an inkling of his later treachery, probably raising our suspicions and preparing us for his corruption—disclosing nothing, but bracing us for the disclosure. But then, why should the text bother to forewarn us, arousing suspicions about Tito?

Prolepsis is an odd device, entailing that we look backward from the perspective of the future, to see that in the past, a mysterious moment actually pointed towards unknown future events, which were then later realized. But this device, in the plotted text, serves an important purpose: Piero's suspicions about Tito may be without epistemological value, but they are about prompting an epistemological *desire*—the dispute makes us crave a resolution, it makes us want to *know* whether Tito will become a traitor. Foreshadowing thus provokes readerly anticipation, the suspense that guides thrillers and detective plots, prompting us to wait for the truth to emerge. It is a perfect device for the realist text. Indeed, proleptic desire implicitly guides us, as readers, to put our faith in the truth-telling powers of narrative.

It is important, too, that the recurring debate over Tito's character alerts us to the fact that his development is of particular interest to the narrative: what will Tito become? This question, we find, is a focal ethical and epistemological question for this narrative. How does someone become a traitor? How is it that a person can come to commit 'the basest deeds' (588)? As I suggested earlier, it is moral knowledge—not only Romola's passage to ethical maturity, but also Tito's path into iniquity—that constitutes the central epistemological fruit of this narrative.

Foreshadowing, then, is about provoking a desire for this very knowledge. And the epistemological failures of the visual, here functioning as foreshadowing devices, facilitate the path to empirical understanding. The argument between Piero and Nello about Tito's face, with its two clear and mutually exclusive positions, offers us alternative outcomes, only one of which can come true. When one is positively disproved, we seem to have a decisive answer. Encouraged into suspicion, urged to test the too-easy correlation between appearance and essence, we are prepared by the mysteries of the visual for the eventual disclosure of the truth.

It is worth noting, too, that at several points in the text, Romola is strikingly similar to the reader who encounters foreshadowing in the novel: she reads a set of signs, intuits the fact that they are meaningful, and then establishes the truth that lies behind them simply by waiting for further information. For example, Piero paints an imagined picture of Tito's terrified face *before* he witnesses an actual instance of Tito terrified. '[Tito] saw himself with his right hand uplifted, holding a wine-cup, in the attitude of triumphant joy, but with his face turned away from the cup with an expression of such intense fear in the dilated eyes and pallid lips, that he felt a cold stream through his veins, as if he were being thrown into sympathy with his imaged self' (191). Romola is struck by the picture, which she comes across by surprise, and she characterizes it as a 'fact'—something which reveals a real connection between Tito and Baldassarre, but one which is not at all intelligible: 'the facts of the armour and the picture [suggested] some external event which was an entire mystery to her' (280). In using this 'prophetic' picture as factual evidence, Romola is hardly relying on standard documentation. Yet she is not wrong; there is a crucial connection between the two men. And if Piero has unwittingly predicted Tito's real fear, his vision is acute enough to recognize a real source for it in Baldassarre. The painter's truth-telling is so trustworthy that he is unconsciously correct even in this prophetic case. We might say that the verisimilitude of Piero's work is enough to raise suspicions in Romola's mind, and these suspicions will be justified. But it is crucial that Piero's vision is always shown to have been revealing after the fact, without being capable of producing positive knowledge in the present. On seeing the picture, Romola, after all, remains unenlightened.

In other words, the world that Romola interprets is remarkably like a novel, and reading the real is all too much like reading a narrative. She takes visual signs to be meaningful, though their meaning is inscrutable in the present, and she trusts them to become legible over time. Romola learns to be wary and sceptical from Piero's pictures, just as the reader does. Both the novel's protagonist and its readers grasp the hypotheses offered to us by the visual, and wait for time to show us which hypothesis successfully matches our experience.

Foreshadowing, then, is a way of affirming the truth-value of narrative as a form. We do not know how to interpret a meaningful moment in the present and, since the solution to the mystery is withheld, we read on to find out how it should have been read. In the texts of plotted desire, we learn to wait for knowledge.

The hazards of prophecy

The stuff of empirical realism is narrative prolepsis, wary scepticism and the desire for tested truth. But Florence, in 1492, is brimming with prophetic voices and superstitions. And a number of prophecies, like Piero's paintings, seem to come true, apparently confirmed by narrative events. The prophets proffer hypotheses about what is to come, and we wait to see which of these will fit the experience of the text. Early in the novel, for example, Romola's visionary brother prophesies that her marriage will bring disaster, and he is later proven right. Like Piero's hypothesis, Dino's prophecy is justified by the passage of time.

Curiously, however, when Romola realizes that Dino's prophetic dream has been fulfilled, she denies it all legitimacy:

> What had the words of that vision to do with her real sorrows? That fitting of certain words was a mere chance; the rest was all vague—nay, those words themselves were vague [...] What reasonable warrant could she have

had for believing in such a vision and acting on it? None. True as the voice of foreboding had proved, Romola saw with unshaken conviction that to have renounced Tito in obedience to a warning like that, would have been meagre-hearted folly. Her trust had been delusive, but she would have chosen over again to have acted on it rather than be a creature led by phantoms and disjointed whispers in a world where there was the large music of reasonable speech, and the warm grasp of living hands. (328)

The phantoms of prophecy are convincing only by a coincidence—they are vague, and the fitting of Dino's words to subsequent events is 'a mere chance'. Experience might seem to validate Dino's vision, but Romola, in retrospect, remains unconvinced of the truth of visions and seeks the value of life in the world: human reason and human warmth, in place of disconnected prophecies. Again like a good realist, Romola prefers the reality of human experience to a faith in the broken whispers of an unseen world.

But there are epistemological questions posed by this interpretative dismissal of the prophets: if Dino's vision is an accidental, inauthentic correspondence between words and the world, what is the proper, grounded, authentic way of seeing? If prophetic pronouncements are vague correlations between predictions and events, what would be an indisputable link between interpretation and the real? And what would constitute a 'more reasonable warrant' for action than the voices of the prophets?

Prophecy fails to offer a valuable knowledge of the real. But it fails on curious grounds. As Romola says, her brother's prophecy does correspond to events, but it does not correspond in any *essential* way. True as the voice of foreboding might prove, Romola dismisses it as unreal, vague and coincidental. Prophecy fits experience, but only by *chance*. Thus unlike the other failed paradigms that Romola comes to reject—the 'special ties' of state, marriage and religion—prophecy is never discredited by the events of lived experience. The other models collapse when they do not correspond to the real. Prophecy fits the real—but is dismissed none the less.

We do not have to look far for reasons to distrust the visionaries, since we encounter doubts about the validity of prophecy within the novel itself. According to Nello, for example, the trouble with prophecy is that conflicts among prophetic visions prove that they cannot all be justified, and there is no way to tell which of the prophetic voices is sound until events happen that correspond to one rather than another. 'With San Domenico roaring *è vero* in one ear, and San Francisco screaming *è falso* in the other, what is a poor barber to do?' (19). Only temporal passage will tell which prophet is right. It is impossible to judge the validity of prophecy in the present.

The second interpretative doubt that haunts and unsettles the persuasive force of religious predictions is a more radical scepticism, involving misgivings about the validity of prophecies that do indeed seem to have come true. Nello, like Romola, claims that religious visions are persuasive only in a self-justifying fashion:

> [T]here is as wonderful a power of stretching in the meaning of visions as in Dido's bull's hide. It seems to me a dream may mean whatever comes after it. As our Franco Sachetti says, a woman dreams over night of a serpent biting her, breaks a drinking-cup the next day, and cries out, 'Look you, I thought something would happen—it's plain now what the serpent meant'. (266)

Perhaps, that is, the event will always be capable of confirming the prophetic voice, since both are vague enough to be stretched to fit the other. Hence the trouble with prophecy is that it relies on an interpretative ambiguity for its persuasion. The passage of time might validate any hypothesis if the audience were willing simply to wait indefinitely, and to 'stretch' predictions to fit subsequent phenomena. The very imprecision involved in interpretation—the elusive problem of matching meaning to experience—thus becomes all too clear.

In this particular scene, Nello is responding to the report of a prediction uttered by Camilla Rucellai, that the scholar Pico della Mirandola 'would die in the time of lilies'. When he dies in November—'not at all the time of lilies'—Camilla appears to have been discredited (265). But she replies with the assertion that her vision should be interpreted metaphorically, rather than literally: 'it is the lilies of France I meant, and it seems to me they are close enough under your nostrils' (265). Thus the complexity of interpretative validity—the 'fitting' of words to events—is made even more suspect by Camilla's metaphorical interpretation, which carefully upholds her own prophetic authority. With metaphors to come to the rescue, perhaps every prophecy, after the fact, could be made to seem true.

If there are various ways of stretching predictions to validate the visions, the visions themselves also present epistemological difficulties. The prophet may offer more than one future alternative: Savonarola, for example, threatens a scourge if Florence does not purify itself, and glory if it does. But if there are two possible outcomes to a prophecy, we are faced with a serious *ex post facto* epistemological problem: if we manage to prevent the realization of a particular outcome, we will never know whether the imaged future would have come true if we had not done as we were directed. Dino's dream is also an example of this kind of prophecy: Romola claims that she would not act on her brother's warning if she had the choice again, despite the fact that his prediction has come true. After all, if she had acted on the basis of the dream, she would never have learned the crucial lessons of her own experience—the collapse of the marriage tie and its eventual displacement by a more fitting moral law. Indeed, according to the paradoxical logic of warnings, if Romola had in fact averted the disastrous marriage predicted by her brother, she would never have known whether or not the warning itself was justified. Prophecies therefore frustrate the task of *Bildung*—the individual's path to understanding and maturity. Visions fail to draw connections between 'experience' and interpretation, between cause and effect, but claim interpretative mastery—leaving their listeners dependent on the prophets. Prophecy leaps over the intervening time between prediction and event and ignores the links that bring particular events to pass.

The other type of prophecy, exemplified by Camilla Rucellai's prediction, always comes true, but not necessarily in a literal way. Thus we confront the interpretative problem that Nello describes: if words can be stretched like a bull's hide to fit the event at hand, how can we be sure that a particular prophecy is really being fulfilled? How do we know when and how to connect events in the present with prophecies in the past?

With prophecy, we face either an epistemological problem, or a hermeneutic one: we do not know for sure whether a prophecy has 'really' been fulfilled, and we have no firm, convincing way, even once time has passed, of distinguishing valid prophecy from vague, coincidental assertions made after the fact. Thus Nello and Romola can be seen to share a sceptical interpretative model: namely, that the fitting of present experience to cloudy, dream-like premonitions in the past is always potentially a process of distortion, an interpretation after the fact, perhaps tailored to establish the very validity of the premonitions.

But again, if the 'fitting of certain words' can be 'a mere chance' and meanings are infinitely stretchable, how might we ever establish 'real' links between interpretation, experience and knowledge? If there are 'chance' conjunctions of words and meanings, are there also deliberate conjunctions, legitimate and true correlations between words and meanings? And how might we tell one from the other?

Knowledge, free will and narrative suspense

Instead of putting our faith in the erratic interventions of providence, we learn from the text to study the duplicable laws of the world. The novel offers us empirical law as an alternative to the slippery persuasiveness of prophecy. Romola dismisses her brother's vision because 'she had the vivid intellect and the healthy human passion, which are too keenly alive to *the constant relations of things* to have any morbid craving after the exceptional' (162, my emphasis). Here, the uniform relations of things gains clear precedence over the exceptional and inexplicable, as if prophetic visions are worthless precisely because they do not describe *repeatable* links between one event and the next.

Eliot is not the first to oppose the empirical to the miraculous. Her text takes its place in a tradition of religious scepticism, including the work of David Friedrich Strauss, whose *Life of Jesus Critically Examined* Eliot herself translated. Strauss rejects the truth of the Gospels wherever the texts are marked by miraculous interventions which interrupt the laws of nature: this is enough to establish aspects of the biblical text as untrue, because, as Strauss claims, 'the absolute cause never disturbs the chain of secondary causes by single arbitrary acts of interposition, but rather manifests itself in the production of the aggregate of finite causalities, and of their reciprocal action'.[7] Assuming that God would never hinder the usual course of events because the laws of nature are His own work, Strauss, like Romola, dismisses the 'exceptional' in favour of the 'constant relations of things'. This may be a circular argument, but it certainly affirms the laws of ordinary causality.

Thus Eliot, like her sceptical precursor, aims to persuade us of a set of real, repeatable, empirical patterns, deducible from common experience. But what are these patterns? The narrator explains that the alternative to arbitrary divine power in the world is the force of the human will. 'Tito was experiencing that inexorable law of human souls, that we prepare ourselves for sudden deeds by the reiterated choice of good or evil which gradually determines character' (224). If the prophets believe in the dictates of a divine purpose, the narrator favours the principle of human agency. The laws of the world are worldly laws.

This statement of 'inexorable law' also implies a clear model of subjectivity: a chronological history of choices which steadily defines a coherent self. Felicia Bonaparte argues that Eliot consistently replaces the conventional essentialist self, untouched by its actions and circumstances, with a selfhood that is coterminous with its actions. There is no ontological distinction, for Eliot, between the choices a character makes and character itself.[8] Indeed, coherent novelistic characters may always be the result of repeated actions or attributes, as Shlomith Rimmon-Kenan affirms: 'The repetition of the same behaviour "invites" labeling it as a character-trait'.[9]

It is true that Tito and Romola can be identified and differentiated as character-types on the basis of the ways they come to their conclusions about appropriate action in the world. These two figures repeatedly make particular kinds of decisions, and depend on distinctive sets of arguments, which increasingly distance them one from the other. Tito's first treacherous acts precipitate events that call for further choices, and once he has begun to deceive, he becomes more and more wedded to his treachery. As the narrator puts it: 'Our lives make a moral tradition for our individual selves, as the life of mankind makes a moral tradition for the race' (353). Here, a sequence of moral choices makes the self just as it makes the larger group, gradually circumscribing character and determining future choices. Put simply, character is formed in the act of decision-making, and these decisions, as the novel shows, bring significant consequences. Choice is a force in the world.

At the beginning of the novel, Tito has not yet decided to sacrifice his adopted father for the sake of his own comforts, and yet he has a strong preference for avoiding suffering and enjoying pleasure and, as the narrator tells us, 'an innate love of reticence' (94). He has characteristics already in place, apparently, that will lead to his eventual treachery and duplicity. As this example proves, however, the 'innate' is no fixed trait: it is a drive of desire, an 'impulse', an inclination. And importantly, throughout *Romola*, we find Tito caught in a moment of indecision, in the uncertain time before he makes a choice, weighing the arguments for and against a particular action.

Character, then, involves not compulsion—the subjugation of action to a prior, essential, constraining self—but *self-persuasion*, the need for argument to guide or to rationalize action. And this primacy of debate—the need, even for a pleasure-seeker like Tito, to weigh the grounds of his decisions— suggests that arguments may indeed sway actual choices. The consequent sense that there is more than one real and plausible alternative would imply that individuals might be capable, always, of making their choices otherwise. Implied throughout is the didactic suggestion that we are all capable of behaving differently. What Dino's prophecy most importantly disregards, in this causal context, is that what actually brings about the disastrous marriage between Tito and Romola is not divine intervention, but a conflict between two ways of making choices, a conflict between Tito's repeated pursuit of pleasure and the scrupulous choices of his more duty-bound wife.

In one example, Tito deliberates over whether or not to tell Tessa that their marriage is a sham. The very tension of the moment before he settles on a single choice is presumably part of the anticipation and interest that push us to read on. It is a moment of plotted uncertainty. 'Tito felt the necessity of speaking now; and, in the rapid thought prompted by that necessity, he saw that by undeceiving Tessa he should be robbing himself of some at least of that pretty trustfulness which might, by and by, be his only haven from contempt' (153). In this moment of 'rapid thought' we recognize Tito's desire to bury the past and secure the future, which has been with him from the outset. But this is also a character in the process of formation: indecisive for this instant, he seems to be capable of choosing another course. And thanks to the central place of self-persuasion in the act of decision-making, Tito's choice does not appear, even in retrospect, to have been the only possible outcome. His 'character' is not discernible, as such, until he has made numerous such decisions. In short, we are not surprised to find Tito sinking into iniquity, since he has already begun to do so, but since his character becomes recognizable only through his *repeated* decision to avoid pain and discomfort, his initial choices are not constrained by a prior, fixed nature.[10]

It is in these moments of individual deliberation that the narrative produces a sense of openness, of indeterminacy. Or, as Gillian Beer puts it: 'The idea of a future foregrounds the insufficiency of determinism'.[11] The novel clearly needs its sense of an open future in order to keep its readers' interest, relying on the workings of suspense. On a more ideological level, too, these moments reveal that character is not fixed, since humans are free to choose one of many possible moral 'traditions'. Instead of disclosing the truth behind Tito's features, the novel charts the development of character, which might, in each case, take numerous possible routes. Thus Piero's reading of Tito as a plausible traitor, early on, is predictive in the sense that he can foresee a probable moral path for a face like Tito's, and the picture is also true in the sense that Tito does indeed pursue that course. But Piero's interpretation is valid in a more crucial way as well: it is right about Tito's *potential* for treachery, whether or not the character ever comes to realize that potential. In other words, Piero's picture does tell the truth in the present, because it is itself the *truth of promise*—of possibility. In effect, there is no 'truth' of character in the present: character is moulded by action, it is a history of choices rather than a fixed entity. Tito, free to choose his own future, may truly become either traitor or saint. Thus it is not only that we come to knowledge through plotted narrative, but that valuable knowledge is itself narrative in form: the making of the self out of its choices.

Our moments of suspense as characters try to make their choices, then, are the places in which the future necessarily becomes the site of meaning and knowledge, and narrative gains its temporal interest, its impulse towards futurity. Plotted suspense suggests that Tito is free to make himself into a range of moral selves. Consequently, in the barber shop, Tito's character is essentially potential—it is still open and capable of change. And Piero is therefore doubly right: Tito might either come to have the heart of a hero or the soul of a traitor, but he has neither as yet. Subjectivity is not fixed essence, buried beneath signifying appearance: it is possibility, evolution, agency. In this way, painting, fixed in time, reproduces visual signs that could never be indices of shifting, mutable character. The static tokens of appearance are not legible keys to emergent selfhood.

It is my basic contention, then, that Eliot's version of novelistic suspense is presented as an educational alternative to visions, and one that relies on the central element of individual moral freedom. In the final chapter, when Romola has come to her serene, untroubled law of universal sympathy, there is no further need for self-persuasion and consequently no further need for plotted suspense. She has found a law that indeed fits the realities of her life and contains no internal tensions or contradictions. But the operations of plot are not the only factors to suggest that moral freedom is central to the text of *Romola*. The novel's didactic epilogue also seems to imply that it is indeed possible to choose a moral course rather than an immoral one, and that a proper moral education might come from hearing exemplary narratives and choosing one path rather than another. There, Romola lectures her adopted son Lillo about the dangers of his father's values, and she attempts to persuade him by telling him the story of Tito's life. In this moralizing narrative, she emphasizes that the end is the result of accumulated choices based on a particular set of values and preferences. This is a narrative in which selfish desires lead directly to evil: 'because he tried to slip away from everything that was unpleasant, and cared for nothing else so much as his own safety, he came at last to commit some of the basest deeds' (588). The mature Romola thus passes on her knowledge of cause and effect in order to convince Lillo to resist a life of pleasure-seeking: she wants him to choose the path of moral responsibility. Telling stories is intended to persuade readers to opt for one set of choices over another.

Romola learns what it takes to make a murderer and an adulterer, just as she learns to forge a path of duty and human sympathy and, at the very end, she communicates this knowledge in the form of narrative. Everywhere in this text, it would seem, is the implication that narrative is the proper vehicle of knowledge. And plotted desire, which guides us to valuable knowledge, is predicated, here, on the sense of openness, mutability and moral freedom.[12]

With its epistemological questions to pique the reader's interest, this text relies on narrative form as a vehicle for telling its truths about responsibility and agency. We have seen that plotted knowledge comes about in two ways: first, as we saw earlier, is the knowledge that follows *empirical questions*—as in the debate about Tito's features; and second are the moments of *individual deliberation*—as when Tito tries to decide whether or not to illuminate Tessa about their marriage. It is my contention, however, that these two kinds of suspense are in fact two sides of the same epistemological coin, and both involve the conflation of ethics and epistemology that I suggested earlier: to know the truth of character lying behind Tito's features is to know what choices he will make. The suspense prompted by painting and the suspense surrounding the act of decision-making alert us to precisely the same question: namely, what will Tito become? In two ways, then, suspense, the prompting of epistemological desire, leads directly to the knowledge of free will and individual moral responsibility.

The logic of plotting

Surprisingly, perhaps, the plot of sceptical realism has brought us to a knowledge of bourgeois morality—which suggests that it might not be so sceptical after all. In order to unravel this logic of plotting, let us return, yet again, to our first example of foreshadowing—the representation of Tito as Sinon the traitor. There may be many convincing readings of the scene's significance, of course, but the terms of the actual debate are clear: either beautiful faces are always signs of lovable souls, or beautiful faces can come to hide traitors. Two alternatives are represented; only one of the two will be borne out by the events of the narrative. If we read two alternative ways of seeing and return to re-read the scene with the knowledge that only one of those alternatives fits the evidence provided by the novel, we have presumably learned something.

But have we? After all, the temporal relationship among these interpretative moments is more complex than a simple return to a remembered past might suggest, since within all plotted narratives, 'the future is covertly converted into retrospect. The future we are about to read has already been inscribed by the author and experienced by the characters'.[13] Thanks to this quirk of narrative, we know that the discussion between the painter and the barber has been selected for us as worthy of notice—as interpretable—from the perspective of the future, the implied time of writing rather than the actual time of the debate. The initial conflict between Piero and Nello, written in the past tense, implies that the scene has been chosen, later, as significant. But its truth is unavailable to the reader in the present, who must commit to memory cryptic signs whose later plenitude of meaning we simply take on faith. Peter Brooks calls this process of reading the 'anticipation of retrospection'. The peculiar expectation that the present will be explained by the future is actually intrinsic to narrative, Brooks claims, since in storytelling, 'If the past is to be read as present, it is a curious present that we know to be past in relation to a future we know to be already in place, already in wait for us to reach it'.[14] We readers become suspicious about Tito at an early moment because we assume that the debate is being represented within the novel *for a reason*. The time of writing, which is the knowing future beyond the novel's closure, suggests that we take the present, written as past, meaningfully. But then, like the prophet's audience, we do not know exactly what the present means while we are reading, and the knowledge to be gleaned from the scene is not disclosed to us until later.

Expectant, we are dependent on narrative time to confirm or deny our misgivings, but, since plotted narratives are always told from the perspective of the future, our dawning suspicions are, ironically, themselves prompted only by the events to come, meanings in the present that are actually prompted by the future. As Christopher Norris explains:

> 'Causes' in the novel are brought into play by the need for some solution
> or (apparently) antecedent fact which explains and unravels a complicated
> plot. In this sense causes are really *effects*, since they spring from a given
> complex of events which creates them, as it were, in pursuit of its own

coherence. Effects are likewise transformed into causes by the same curious twist of logic.[15]

Perhaps any causal narrative, anticipating retrospection, has to reach its conclusions before it can take on meaning. And although it sounds topsy-turvy, we can say that Piero posits an intriguing, generalized way of reading beautiful faces in the world precisely *because* this view will later be validated by the novel's events. Narrative, like the prophets it spurns, *already knows the future in the present.*

Thus the thorny epistemological problem, in *Romola*, concerns the relationship between time and meaning. If the treacherous world of surfaces—the split between appearance and truth—prompts the desire for more certain knowledge, it also, as we have found, calls for a healthy scepticism. But plot is not a sceptical form. If the text asserts the legitimacy of suspicious testing and experiential knowledge, it does so by setting up questions that the novel has already *arranged to be answered.* Consequently, far from truly being invited to be sceptical readers, we are reading a narrative that catches us with the 'snares' of plotted desire in order to capture our faith in its conclusions. Indeed, if the novel dictates *both* the theory and the evidence, we could not be as active, in plotted texts, as some reader-response critics would like us to concede.[16] Rather than proposing our own hypothetical meanings and looking to the text for answers, we are reading a narrative that establishes the questions and then provides 'empirical' responses to them. Carefully deployed plotted suspense in *Romola* effectively trains us to put our faith in narrative as a vehicle of truth, and hence, in this case, to recognize the importance of individual moral responsibility. But if this ethical conclusion actually *guides* the narrative from the outset, then plot begins to look more closely allied to ideology than to knowledge.

And if prophecy and plot are truly analogous forms, then the novel's critique of prophecy can be turned back on its own form. Let us return, for a moment, to Dino's prophecy. The novel uses this dream as it would other kinds of foreshadowing, prompting us to wait for knowledge. But it then disputes the value of the knowledge that emerges, claiming that it is arbitrary, merely coincidental. Romola rejects the validity of the prophecy just as it is being fulfilled. 'True as the voice of foreboding had proved, Romola saw with unshaken conviction that to have renounced Tito in obedience to a warning like that, would have been meagre-hearted folly' (328). On the one hand, then, the novel validates the prophecy, in the sense that Dino's dream does come true—the marriage between Romola and Tito is indeed a disaster, as Dino has forewarned, as we readers expect, and as Romola recognizes. The dream is then validated by the events of the text. On the other hand, Romola denies the significance of the dream, even once it has been confirmed. The text thus presents Dino's vision as a moment of explicit and deliberate prolepsis—a prophetic dream—and later events show that expectations prompted by the dream are right. But, apparently *arbitrarily*, the narrator and character discount the dream. The prophecy functions as if it were another example of epistemological foreshadowing, but the novel affirms a surprising, contradictory interpretation of this mode of producing meaning—which goes against the customary connection between signs and meanings in the unfolding of plotted time. It would seem that this narrative, when it comes to prophecy, actually invalidates the production of narrative meaning.

What does it mean for the novel, then, to suggest that its own details are meaningless? To raise suspicions and confirm them, only to deny the validity of some of these narrative messages? Or to put this another way: what does it mean to remember and to forget—specifically within a narrative?

Crucial both to the epistemology of narrative and to the ethical education this narrative recommends is the connection of past to future. Our two major characters represent two antithetical ways of remembering: Tito tries constantly to bury the past, or to conceal it, while Romola attempts both to make sense of the past and to value her initial ties, her originary duties. Unwilling to remember, Tito is also conspicuously unable to learn, while Romola, faithful to her promises and vows, learns both to understand and to work through the past. Immediately after the betrothal, Romola tells Tito that she remains frightened by her memories of Dino's dream. In response to this reborn memory, Tito locks Dino's crucifix into the casket painted with the glorious images of Tito as Bacchus and Romola as Ariadne, telling her that he has 'locked all the sadness away' (204). But Romola remains unconvinced: 'it is still there—it is only hidden', she murmurs (204). Tito still urges her to forget: 'See! they are all gone now! [...] My Ariadne must never look backward now—only forward' (205).

Here, as elsewhere, Tito denies the very temporal continuum that is the logic of the novel—a narrative system which relies on connections of past to present for its meanings. The play between past and future is a fundamental part of the temporal continuum of meaning that makes up the plotted whole, in which particular events are not read in their specificity but 'point beyond themselves to a coordinating system'.[17] And so indeed the past persistently returns, much as Tito tries to bury it. According to the paradoxical logic of plotted narrative, the past *must* return, since it is mentioned only in its relation to subsequent unfolding, the causes included for the sake of their effects, the choices for the sake of their consequences. Tito's rejection of duty and responsibility is thus intimately intertwined with the refusal to remember, ultimately futile attempts to prevent the past from influencing his present. His desire to bury the past is something like denying the most fundamental structure of narrative meanings, which necessarily entail links between past and present simply in order to preserve comprehensibility. Implicit, then, is again the alliance of plotted narrative and bourgeois morality: knowing that the past has an ineluctable claim on the present is both the substance of individual responsibility and the very fabric of realist narrative.

'You have changed towards me', Tito says to Romola, 'it has followed that I have changed towards you. It is useless to take any retrospect. We have simply to adapt ourselves to altered conditions' (418). Aside from the fact that this is not the whole story—since it is Tito, after all, who first changes towards Romola, rather than the reverse[18]—what is most telling is Tito's dismissal of the use of retrospection in favour of adaptation: one must change to suit the circumstances, but without looking backward. This is the opposite of Romola's empirical education, which moves towards final knowledge by containing the results of past trials within the present. It is also the survival of the fittest with a vengeance. For Tito, the extinction of earlier forms is relentless and unsentimental, and the future alone holds a monopoly on interest and value.

In short, Tito tries to bury the past that generates or informs subsequent moments. Romola knows that this forgetting is impossible, because memories simply do not disappear. And of course the difficulty of forgetting is particularly important within a narrative sequence, where our readerly presumption is that details are included only if they are worthy of being remembered. Thus Tito's insistence that Romola forget Dino's crucifix ironically functions as a *reminder* for the reader. The fact that the narrator describes his concealment of the crucifix means that the symbol is kept there, in the casket, for the future, a fact that is distinguished for us by its inclusion in the narrative. And indeed Romola will later un-bury the crucifix, as this moment presumably leads us to suspect. We might even say that in this scene Romola actually reaffirms the importance of foreshadowing in the novel: she argues that we cannot forget earlier signs and symbols. Just as Tito's burial of the crucifix within the casket simply preserves the symbol for future use ('it is still there, it is only hidden'), Dino's prophetic dream cannot be forgotten by the reader, but is only hiding in the memory—like the crucifix, it is still there, in the novel's pages.

If Romola is concerned to remember past images and ties, and Tito entirely dismisses the value of the past, we might formulate a simple dichotomy to describe the difference between their perspectives: the moral and responsible heroine recognizes the importance of the past, and traces a path that connects the experiences of the past with choices in the present, making her a perfect student of narrative. By contrast, her masculine counterpart, in pursuit of pleasure, neglects and betrays past bonds, and keeps his eye entirely on the future, unable to construct true narratives to account for his experiences. Thus it is Romola who tells the story of Tito's life to his own son at the end of the novel, Romola who understands temporal links between choices and their consequences. Her husband's inability to make the proper connections between past and present makes him unable to grow into moral maturity, unable, therefore, to gather knowledge and equally unable to construct true narrative sequences that make valid sense of the ways of the world. As always, ethics, epistemology and time-bound narrative unite in Eliot's novelistic world.

But the place of Dino's dream in the novel functions as a way of unravelling the narrative's own persuasive structure: Romola tries, in the exceptional case of her brother's prophecy, to forget the past, to dismiss a moment that has been chosen as meaningful within the narrative, and her dismissal is corroborated by the narrator. But the image returns, again and again—as irrepressible as Tito's denials of Baldassarre. 'Still, the images of the vision she despised jarred and distressed her like painful and cruel cries' (162). In other words, there is no way to reject the images of the memory, no matter how unfounded they might be. Later, the narrator represents this process as an insistent, irrevocable return: 'She could not prevent herself from hearing inwardly the dying prophetic voice [...] She could not prevent herself from dwelling with a sort of agonized fascination on the wasted face' (328). This denial and return might lead the reader to believe that Romola is actually *mistaken* to dismiss the quintessentially narrative voices of prophecy. Perhaps they cannot be forgotten because, like old ties, they have a valid claim on the present. Mary Wilson Carpenter's apocalyptic reading of the novel is based, in part, on this assumption:

> [I]f Dino's prophecy, despite its accuracy, is not worth heeding, why is it given such importance in the narrative? Or to put it another way, if the prophecy is only part of a world of 'phantoms' and 'disjointed whispers', why should Dino nevertheless appear to have been correct in his prediction of events?[19]

Carpenter frames the question perfectly. But rather than proposing an intricate symbolic scheme to account for the workings of the novel, as Carpenter does, I would contend that it is at this point that the realist narrative reaches its crucial tension. In the novel's attempts to dismiss the voices of prophecy, the form and the ideological aims of the text come into conflict.

Narrative truth and the question of alternatives

If the power of prophecy is included in the text for any constructive reason, it is, according to the narrator, because it allows Romola to sympathize with those who succumb to the force of visions. The protagonist returns, again and again, to memories of her brother's dream, but not to emphasize their truth-value:

[T]he persistent presence of these memories, linking themselves in her
imagination with her actual lot, gave her a glimpse of understanding into
the lives which had before lain utterly aloof from her sympathy—the lives
of the men and women who were led by such inward images and voices.

'If they were only a little stronger in me', she said to herself, 'I should
lose the sense of what that vision really was, and take it for a prophetic
light. I might in time get to be a seer of visions myself' [...] Romola
shuddered at the possibility. (328-9)

Thus we learn that prophecies are powerfully persuasive but ultimately
fallacious. It is this rationalist theme, however, that is necessarily undercut by
the *non-rational* structure of narrative, which cannot distinguish true from
false temporal patterns within the temporal continuum that makes narratives
persuasive. Roland Barthes asserts that this is a quintessentially narrative
problem; he writes: 'Everything suggests [...] that the mainspring of narrative
is precisely the confusion of consecution and consequence, what comes *after*
being read in narrative as what is *caused by*; in which case narrative would be
a systematic application of the logical fallacy denounced by Scholasticism in
the formula *post hoc, ergo propter hoc*'.[20] The classic text, which conflates
consecution and consequence, creates suspense by ambiguous connotative
signifiers, which produce a sense that there are resolutions to come,
conclusions to be born of the narratable flux of the text; and if they do come
as expected, they necessarily take on *narrative* validity, whether or not a
voice—even an authoritative voice—dismisses them in no uncertain terms.
With Carpenter, then, we can always ask: if the vision has no significance,
why does it come true?

I have argued that foreshadowing in the novel is a way of asserting the
truth-value of narrative as a form; we cannot tell how to interpret a
meaningful moment in the present, and we need to read on to find out how it
should have been read. And this epistemological process is dangerously
similar to arbitrary prophetic authority: neither offers us valid proof of *actual*
connections between hypothesis and event, and both persuade us simply by
claiming a link between interpretative suggestions and later events.

Perhaps, given this structural analogy, we might face the same
interpretative dilemmas with the novel as we did with the visionary.
Remember, for example, that conflicts among visionaries made it impossible
to tell which was the better seer. It was one of the text's own criticisms of
prophecy that the prophets disagreed with one another, producing differing
visions that they then proceeded to defend on their own interpretative
grounds. With the Franciscans predicting one outcome, and the Dominicans
another, both aiming to validate their predictions after the fact by some
intricate interpretative 'stretching', only prior faith in one or the other would
allow us to choose to believe one rather than the other. The same is true of

narrative. After all, there are other narratives out there, equally concerned with the problems of appearance and essence, of truth and morality. And perhaps if we turned to other narratives with different outcomes to the same debates as those we find in *Romola*, the 'knowledge' we have gathered in this narrative would begin to look dubious indeed. What, after all, would make one fictional plot more persuasive than another?

But we do not actually need to turn our attention as far afield as other novels to find alternatives to the empirical lessons taught to us by this text. There are alternative narratives implied within *Romola* itself. As we have seen, the novel relies on its sense of openness, of numerous possible paths, for its interest. Without that sense of possibility, plotted narrative would not exert its powers of seduction, which always rely, to some extent, on the workings of suspense, on the understanding that there are many potential paths a narrative can plausibly take. The suspense crucial to our desire for knowledge actually requires that there be more than one plausible outcome to any narrative mystery. Thus within *Romola*, suspense actually reaffirms the viable *multiplicity* of outcomes. Tito almost undeceives Tessa about their marriage, and thus almost remains faithful to Romola. As we saw earlier, in his moment of deliberation both options seem truly possible. But if he had decided to be faithful to Romola, his beauty would indeed have been a sign of his goodness, Piero would have been wrong, and we readers would have had no reason to cast off Romola's proverbial correlation between outer and inner beauty. Surely the novel invites such speculations, and the fact that he chooses the immoral path within the novel does not make the experience of the text conform to the 'real' more than it would if he were allowed to follow the moral course. Crucial to the ideological lessons of the novel, he must be entirely capable of choosing the moral direction.

Given the necessary openness of suspenseful narrative, then, it must be possible to write *equally* convincing narratives to support *conflicting* general claims. Thus the condemnation of prophecy on the grounds of its conflicting declarations—its profusion of *epistemologically* undifferentiated possibilities—can be turned back on the plotted text.

As we have seen, the text also suggests that it is not valid to assert the legitimacy of religious prophecy simply because it happens to come true subsequently, for two reasons: on the one hand, the fulfilment of the prediction might be an accidental, inauthentic connection, in no way proving the validity of the prophecy; and on the other, interpretations can always be stretched, after the fact, to confirm the prophetic voice. But how does the narrative establish the validity of its own empirical knowledge? We have seen that plot works in part by setting up cryptic suggestions and unresolved debates which, since narrative is told from the perspective of the future, are actually incorporated for the sake of their later resolution. Thus our 'empirical' conclusions, which seemed to involve the testing of interpretative paradigms against the hidden realities of the world, were in fact there *before* they were ever arranged to be tested. The debate about Tito's features alerted us to his later treachery because, as all readers of plotted narrative know, mysteries are there to be solved. We might say, in this context, that Tito, far from being a free moral agent, is absolutely destined to a treacherous future, and we, far from being autonomous and sceptical readers, have acquired a knowledge that is as preordained as the miraculous interventions of the divine will.

This brings us, then, to the union of narrative, epistemology and ethics—the lesson that Romola learned, that we were meant to learn and that Tito did not learn at all—namely, that moral maturity calls for an understanding of the power of the human choices in the world. In place of arbitrary divine predestination, the text favours an empirical causal model that affirms the force of moral agency: 'the inexorable law of human souls, that we prepare ourselves for sudden deeds by the reiterated choice of good or evil which gradually determines character' (224). Importantly, the text simply states this law, and then offers substantiation of it: both Romola and Tito follow precisely this pattern. But although crucial to the lessons of the text, this rule of character is never itself subject to sceptical hypothesis, test, or proof: it guides all of the valuable moral knowledge that we acquire, but it is never the object of empirical testing. The novel suggests that it is not valid to assert the legitimacy of religious prophecy simply because it happens to come true subsequently. But is it ever valid to assert the legitimacy of a *novel's* events, simply because its hypotheses are validated by the unfolding of its own plot?

This is of course a question of correspondence, that quintessentially realist problem. How can we tell whether our hypotheses and representations really *fit* the world? Is it possible that our surmises about cause and effect in the novel are in fact only accidentally correlated with experience? The sceptical philosopher David Hume argued in the eighteenth century that a knowledge of essential causality is never truly possible—only the derivation of consequence from succession and contiguity: 'the inference we draw from cause to effect, is not deriv'd merely from such a penetration into their essences as may discover the one upon the other'.[21] If Hume is right, then it is effectively impossible to distinguish between true causal patterns and deceptive, self-justifying ones. Narrative meanings cannot offer us proof of actual, grounded connections any more successfully than the prophets. In *Romola*, the monk's vision occurred and the event that followed it may seem to correspond to that vision, but according to Romola, our proxy within the text, there is no causal link between the two. All too similarly, however, the debate about Tito suggested that he might turn treacherous, which indeed he did. And a sceptical reader of another ideological bent might contend that events like Tito's treachery are not caused by conscious, individual human choice, as we are told, but by the forces of material production, or by unconscious drives of desire, or by divine fiat. In the context of these other causal models, the novel shows that it is persuasive only within a sequence that it proceeds to explain on the basis of its own, previously established interpretative paradigm. What reasonable warrant could we have for believing in such a vision and acting on it? The text's promotion of the sceptical reader is in bad faith. Within the context of a plotted narrative, bound by its future to certain outcomes, we are hardly free to test the world for ourselves.

Just as prior knowledge of the conventions of painting corrupts the painter of the natural world in Ruskin, a prior faith in the correlation between prophecies and events precludes a 'good' reading of the real in *Romola*. But if the particular narrative path that *Romola* takes traces an equally arbitrary connection between mysteries and their resolutions, then perhaps the persuasiveness of Eliot's novel must rely on a similarly *prior* faith in an ideology of free choice and individual moral responsibility. We readers are actually guided, blind, by a narrative that establishes clear questions and then provides allegedly 'empirical' responses to those questions, based on its own prior theory of causality. Far from free, we too are led by phantoms and disjointed whispers, in a narrative which incorporates its own mysteriously prophetic moments, after having already arranged for their realization. Written in the knowledgeable future, the *Bildungsroman*, like prophecy, allows us readers no independent ways of learning connections in the world. The truth-value of the narrative would therefore *presuppose* a belief in the kinds of causal patterns the novel describes. Hence the validity of the causal model of choice and its consequences is, like prophecy, authoritative and self-justifying, confirmed only by the evidence that the text describes.

Romola herself, unwilling to accept the interpretative stretching involved in this form of persuasion, simply rejects the truth-value of the visionary even once it has come true. She refuses to believe in prophecy despite the fact that its visions are realized. And perhaps we—who have learned from the plot to be sceptical readers—should, like her, resist plotted authority and insist on a rebellious reading, That is, we can turn our wary eyes on the plotted text itself. With revolutionary gusto, we can encourage readers of the *Bildungsroman* to imitate the sceptical protagonist, to *take* the very same freedom in interpretation that Romola does when she refuses to be persuaded by the authoritative voices of prophecy. Rejecting the causal model implicit in the text, we can simply dismiss the novel's lessons, claiming that they represent an arbitrary connection between interpretative possibilities and narrative unfolding. The law of narrative might be sacred, but the rebellion might be sacred too.

Notes

1. See, for example, Leo Bersani, *A Future for Astyanax: Character and Desire in Literature* (Boston and Toronto: Little, Brown, and Company, 1976). Bersani writes: 'Realistic fiction serves nineteenth-century society by providing it with strategies for containing (and repressing) its disorder within significantly structured stories about itself' (p. 63).
2. Robert C. Holub, *Reflections of Realism: Paradox, Norm, and Ideology in Nineteenth-Century German Prose* (Detroit: Wayne State University Press, 1991), p. 15.
3. I am borrowing these terms from Roland Barthes, *S/Z*, trans. Richard Miller (New York: Hill and Wang, 1974), pp. 75-6.
4. Susan Winnett argues that the story Romola tells Lillo in the Epilogue is a reading of the novel as a whole: see 'Coming Unstrung: Women, Men, Narrative, and the Principles of Pleasure', *PMLA* **105** (May 1990), p. 515.
5. Barthes, p. 100.
6. This lesson marks *Romola* as anti-conventional if we look to the many Victorian novels that rely on the correlation between visual appearance and moral essence. To give just two examples, in *Agnes Grey* (1847), Mrs Bloomfield's brother has a face which gives away his character: 'a nose that seemed to disdain the earth, and little grey eyes, frequently half closed, with a mixture of real stupidity and affected contempt'. Anne Brontë, *Agnes Grey* (Oxford: Oxford University Press, 1991), p. 42. And even Dinah Morris, in *Adam Bede* (1859), bears clear marks of character on her visage: 'The eyes had no peculiar beauty beyond that of expression, they looked so simple, so candid, so gravely loving'. George Eliot, *Adam Bede*, ed. Leonee Ormond, (London: Everyman, 1992), p. 22.
7. David Friedrich Strauss, *The Life of Jesus Critically Examined* [trans. George Eliot], (London: Chapman, 1846), vol. 1, p. 88. Similarly, Ludwig Feuerbach too condemns the spiritual authority of the Christian Church as arbitrary: 'Moral rules are indeed observed [by religious believers], but they are severed from the inward disposition, the heart, by being represented as the commandments of an external lawgiver, by being placed in the category of arbitrary laws, police regulations'. Ludwig Feuerbach, *The Essence of Christianity*, trans. George Eliot (New York and London: Harper and Row, 1957), p. 207.
8. Felicia Bonaparte, *Will and Destiny: Morality and Tragedy in George Eliot's Novels* (New York: New York University Press, 1975), pp. 48-62.
9. Shlomith Rimmon-Kenan, *Narrative Fiction: Contemporary Poetics*

(London and New York: Methuen, 1983), p. 39.

10. It is telling that a contemporary reviewer is unable to decide whether Tito is wholly a victim of circumstances or wholly responsible for his own demise: 'There is, first, the picture of a man falling into falsehood, and made positively, though gradually, worse, not only by contact with evil, but by the companionship of unrelenting truth and purity, which perpetually reminds him of the barrier between himself and innocence which he has built up'. First he 'falls'—an ambiguous moral term, implying neither total responsibility nor total compulsion—but then he has been 'made worse', which suggests that he has been forced into evil. And he also seems to have 'built up' his own guilt. 'Romola', an unsigned article in *The Saturday Review* 16 (25 July 1863), p. 125.

11. Gillian Beer, *Darwin's Plots: Evolutionary Narrative in Darwin, George Eliot, and Nineteenth-Century Fiction* (London: Routledge and Kegan Paul, 1983), p. 185.

12. Critics have largely agreed that human choice is crucial to Eliot's epistemology: Felicia Bonaparte explains that there is no escaping the 'web of events', which connects each action to a larger whole (*Will and Destiny*, p. 55); and Elizabeth Deeds Ermarth argues that '[T]he far-reaching consequences of every action and the growing weight of conditions that the sum of actions entails are [...] powerfully present facts'. See her 'Incarnations: George Eliot's Conception of Undeviating Law', *Nineteenth-Century Fiction* 29 (December 1974), p. 273. John R. Reed also argues that 'Eliot wanted to represent a world governed by the laws of invariant causation unaffected by any supernatural power'. *Victorian Will* (Athens, Ohio: Ohio University Press, 1989), p. 309.

13. Beer, p. 185.

14. Peter Brooks, *Reading for the Plot: Design and Intention in Narrative* (Cambridge, MA, and London: Harvard University Press, 1984), p. 23.

15. Christopher Norris, *Deconstruction: Theory and Practice* (London and New York: Routledge, 1982), p. 133.

16. See, for example, Norman Holland, *The Critical I* (New York: Columbia University Press, 1992), pp. 21-2. Holland argues that a hypothesis about the text is proposed by the reader based on his or her own 'identity theme', tested against the evidence, and then rejected or affirmed.

17. Elizabeth Deeds Ermarth, *Realism and Consensus in the English Novel* (Princeton: Princeton University Press, 1983), p. 42.

18. Indeed, four serial issues earlier, the narrator tells us: 'this morning for the first time [Romola] admitted to herself not only that Tito had changed, but that he had changed towards her' (280).

19. For Carpenter, prophecy provides an important way of reading events,

which prompts her to read the whole novel as a text that employs a prophetic 'method'. Mary Wilson Carpenter, *George Eliot and the Landscape of Time* (Chapel Hill: University of North Carolina Press, 1986), p. 76.

20. Roland Barthes, 'Introduction to the Structural Analysis of Narratives', in *Image, Music, Text*, trans. Stephen Heath (London: Fontana Press, 1977), p. 94.
21. David Hume (1739), *A Treatise of Human Nature* (Harmondsworth: Penguin, 1985), p. 135.

CHAPTER NINE

'An Imperceptible Start':
The Sight of Humanity in *Romola*

CHRIS GREENWOOD

> The lustre of good fortune was upon him; he was smiling, listening and explaining, with his usual graceful unpretentious ease, and only a very keen eye bent on studying him could have marked a certain amount of change in him which was not to be accounted for by the lapse of eighteen months. It was that change which comes from the final departure of moral youthfulness—from the distinct self-conscious adoption of a part in life. (217)

I

In the Proem to *Romola*, one of the most beautiful passages of her prose, George Eliot writes of the 'angel of the dawn' casting light upon

> the night-student, who had been questioning the stars or the sages, or his own soul, for that hidden knowledge which would break through the barrier of man's brief life, and show its dark path, that seemed to bend no whither, to be an arc in an immeasurable circle of light and glory. (1)

Together, the novel and the Proem set out to demonstrate that human nature itself is one of the constituent arcs of this immeasurable circle, transcending the historical particularities of individual lives ('the barrier of man's brief life'). But who can gain access to this 'hidden knowledge'? Tito Melema's duplicities successfully convince his contemporaries whilst remaining transparent in the eyes of the historically distanced narration—and thus Tito becomes the author's figure for both the elusive nature of this transcending arc and for the inevitability of its discovery in the face of dedicated study and gifted perception. In the main body of the novel—exemplifying the Proem's thesis—'hidden knowledge' repeatedly breaks 'through the barrier of' Tito Melema's 'brief life' before our eyes, teaching us, at our distance, that his 'dark path' is just as much an arc in this transcending circle as any result of the night-student's virtuous searchings. Enlightenment must include a knowledge of darkness.

The moments when Tito's dark past breaks into view are crucial narrative impulses, and they constitute the narrative's dramatic appeal. The suddenness of these moments, the anxiety and shame that they exemplify, sustain the work's otherwise dry philosophical, moral and historical investigations with an emotional correlative. By rendering Tito's emotions opaque to his contemporaries whilst clearly advertising his fraught condition to the reader, Eliot works hard both to generate suspense and to exemplify a philosophical stance: the action of the central character is a matter only fully available to acute, disinterested observation.

For example, when the barber, Nello, accidentally causes a sudden start in Tito the scene is typical of the way in which momentary outbreaks of guilt or shame suggest to us that Tito is hiding something:

> 'your Christian Greek is of so easy a conscience that he would make a stepping stone of his father's corpse'.
>   The flush on the stranger's face indicated what seemed so natural a movement of resentment, that the good-natured Nello hastened to atone for his want of reticence. (37)

Here it is crucial that Nello fails to interpret correctly the brief blush with which Tito responds to his heavy banter. That it is the narration which has to catch Tito suffering from 'slight, almost imperceptible start[s]'(70), thrills and flushes of guilt when other characters innocently mention ransoms, fathers or abandonments affirms the idea that 'human nature' is an arc in the great transcendental circle of knowledge, beyond the ken of the individual limited by quotidian concerns. The 'good-natured Nello', after all, seeks to explain Tito's blush as the result of his own fault. According to Nello, Tito's behaviour is a reaction to an aspect of his own self, 'his want of reticence'. By locating Tito's guilt as a fact that the average self-absorbed human being cannot discern, George Eliot confers upon it the status of that 'hidden knowledge' sought after by the 'night-student', both in himself and in the writings of the sages.

Throughout the novel a series of fleeting reactions, taken together, act to ground George Eliot's description of human nature as something not immediately visible in its entirety but, nevertheless, when submitted to the action of disinterested and prolonged scrutiny, wholly present in the human scene, across all of time. Locating Tito's guilty secret as a set of visible events, George Eliot asserts the positivistic creed that all is open to the perceptive, regardless of historical particularity. In a review of Mackay's *The Progress of the Intellect* she describes

> the pleasure of perceiving identity of nature under a variety of manifestations—a perception which resembles an expansion of one's own being, a pre-existence in the past.[1]

To be fully human, George Eliot implies, is to exist across time. One becomes more human, as the Proem to *Romola* clearly demonstrates, by paying attention to tradition, by studying and becoming aware of the works produced not by individual humans but by the action of human nature *in* individuals. This human nature, to the educated, attentive eye is everywhere, always.

As the novel progresses it turns out that no matter how skilfully the Greek can disguise his treachery it remains available for discovery. The question the text poses is not the one implicitly posed and answered by one of its characters, Niccolo Machiavelli: whether Tito's conscience can successfully obliterate his crime so that it simply does not matter to him. Rather it is a question of suspense: how long can the crime remain unperceived in a world where all is open to the attentive seeker? This philosophical formula serves the dramatic needs of the novel. Despite the fact that Tito may wish to hide his sinful acts as if to exclude them from the plane of existence, George Eliot's narration repeatedly presents the irruption of his sins, in fits and starts, as all too clear. Which is to say that his actions will out and that, to the attentive student, they are as much visible points on the circumference of the 'immeasurable circle' as the sayings of a saint. This perceptibility is not only a dramatic necessity but a philosophical position.

Throughout *Romola* George Eliot plays a double game in order to render Tito's dissembling an observable facet of human nature. Whilst she opens up his treacherous nature to the reader through a series of involuntary reactions to accidental stimuli, she keeps it concealed from her cast of characters. The reader's suspicions grow as a list of shocks are recorded on Tito's body, shocks clearly remarkable for the specificity of their cause and their frequency within the time-frame of reading—rather than in the time-frame of the character's existence. On the other hand, the characters, because they are each of them only intermittently present in the text—compared to the narration's near omniscience—see isolated events and as a result detect nothing worth committing to memory. In this work dramatic irony is a device which operates to validate the argument of the novel, that human nature is ahistorical, present to the attentive seeker, across the whole of time.

When any of the characters, their vision limited by contingent concerns, actually spots the movement of thought across Tito's face, they are likely to attribute it in a manner that accords with their own desires, neglecting to remember it as anything unusual. Where the text's historical overview guarantees dispassionate observation, 'an expansion of one's own being, a pre-existence in the past', the perspective of the characters leads to a perception of events clouded by their own preoccupations. Romola can see through the schemer only once she has gained the experience of a continued observation of Tito's body and has studied the mortification of the self. She begins by seeing Baldassarre's shadowing Tito like the 'ghost of his conscience'.[2] Gradually, through a combination of faith and clear-sightedness she comes to know the real relation between Tito and his ghost. Otherwise, everyone seeks to explain Tito's reactions in ways that match their desires:

> 'and you had, doubtless, a father who cared for your early instruction—
> who, perhaps, was himself a scholar?'
>   There was a slight pause before Tito's answer came to the ear of Bardo;
> but for Romola and Nello it began with a slight shock that seemed to pass
> through him, and cause a momentary quivering of the lip; doubtless at the
> revival of a supremely painful remembrance. (61)

To us, who have already witnessed one too many of these 'slight shocks',
there is a story in Tito's quivering lip, a story his body is clearly trying to tell.
But to the young, as yet inexperienced Romola, there is only confirmation of
her desires:

> A girl of eighteen imagines the feelings behind the face that has moved her
> with its sympathetic youth, as easily as primitive people imagined the
> humours of the gods in fair weather: what is she to believe in, if not in this
> vision woven from within? (68)

In such moments George Eliot's narrative technique investigates the
relationships among vision, memory, will and perception. Her descriptions of
contingent perspectives in the novel, of characters tending to see what they want
to see, are contrasted against a perspective on Tito's behaviour that is measured
against a far larger scale—that of history. The visual demonstrates, in its
relentless clarity, how easily distracted we are from the evidence our eyes
provide us.

   George Eliot's characters perceive the world according to the operation of
their wills. There is scant likelihood of their remembering anything other than
their own concerns. In the initial example, when Tito recoils at the jesting
reference to the easy conscience of Christian Greeks, Nello sees a fine subject
upon whom to operate his skills as a barber, coiffeur, raconteur, gossip and
intermediary. Hence he is persuaded by his easily won good heart that the
source of Tito's blush is innocent, a justifiably resentful reaction to his banter.
Pages later Piero di Cosimo enters the shop, Tito's shave complete, his nature
less fully concealed by beard and ragged locks, and causes another shock to the
Greek's sensitive frame:

> 'Young man, I am painting a picture of Sinon deceiving old Priam, and I
> should be glad of your face for my Sinon, if you'd give me a sitting'.
>   Tito Melema started and looked round with a pale astonishment in his
> face as at a sudden accusation. (42)

Piero sees, as he points out, what he is looking for, a 'face, informed with rich
young blood, that will be nourished enough by food, and will keep its colour
without much help of virtue'. Rather than detecting some guilty reaction,
Piero sees what he wants: the perfect model for the treacherous Sinon, a face

that gives little away. Despite the fact that Eliot has given the artist the extraordinary power to spot the truth, Piero's intimation of Tito's nature, like Nello's gossipy version, becomes a facet of the speaker's will, a story not that he has perceived, but that he has deliberately looked for.

The stories that the characters tell themselves are not good histories of the events that motivate Tito's features. Characters extrapolate from individual moments the stories they want to tell, pertinent only to the history of their own lives. Hence, four hundred years distant, in a broader history, Tito's face is the opposite of that impassive visage required by Piero. It tells and tells repeatedly, concealing very little from those who are permitted the perspective to regard it dispassionately.

The story that the body tells is part of what the Proem identifies as the 'great-river courses which have shaped the lives of men [...] the life-currents that ebb and flow in human hearts, [...] the same great loves and terrors [...] the broad sameness of the human lot' (3). Tito's treachery, a result of the ease his soul craves, is but an example of one of the life-currents flowing throughout human history. It is not unusual. George Eliot is keen to show that this sameness cuts across the history of humanity. She dissects this history as if it were a whole, for autopsy, and permits herself to write a novel about people in late fifteenth-century Florence in order to instruct the readership of mid-nineteenth-century Britain. As she says in her review of Mackay, responding to a dogmatic Auguste Comte, it may be

> better to reason justly on some point of immediate concern [...] than quote
> Aristophanes [but] it is a mistake to suppose that the study of the past and
> the labours of criticism have no important practical bearing on the present.
> (353)

Reading *Romola* as a dissection of humanity, as an act of dehistoricized forensic science, lends credence to the common complaint that the novel's opening chapters are laborious and that some of its characters seem overly wooden, and suggests that late fifteenth-century Florence is reduced to the status of a corpse upon the author's examination table. From this one might argue that only what she regards as essentially human receives the full attention of George Eliot's passion, that the history of Savonarola's rise and fall is a mere backdrop against which her characters act out an anachronistic morality. She might be said to have tried to transplant that which she understood to be human from the life of her own time into a setting which rejected it.

Such an argument works only in the context of a distaste for the humanist belief in the existence of a human nature. Emphasizing the absence of determining historical influences, of a proper expression of human beings as products of their time and place, this position argues implicitly for the material human being, shaped by subject positions constructed from

contemporary materials. Such a historicizing stance must refuse to recognize
the deliberately juxtaposed similarities among the distinctly individual Bardo,
Tito and Savonarola. It must also refuse to take account of the sheer artistry of
the characters' relations, failing to spot, for example, that Savonarola's
failings echo those that condemn the still more corrupt Tito. Of course George
Eliot was well aware of such arguments, they are far from new. Her *Romola*
is, in one of its manifestations, a protracted defense of the humanist's sense
that love, passion, power and treachery are broadly constant across the history
of humanity. They are responses to the 'undeviating law in the material and
moral world'[3] sensed by writers of history, writers with the synthesizing
power of a Mackay.

What follows is an account of this defence. By burying the essential
constituents of human nature within her story, like organs hidden beneath the
skin, and by indicating and justifying the care with which such precious
resources are concealed and protected, George Eliot draws attention to just
how superficial the materialist position truly is. The ebbs and flows upon
which her Proem discourses, repeated as they are within the main body of her
text by the ebbs and flows of the Florentines' political fashions, are those
forces which it accuses the determinist of overemphasizing. The guilty fear,
on the other hand, that causes those sharp observers, Bernardo Del Nero and
Piero di Cosimo, to perceive the distortions of Tito's beautiful frame as
suspicious, is an aspect of the human nature that the talented dissembler
strives to keep well hidden.

George Eliot's argument in this novel is that there are essential human values
that run throughout history because history is a matter of the human beings
through whom these values flow. If these values are sometimes hard to detect
that is because, very often, people conceal them so effectively.

II

On 26 June 1862 Anthony Trollope wrote a sparkling letter of appreciation
about *Romola*. In it he exclaimed that 'the character of Romola is artistically
beautiful,—a picture exceeded by none that I know of any girl in any novel. It
is the perfection of pen painting'.[4] In asserting George Eliot's achievement
thus Trollope ascribes to painting the ultimate power of characterization, a
power greater, certainly, than that of the novel, and confers upon the author of
Romola the compliment that her art transcends the boundaries of its medium.
In 1882 Henry James was equally capable of regarding art as a category that
transcended the contingencies of the media. He wrote:

> If all art is supposed to be one and if its different manifestations, to the
> truly penetrating eye, are supposed to minister a mutual light, there should

be no great violence of transition in passing from the exhibitions to the theatres.[5]

Suggesting that art is a category separate from the art form, James identifies the same visual quality as Trollope. The 'truly penetrating eye' is both the artist's resource and that to which he has to respond.

George Eliot was equally concerned with harnessing and emphasizing the visual because she believed that the mind functioned best when it visualized the objects of its attention, preferably from a memory of an actual encounter, rather than from an imagined impression. Her essay on Riehl, the German social historian, introduces its subject with a discussion of 'the picture-writing of the mind', a phrase which denotes 'the images which are habitually associated with abstract or collective terms'.[6]

All three writers remark upon the appeal to the mind that art makes through the eye. If Trollope seeks to make explicit the transfer of this power to writing, James implies it in that he supposes 'all art [...] to be one'. Where Trollope's letter is brief (it rests only on the effect of Romola's characterization) the lengthy introduction George Eliot provides in her essay on Riehl examines the implications of 'picture-writing'. One example scarifies the visionary politician who lacks the precise mental imagery for his dreams of great projects to become real. The politician envisions a global railway without actually observing one:

> He may talk of a vast network of railways [...] But it is evident that if we want a railway to be made, or its affairs to be managed, this man of wide views and narrow observation will not serve our purpose.[7]

The ability to manage and to make railways should properly be gleaned from a visual familiarity with them. Observation amounts to practical knowledge. Making an explicit link with the artist the essay goes on to state that the best quality, indeed the definition, of the competent engineer-manager lies in the possession of an extraordinary power of observation. 'Wide views and narrow observation': could this be the chattering Nello or the visionary Savonarola? At any rate, observation is the hero of the essay.

Elsewhere in George Eliot's work, characters who envisage things are far less likely to achieve happiness and success than those who actually see things. The narrow-sighted visionary whom George Eliot conjures up to contrast with the practical observer is recognizable to us all in the figures of Mordechai, Casaubon and Bardo. And if Bardo has become blind through a lack of attendance upon the world, so too has Fra Girolamo. The contrast effected between Fra Girolamo, blinded by his own need for power over men, and a man who observes carefully for a living, Piero di Cosimo, could not be greater. It is a precise demonstration in fiction of George Eliot's belief that one must watch real things that occur in the present carefully, setting aside one's own desires, if one is to catch a glimpse of human nature.

Therefore, when we are introduced to Bardo and Romola in Chapter 5, 'The Blind Scholar and His Daughter', the passage concludes

> Nonnus [...] introduces Actaeon exclaiming that he calls Teiresias happy, since, without dying, and with the loss of his eyesight merely, he had beheld Minerva unveiled and thus, though blind, could for evermore carry her image in his soul. (94)

Where Teiresias has witnessed immortal beauty and has been able to internalize the sight, Bardo has pored over a thousand books, envisioning rather than seeing. His Miltonic characteristics, vanity and an insensitivity towards the needs of his daughter, the 'Milton blindness' that George Eliot wrote of as obscuring levels and levels of attention, stifle his ability to live in the world.[8] Bardo is a failed visionary noticing not what is about him, nor producing anything of value, only allowing his selfish concerns to lead him into blindness. His demise—figured by the impracticality of his academic projects and the sale of his library, as well as by his blindness—is compared implicitly, if rather harshly, with Actaeon's: men who hunt after knowledge for selfish ends. The Proem's virtuous 'night-student', by contrast, searches disinterestedly, seeking to 'break through the barrier of man's brief life'. Thus Bardo's admission that 'blindness acts like a dam, sending the streams of thought backward along the already travelled channels' (98), expresses George Eliot's moral and philosophical position regarding vision. The trope of blindness shows that the old scholar's self-concern causes him to fail to notice even those who are closest to him.

Bardo's blindness also represents the scant attention he has ever paid to the world. The visual memories he chooses to dwell upon are of his books and the words in them, rather than of, say, the sight of his daughter, a beauty approaching that of Minerva.

> it was evident that the deepest fount of feeling within her had not yet wrought its way to the less changeful features, and only found its outlet through her eyes.
> But the father, unconscious of that soft radiance, looked flushed and agitated as his hand explored the edges and back of the large book. (50)

That it is his daughter's eyes, to George Eliot the 'most changeful' of the human features, that Bardo cannot see indicates both Romola's restraint in hiding her response to his insensitivity and the general thesis of the novel that the signs of human nature are always present to the attentive eye. In his inability to write a whole text and in his inattentive relationship with his daughter, Bardo is also the opposite of Baldassarre, a man 'whose sense of vision was instructed with large experience' (340). Bardo is the visionary politician, dreaming of impractical schemes, whilst Baldassarre, the scholar who risked his life travelling to occupied Greece just for a sight of the

Pantheon, is his opposite, the engineer-manager possessed of a visual knowledge of his subject.

III

Henry James remarked that George Eliot's 'figures and situations are evolved, as the phrase is, from her moral consciousness, and are only indirectly the products of observations'. Hugh Witemeyer, countering James, establishes that her 'figures and situations' 'are not abstract or indirectly observed in any visual sense of the terms; on the contrary, they are highly particularized and often modeled upon specific, identifiable pictures'.[9] And in fact, *Romola* takes the power of observation so seriously that the novel actually matches the political and social hierarchy of its characters to their ability to 'read' pictorially described situations. The text sets characters apart morally, intellectually, politically and socially on the basis of their willingness to respond to framed images. The less they are able to understand what they see, the less power they have. Hence Baldassarre's power to threaten Tito fluctuates with his ability to match present sights to those in his memory.

The novel sets the narration apart from the characters on the same grounds. There is a kind of observational hierarchy: at its foot stand Tessa and Baldassarre, understanding very little of what they see, powerless and deprived in the face of a baffling and deceptive visual scene. At the other end of the scale, beyond even the visually skilled Bernardo del Nero or Piero di Cosimo, is the narration itself, defining the limits of observation. The narration's pronouncements are authoritative because it can see more clearly than any of the cast. It is to be believed because it claims the highest power of sight.

But the narration's authority becomes suspect if James is correct about George Eliot's partial commitment to reproducing her observations of daily life in her novels.[10] If the narration chooses the visual scenes on its own terms, it stands less as an authority and more as an arbitrary political power, something more authoritarian than authoritative, imposing interpretations and hierarchies in order to enforce its rule. Indeed it could be said to base its power in deception. Characters become more or less powerful only because the narration can show the extent to which they have missed, or misread, clear visible signs of 'human nature'. Most importantly, their ability to see this essence clearly is directly linked to their social position.

Patently, or according to Witemeyer's research, what the narration observes is no such thing. It places before its characters' eyes a series of scenes from works of art, ordered and valued by a tradition of appreciation four hundred years older than any of these unfortunates. In other words, a distanced, nineteenth-century critical perspective reproduces scenes from Renaissance paintings, posing them as depictions of human nature, and then ranks the characters in so far as they are blessed with its perspective. But if Witemeyer can identify the observations upon which the novelist based her writing as works of art, George Eliot's characters are not so blessed. For them these scenes have no interpretative frame. They are momentary, barely available to observation at all, unavailable to scrutiny. That it is only Piero di Cosimo who comes anything like close to catching all there is to know about Tito, having observed him with a telling eye, is an expression of exactly the kind of privilege George Eliot accords to the schooled artistic vision—her own. After witnessing the beautiful Greek a number of times he recognizes the painted 'type', which Tito cannot prevent himself from representing. In other words, Piero comes the closest of all the characters in the novel to identifying the works of art that his author drew on to produce the treacherous Greek.

One of the pictorial set pieces occurs at the novel's outset:

> Under this loggia, in the early morning of the 9th of April 1492, two men had their eyes fixed on each other: one was stooping slightly, and looking downward with the scrutiny of curiosity; the other, lying on the pavement, was looking upward with the startled gaze of a suddenly awakened dreamer. (10)

As in many oil paintings, the description connects the two characters via their line of sight. It also pays attention to their relations through the means of posture and location. We are given the condition of the light and a sense of proportion and scale from the 'loggia' and 'pavement'. The dynamics of the description, the capture of a 'startled gaze' in process—a start that will be associated with this figure throughout the work—and the active voice with 'stooping', produce the 'frozen moment' beloved of painters of dramatic canvases.

Two particular phrases serve to intensify the significance of the rapture that holds the two figures, rendering it enigmatic, open to rational explanation, opening up the image to narrative. One is 'the scrutiny of curiosity' and the other is 'the startled gaze of a suddenly awakened dreamer'. Both remarks interpret the pictured scene, hinting at the possible thoughts of the depicted figures from visual details. The author's own general remarks upon narrative are pertinent here. In her essay, 'Leaves from a Note-Book', speaking of 'the superior mastery of images or pictures in grasping the attention' she claims that

> the desire for orderly narration is a later, more reflective birth. The presence of the jack in the box affects every child: it is the more reflective lad, the miniature philosopher, who wants to know how he got there.[11]

The surprising sight grabs the attention and, in the 'more reflective', induces curiosity. Phrases like 'the scrutiny of curiosity' which the narration includes to reveal the meanings of its surprising sights imply the need for active, reflective interpretation of visual details, the need to discover the narrative that has produced the scene. Throughout *Romola* pictorial moments seem to interrupt the narrative flow but in fact they serve to reintroduce narrative continuity.

What of a hierarchy of observation in this 'frozen moment'? The image has Tito lying, Bratti standing. Bratti makes a remark, Tito reacts sharply, but Bratti shows no perception of it.

> Something like a painful thrill appeared to dart through the frame of the listener, and arrest the careless stretching of his arms and chest. For an instant he turned on Bratti. (10)

Bratti's failure to react to this 'thrill' begins to establish the powers of observation accorded to the narration. The text focuses on visual details that the characters do not notice and implies the need for explanation. The start that passes through Tito's frame occurs time and time again in the text. The number of times Tito shudders at significant remarks make one worry for his delicacy but, as Piero notes at the outset of the novel, if it is a wonder Tito is not a nervous wreck, that is because his face when well-fed 'will keep its colour without much help of virtue' (42). His deceitful nature is itself the source of the wonder that serves the narrative, keeping any nerves well hidden, sustaining the enigma of Tito's past.

Chapter 6, entitled 'Dawning Hopes', gives us another of the Greek's reverberations and in doing so emphasizes clearly my notion of the observational hierarchy within the text. This passage gives us much of the exchange of glances between Tito and Romola. Romola and Tito look at each other and see not what is there but what they want to see there:

> 'Ah, then, they are fine intagli', said Bardo. 'Five hundred ducats! Ah, more than a man's ransom!'
>
> Tito gave a slight imperceptible start, and opened his long dark eyes with questioning surprise at Bardo's blind face, as if his words—a mere phrase of common parlance, at a time when men were often being ransomed from slavery or imprisonment—had had some special meaning for him. But the next moment he looked towards Romola, as if her eyes must be her father's interpreters. She, intensely preoccupied with what related to her father, imagined that Tito was looking to her again for some guidance, and immediately spoke. (70)

The narrative stills, diverting its attention from listening to conversation to picking out the movement of its characters' eyes. Tito's first glance is to Bardo, an attempt to divine in the man's dead eyes his meaning, as if he has briefly forgotten the scholar's blindness. He is then forced to look to Romola in the hopes that her eyes will speak for her father. This second look is questioning, as in everyday life as in a fine painting, but the question asked is missed by Romola, she sees something different, a plea for 'guidance'. So both Tito and

Romola misinterpret visual signs on the strength of their own preoccupations. Fortunately for us however, we ourselves are guided by the narration's miraculously observed 'imperceptible start'. Whilst Tito and Romola, 'intensely preoccupied', see what their selves will them to see, we see what the observant see.

Of course, to perceive an 'imperceptible start' is impossible. Yet its brief passage across the Greek's frame is the site of the text's efforts to locate human nature within its boundaries. Only the artist, the Piero di Cosimo or George Eliot, is capable of performing the feat of perception that remarks such an event. When that which the narration notices is beyond the powers of both its characters and its readership, its claim that human nature is available to the night-student and those of similar perception and knowledge becomes fraudulent. What it detects is available only to a divine eye. A question has to be asked, therefore, of the form that attempts to describe human nature by collocating a dramatic narrative with an historical one. The two aims come into conflict because their subject has to remain simultaneously hidden and revealed. Behind this conflict lies the need to attribute perceptive prowess to the disinterested observer. The one aim, to describe what is common to human beings across history, conflicts with the other, the need to render this account as a mystery, serving the purposes of a dramatic narrative.

Practically this means that the novelist is forced to construct a hierachy of observation. In Tito, Bardo's remark causes first a search of the scholar's face and then the daughter's for traces of a preoccupation wholly his own. In Romola, Tito's glance gives rise to an equally filial misinterpretation. Thus George Eliot implies that the relationship between vision and will produces perception itself. But also it is a consequence of the narrative's reliance upon mystery and suspense. Which is to say that in order to provide its commentary the text has to set the narration's power of sight in tension with the characters'; perception has to be a function of misreading, of visual ironies, and the novel has to be a historical one in order to create the necessary distance between its knowingness and its characters' ignorances. We know that Romola sees less because we know that the narration sees more, just as we know that Bernardo del Nero sees more because his brother, Bardo, sees less. More political power belongs to those who can see, hence more authority, hence the absolute power of the narration.

The entrance of Bernardo del Nero into this scene is a moment we are more likely to encounter in a novel by Henry James. Momentarily the characters form a group but it is not the group that tells, it is the reaction of the seer, told again through the device of shock (in this case 'a keen glance of surprise'), that illuminates the scene:

> He cast a keen glance of surprise at the group before him—the young stranger leaning in that filial attitude, while Bardo's hand rested on his

shoulder, and Romola sitting near with eyes dilated by anxiety and agitation. But there was an instantaneous change (72)

Bernardo, framed by the doorway, frames his relatives and the stranger into a group portrait and learns something. It is George Eliot's fine concentration upon her theme which adds the word 'keen' with its associations of sharp eyesight to Bernardo's 'glance of surprise'. But the narration must also show that what there is to be seen—the 'imperceptible start' of the preceding moment—is missable by the self-concerned so that there stands something to be discovered by these characters and by the readership. The better one observes the closer one is to the truth that the narrative strives to present and occlude at one and the same time: human nature is a question of a proper historical perspective and the constant action of the self is always liable to muddy that perspective. Indeed, as we have just discovered, framing a situation into a picture is the indication of some observational talent—the narrator does it, as do Bernardo and Piero They are figures high up in the text's hierarchy of observation and take their place there in part because they can exclude their own concerns from the action of seeing.

In *Romola* stilled moments show that both characters and the narration have noticed something of significance. But then the authoritarian narration breaks the picture up to show that not all has been noticed, sustaining its position. Certain devices are employed in this process, of which Tito's vibrations are the most prominent. In the previous example, Bernardo del Nero's keen glance espies the growing relation between Tito and his brother's family and with just the same speed Tito breaks the group up, disallowing Bernardo from perceiving anything more. The narrative thus both depends upon pictures and upon destroying the picture's identifying quality: stillness. When all is stilled Tito makes a sudden but slight turn, an anxious movement of the head, or simply thrills and then just as quickly calms, showing us, who have noticed all with the narration, that there is more story to tell.

The device I have concentrated upon most operates most often in the early stages of the novel. As Tito's position in society becomes more sure the risk of accidental discovery loses ground to deliberate exposure at the hands of Baldassarre. Here vision is still at work, the novel's great strength being its extraordinary concentration upon its subject, but in a different way. With the recovery of his imagination Baldassarre's ability to avenge himself increases. When it is at its height 'The Black Marks become Magical':

> he was once more a man [...] whose sense of vision was instructed with large experience, and who felt the keen delight of holding all things in the grasp of language. Names! Images! (339)

It is the return of Baldassarre's internal visual capacity, his ability to create mental images, to 'picture', which allows him to plan and to carry out his revenge:

> He snatched up the book, but the light was too pale for him to read further
> by. No matter: he knew that chapter; he saw the stoning of the traitor
> Aristocrates. (339)

With this image Baldassarre's strength returns. And then, when he cannot
recognize a classical motif, his revenge fails as his vision again fails. The rise
and fall of his ability to observe and to recall from observation is thus
implicated directly in sustaining the narrative.

Conclusion

> 'It is good', sing the old Eumenides, in Æschylus, 'that fear should sit as
> the guardian of the soul, forcing it into wisdom—good that men should
> carry a threatening shadow in their hearts under the full sunshine; else, how
> should they learn to revere the right?' That guardianship may become
> needless; but only when all outward law has become needless—only when
> duty and love have united in one stream and made a common force. (117)

When, in the last serialized section of the novel, Romola is mistaken for a
vision of the Holy Virgin George Eliot completes her fictional essay on the
relationship between the eye and the will. It is specifically as a vision that
Romola gains 'quiet authority'. Her beholders, fully aware that there is only a
resemblance between Romola and their object of reverence, revere her
appearance as the Madonna because the image itself is an enticing, enigmatic
and encouraging one. Indeed Romola's appearance causes the villagers to
reconsider their religion in the manner of the reflective lad or the night-
student. Which is to say that their relationship with her, the needy witnesses of
an inspiring vision, is one that exemplifies the novel's self-conscious
relationship with its readership.

Romola is a novel that provides a set of guiding images aiming to provoke
reflection upon its subject: human nature. The power of the work lies in the
moment when the author's moral philosophy finds itself objectified, in an
image or an action. It is an effort to engage the power that T. S. Eliot
attributed to great poets: both the knowledge of a tradition of metaphor and
the ability to manipulate it in such a way as to express emotions separate from
those belonging to the writer. If George Eliot's philosophical position
regarding the relationship between the eye and the will finds itself stated most
clearly in essays like the one on Riehl, rather than in images, the most
powerful moment in all of her fiction is the one when a set of figures represent
the truth of these moral observations through their interaction. Which is not to
simplify and say that she organized her fictions around a series of didactic
visual encounters, rather it is to indicate that her combination of figures,
themselves individual constituents of her philosophy, could lead to powerful
representations of moral behaviour and an analysis of its sources.

To the extent that this combination is visual and reliant upon careful arrangement of described figures we can assert along with Witemeyer that these moments in her prose are pictorial, or are of a pictorial bent. In Chapter 12 of *Romola* the figures of Tito, Bardo and Romola visually combine in a way that demonstrates the thesis that 'only when duty and love have united in one stream and made a common force' (117) can human beings live without fear (of God, of Nemesis, of guilt). It provides the philosophical tone for the following scene in Bardo's study where the author offers us an image of this 'common force' nearing perfection. When Tito first whispers his love to Romola he introduces himself as the final element in an image of the perfect life. Two beautiful loving creatures assemble themselves at the left and right hand of an old parent. They do their duty in that they pursue Bardo's studies regardless of the scholar's folly, thus exemplifying the two elements that the author identifies as the constituents of life at its fullest. Together the trinity of figures combine to provide us with a portrait of love and duty, an image we may wish to commit to our visual memories:

> Tito took his stand at the *leggio*, where he both wrote and read, and she placed herself at a table just in front of him, where she was ready to give into her father's hands anything that he might happen to want, or relieve him of a volume that he had done with. They had always been in that position since the work began, yet on this day it seemed new; it was so different now for them to be opposite each other; so different for Tito to take a book from her, as she lifted it from her father's knee. Yet there was no finesse to secure an additional look or touch. Each woman creates in her own likeness the love tokens that are offered to her; and Romola's deep calm happiness encompassed Tito like the rich but quiet evening light which dissipates all unrest. (123)

Notes

1. George Eliot, 'Mackay's *The Progress of the Intellect*', *Westminster Review* **54** (January 1851), pp. 353–68.
2. Felicia Bonaparte, *The Triptych and the Cross* (Brighton: Harvester Press, 1979), pp. 49–50.
3. Eliot, p. 355.
4. *The Letters of Anthony Trollope*, ed. N. John Hall with the assistance of Nina Burgis (Stanford: Stanford University Press, 1983), p. 186.
5. Henry James, 'London Pictures and London Plays', *Atlantic Monthly* (August 1882). Collected in *The Scenic Art*, ed. Allan Wade (London: Hart-Davis, 1953), p. 162.
6. 'The Natural History of German Life: Riehl', George Eliot, *Selected*

Essays, Poems and Other Writings, ed. A. S. Byatt (London: Penguin 1990), p. 107.

7.   Ibid.

8.   'I cannot assent to the notion that music is to supersede the other arts, or that the highest minds must necessarily aspire to a sort of Milton Blindness in which the "tiefste der Sinne" is to be substitute for all the rest'. From a letter to John Sibree, Jr, 11 February 1848 (*Letters*, VI, 247).

9.   Hugh Witemeyer, *George Eliot and the Visual Arts* (New Haven: Yale University Press, 1979), p. 104.

10. I think Witemeyer sensibly skirts this sense of James's complaint, preferring to concentrate on what he can prove that she saw rather than dealing with the question of what she didn't see or what she invented for the moral purposes of her fiction.

11. 'Leaves From a Note-Book', *Essays of George Eliot*, ed. T. Pinney (London: Routledge, 1963), p. 445.

CHAPTER TEN

Angels and Archangels:
Romola and the Paintings of Florence

LEONEE ORMOND[1]

One of George Eliot's main aims in writing *Romola* was to create a convincing historical setting for her readers. Evoking late fifteenth-century Florence may have presented her with a more challenging task than the English Midland background of *Adam Bede* or *The Mill on the Floss,* but the novelist was determined to render *Romola* every bit as convincing. For her there could be no doubt about the pivotal role played by environment in defining personality, and the events of her characters' lives take place within a lovingly constructed fictional world. Attempting to render that world as accurately as fiction would allow, she incorporated a mass of precise details to register a particular kind of truth; political, religious, cultural and psychological. George Eliot's admiration for the theories of realism and truth to nature which Ruskin sets out in *Modern Painters,* the third and fourth volumes of which she had reviewed in 1856, may have given her an additional justification for attempting such a narrative method. There is even a telling parallel with the precise rendering of nature and pursuit of sincerity in art which marked the early work of the Pre-Raphaelite Brotherhood, championed by Ruskin in the 1850s.

It has long been recognized that George Eliot's treatment of one particular aspect of her Florentine world picture, that of the visual arts, represents not simply her pursuit of exactitude, but also an important structural device. In contributing explanatory notes for a new edition of *Romola,* I have been drawn into a search for the possible 'originals' of her Florentine paintings and sculptures and fascinated by the ways in which George Eliot uses both real and invented pictures. Why did a novelist with a particular commitment to certain kinds of accuracy devise imaginary paintings and then incorporate them into a novel which also makes considerable reference to identifiable works? Of course, this is fiction and the novelist is free to do exactly what she likes. She employs a similar strategy when she incorporates a fictional character, Tito Melema, into specific historical events like the arrival of the French armies in Chapter 26 or of the French relief galleys in Chapter 43. On both occasions, as Andrew Sanders has pointed out, Tito refuses to 'take the credit for a notable public action', standing back in favour of 'a figure whose name has been recorded by contemporary historians'.[2] George Eliot does not, however, invent literary quotation as she does paintings, preferring to remain close to the actual writing of Romola's period.

I shall begin with a brief glance at some of the ways in which George Eliot incorporated known paintings into her novel. First, however, I should note her considerable debt to the visual arts for her account of the dress and general appearance of the Florentines. We know that she consulted costume books and took ideas from frescoes. As she told her illustrator, Frederic Leighton, restoration works had prevented her from making more than one visit to the Domenico Ghirlandaio frescoes in Sta Maria Novella, with their impressive rendering of the fashions of the later fifteenth century. 'I wish', she told Leighton, 'you would especially notice if the women in his groups have not that plain piece of opaque drapery over the head which haunts my memory' (*Letters*, IV, 43).

In another letter to Leighton George Eliot discussed the possibility that he could draw the head of Piero di Cosimo from a portrait. To her eye, the print of the artist in her copy of Giorgio Vasari's *Lives of the Painters* was featureless. She speculated about finding an image in the Uffizi collection of artists' self portraits (Leighton was on his way to Florence), but in effect abandoned hope that Leighton's Piero could be a true rendering of the original. 'Of Niccolo Caparra', she told Leighton, 'it is not likely that any portrait exists, so that you may feel easy in letting your imagination interpret my suggestions' (*Letters*, IV, 55). One of George Eliot's own 'suggestions' for her account of Caparra's appearance comes from the Ghirlandaio frescoes. Caparra, she notes, 'had often been an unconscious model' to the painter (19). Given his importance to her, it is perhaps surprising that Ghirlandaio, who died in 1494, makes no appearance as a character in *Romola*.

As she told Leighton, George Eliot liked, where possible, to draw upon portraits of her characters for her own account of them. When the narrator refers (for the second time) to Bernardo Dovizi of Bibbiena, the clever outsider who became first tutor and then adviser to Giovanni de' Medici (later Leo X), she notes that he 'now looks at us out of Raphael's portrait as the keen-eyed Cardinal da Bibbiena' (196). A very minor character in *Romola* is thus made visually accessible to a reader who knows the Raphael portrait in the Pitti Palace, Florence.

For another famous face, that of Niccolo Machiavelli, George Eliot turns to the best known of his surviving portraits, Tito di Santi's in the Palazzo Vecchio of Florence: 'He was a young man about Tito's own age, with keen features, small close-clipped head, and close-shaven lip and chin, giving the idea of a mind as little encumbered as possible with material that was not nervous' (166).

The account of the face of Savonarola in Chapter 15 of *Romola* is based upon another well-known portrait, that by Fra Bartolommeo (the best-known version being now in Savonarola's convent of San Marco). As Savonarola takes the crucifix from her brother, Romola sees the Frate with his cowl thrown back: 'They were very marked features, such as lend themselves to popular description. There was the high arched nose, the prominent under-lip, the coronet of thick dark hair above the brow, all seeming to tell of energy and passion; there were the blue-grey eyes, shining mildly under auburn eyelashes, seeming, like the hands, to toll of acute sensitiveness' (160).

At least four Florentine painters of the time make an appearance in *Romola*. With the exception of Piero di Cosimo, who is a major character, these artists are mentioned briefly as part of a larger group, with the assumption that, for an informed reader, their names will add an extra degree of authenticity. We hear of the minor painter Mariotto Albertinelli, who worked closely for a time with Fra Bartolommeo, in Chapter 14, contracting, like Tito, a mock marriage at the Peasants' Fair.

In Chapter 49, there is a glancing reference to Lorenzo di Credi and Fra Bartolommeo, two of the artists known to have fallen under the influence of Savonarola and thought to have burned their early work on the Bonfire of the Vanities. Fra Bartolommeo, as the narrator points out, was known as Baccio della Porta during the period of the novel. He joined the Dominican order as Brother Bartholomew only after the death of Savonarola. For a twentieth-century reader, the missing name from George Eliot's list is that of Sandro Botticelli, also a follower of Savonarola, and now of far greater celebrity than Lorenzo di Credi or even Fra Bartolommeo. In the 1860s, however, Botticelli was almost unknown in Britain, where his fame, urged on by Dante Gabriel Rossetti and Walter Pater, belonged to the later years of the nineteenth century.

As a woman, George Eliot was unable to enter Savonarola's cell at San Marco, but George Henry Lewes had told her with enthusiasm of a 'much defaced' *Madonna and Child* by Fra Bartolommeo which hung there: 'the child more lifelike and noble than any but Raphael's Sistine children' (*Letters*, III, 295). Since Raphael's *Sistine Madonna* was a supreme work of art for George Eliot and Lewes, this was a compliment indeed. Working from Lewes's notes, George Eliot incorporated the Fra Bartolommeo painting into *Romola*, describing the artist as 'that young painter who had lately surpassed himself in his fresco of the divine child on the wall of the Frate's bare cell' (236). Today, there are two paintings of the *Madonna and Child* by Fra Bartolommeo in Savonarola's cell at San Marco, but both were painted for the Hospice of Santa Maria Maddalena in Pian di Mugnone in 1514, after the Frate's death. One was moved to San Marco only in 1867, after Lewes's visit, and the Madonna which Lewes saw can therefore be identified as a half-length with the mother holding the naked child horizontally, his legs in a white veil.

The account of San Marco given by G. H. Lewes also supplied material for the opening of Chapter 64 when Tito, hurrying through the upper corridors of San Marco on his way to Savonarola, glimpses the early fifteenth-century frescoes by Fra Angelico and his school. George Eliot's narration may imply that Tito is startled by the frescoes, described in a passage of unusual lyricism. 'Fra Angelico's frescoes, delicate as the rainbow on the melting cloud, startled the unaccustomed eye here and there, as if they had been sudden reflections cast from an etherial world, where the Madonna sat crowned in her radiant glory, and the divine Infant looked forth with perpetual promise' (529). The reference to the 'unaccustomed eye' suggests that George Eliot is implying a general rather than a particular reading here, that anyone passing that way might experience such an element of surprise at the 'sudden' sight of the Fra Angelico frescoes. Possibly, indeed, George Henry Lewes had reported that this would have been George Eliot's own reaction. However you read the passage, and whether the character recognizes it or not, this angelic world is one from which we are being reminded that Tito, bound on a treacherous errand, is entirely cut off.

There are Fra Angelico frescoes in most of the cells on the upper corridors of San Marco. George Eliot's reference is presumably to those actually painted on the walls of the corridor leading to Savonarola's cell, among them the famous *Annunciation* and the *Sacra Conversazione,* a Virgin and child and saints.[3]

George Eliot would have known paintings by Fra Angelico from the Louvre and from the London National Gallery (where two had just been purchased), as well as from other galleries in Italy. Fortunately for her, however, she *was* able to see a few Angelicos at San Marco, the same ones, as the narrator comments at the opening of Chapter 15 of *Romola,* to which a late fifteenth-century woman would have had access. 'The frescoes I cared for most in all Florence', George Eliot declared, 'were the few that a *donna* was allowed to see in the Convent of San Marco'.[4] Most impressive of all was *The Crucifixion* (Fig. 10.1), generally regarded as the greatest of Fra Angelico's works in the convent, and, fortunately for George Eliot, on the wall of the ancient Chapter House:

> with the inimitable group of the fainting mother, upheld by St John and the younger Mary, and clasped round by the kneeling Magdalene. The group of adoring, sorrowing saints on the right hand are admirable for earnest truthfulness of representation. The Christ in this fresco is not good, but there is a deeply impressive original crucified Christ with St Dominic clasping the cross [*Christ on the Cross Adored by Saint Dominic*] and looking upward at the agonised Saviour, whose real, pale, calmly enduring face is quite unlike any other Christ I have seen.[5]

It is in the chapter-house that Romola sees her dying brother for the last time, and it is in the same place that she pleads unsuccessfully with Savonarola for the life of her godfather. *The Crucifixion,* with its fainting Madonna, strikes Romola as she first enters the room: 'just conscious that in the background there was a crucified form rising high and pale on the frescoed wall, and pale faces of sorrow looking out from it below' (155). One death scene with a sorrowing woman mirrors another. When Romola returns to the chapter-house for her unrewarding attempt to intercede with Savonarola, he, like Pilate before the crucifixion, refuses to follow his better judgement. On this occasion Romola recognizes a parallel between herself and the mourners around the cross: 'Once more looked at by those sad frescoed figures which had seemed to be mourning with her at the death of her brother Dino, it was inevitable that something of that scene should come back to her' (493).

George Eliot's reference to Fra Angelico's *Crucifixion* is a subtle and sensitive one, but straightforward enough for a reader who looks at the work or at a reproduction to see the point immediately. As with the Raphael portrait of Cardinal Bibbiena, the novelist alludes, briefly or at greater length, to an actual painting which she had studied in Florence. For all her scholarly care, she made some mistakes in this practice. As we have seen she placed an anachronistic Fra Bartolommeo *Madonna* on the wall of Savonarola's call and, in the same way, the Filippino Lippi altarpiece of *The Virgin appearing to Saint Bernard,* placed in the Church of the Badia in Chapter 52 of *Romola,* has arrived there too early. Lippi's altarpiece did not reach the Badia for more than 20 years after the period of the novel.

In describing the work of Piero di Cosimo, however, and even more strikingly when she was writing of the *St Michael* in the Church of the Annunziata, George Eliot's plans for her novel compelled her to invent paintings or to move them around in order to fit her structural pattern. According to all available evidence, Piero di Cosimo did not paint a *Bacchus and Ariadne,* and the triptych given by Tito to Romola is, as is well known, an entirely fictional work. The painting and its subject reverberate on a number of narrative levels. Tito intends to pay for it with money raised from selling his adopted father's ring, a symbol of his relinquishment of filial claims upon him. In the context of Tito's marriage to Romola, the subject of Bacchus and Ariadne has an evident meaning. Ariadne, in the myth which Piero illustrates, is abandoned by Theseus and rescued by Bacchus, a parallel with Tito's discovery of Romola, imprisoned in her father's library.

The imagery surrounding Tito in the early part of the novel often continues this Bacchic theme. By the end of *Romola,* however, Tito himself has become the betrayer of the trusting woman, the man who was Bacchus has now become Theseus, and Romola has become a despairing Ariadne on Naxos. Tito's use of the 'Bacchus' triptych to conceal the cross given to Romola by

her brother again moves from realism into symbolism, like Romola's eventual
rescue of the cross from its pagan setting. As Hugh Witemeyer puts it, the
triptych is 'a false pastoral fancy portrait'.[6] and it is doubtful whether the real
Piero di Cosimo would have painted it. The other works attributed to Piero in
the novel, 'Sinon deceiving Priam', 'Oedipus and Antigone', respectively
show Tito as a traitor and Romola as a dutiful daughter, parallels directed to
the morality of the novel. In these fictional paintings Piero's gift of seeing into
his subjects' true being adds another level of commentary. Like the novelist,
the artist can interpret and exemplify the hidden truths of human nature.

George Eliot invents, not only the 'Bacchus and Ariadne', but a whole
series of works by Piero di Cosimo, an artist whom, after reading his life by
Vasari, she chose to play a part in her novel. Hugh Witemeyer speculates that
she also chose Piero because he was sufficiently little known for her safely to
invent an *oeuvre* for him.[7] In his fictional studio, there is just one 'real' work,
the *Venus, Mars, and Cupid*, then in the Kaiser-Friedrich-Museum in Berlin
and now in the Dahlem Museum. Giorgio Vasari, who owned the work,
describes it in some detail in his *Lives of the Painters*, and (although she may
have seen it in Berlin) this is probably George Eliot's source for her account
of it. The *Allegory* by Piero, with the three masks of 'a drunken laughing
Satyr, another a sorrowing Magdalen, and the third, which lay between them,
the rigid, cold face of a Stoic', has attracted much attention from critics of the
novel, but the real Piero never painted it: 'The masks rested obliquely on the
lap of a little child, whose cherub features rose above them with something of
the supernal promise in the gaze which painters had by that time learned to
give to the Divine Infant' (33).

A good deal has been written about the imaginary works by Piero di
Cosimo in *Romola,* but far less about the painting representing *St Michael*
which Tessa sees, and before which she prays, in the Church of the
Annunziata. As Andrew Brown has pointed out, there in no such work in the
Church, and I am inclined to agree with him that what George Eliot had in
mind was the figure of St Michael in Perugino's *Assumption of the Virgin* in
the Accademia Gallery in Florence (634-5). There is an almost exact copy of
the Saint Michael figure in the left-hand panel of the triptych of *The Virgin
with Saint Michael, Raphael and Tobias* in the National Gallery, London, a
painting bought for the Gallery from the Charterhouse of Pavia by Sir Charles
Eastlake in 1856 (Fig. 10.2).

George Eliot's reference to an imaginary fresco in the Annunziata, and to
Tessa's confusion of the Archangel with Tito, is one of a series of references
to St Michael in *Romola*. The first comes near the opening of the novel when
Bratti finds the shipwrecked Tito and asks him: 'But how comes a young man
like you, with the face of Messer San Michele, to be sleeping on a stone bed
with the wind for a curtain?' (11). Bratti refers here to the general

iconography of St Michael as handsome, young, and in armour. In August 1860, George Eliot had read Anna Jameson's *Sacred and Legendary Art* of 1848, with its section on representations of St Michael. For Jameson the Archangel 'is young and beautiful, but "severe in youthful beauty", as one who carries on a perpetual contest with the Powers of evil'.[8]

References to St Michael are more frequent in *Romola* than references to Bacchus, and the image of the warrior saint acquires increasing force through the novel. When Tessa gazes at the altar-piece, she sees the Archangel Michael as Anna Jameson sees him: 'in his armour, with young face and floating hair' (148). If St Michael is a thing of wonder for Tessa, Tito is even finer: 'very much more beautiful than the Archangel Michael, who was so mighty and so good that he lived with the Madonna and all the saints and was prayed to along with them' (148-9). Tessa not only thinks that her 'husband' looks like St Michael, but she also speculates on more than one occasion that St Michael is Tito's guardian angel, as Tito is hers.

We know that this is a false image, and that, however beautiful Tito may be, and though he rescues Tessa from attack, he only *seems* to be like an Archangel. Angels and Archangels, as George Eliot would have been aware, are rather different from saints, not least because they are not, and have never been, human. In her terms, a lack of humanity was not necessarily a virtue, and George Eliot's fictional 'angels' are likely to be human beings, not celestial spirits. In *Silas Marner,* for example, she describes the effect of a child upon an erring or endangered adult in terms of an angelic visitation:

> In the old days there were angels who came and took men by the hand and led them away from the city of destruction. We see no white-winged angels now. But yet men are led away from threatening destruction: a hand is put into theirs, which leads them forth gently towards a calm and bright land, so that they look no more backward; and the hand may be a little child's.[9]

Angels and saints are one of the features of the Eve of San Giovanni procession in Chapter 8 of *Romola,* when the narrator describes the processional floats, undercutting the fantastic effect by noting that the figures may have looked like Perugino's angels and cherubs but were in fact constructed from humbler material: 'The clouds were made of good woven stuff, the saints and cherubs were unglorified mortals supported by firm bars' (82).

St Michael the Archangel was a cult figure during the Middle Ages, and was still popular at the date of *Romola's* action. Traditionally presented as a warrior fighting for the chosen people, St Michael was often shown by artists as a protector who conducted the souls of the dead to God or as one who weighed those souls in the balance.

Mythologically, St Michael is related to the classical god Hermes or Mercury, who performed a similar function as a conductor and protector, a role which Christianity took over and bestowed upon the Archangel. In *Romola*, there is a statue of Hermes in Nello's garden, but it is a female character, Romola, who plays his traditional part, coming as a rescuer to the plague-stricken village or to Tessa and her children. There is a circularity here typical of the Renaissance. Pagan and Christian symbols come together as Michael, Hermes and Bacchus blur into one another.

Tito is, of course, not a rescuer but a destroyer. Mocking his wife's grief for her godfather, he asks her whether her adherence to Savonarola has not led her to understand that 'Messer Bernardo del Nero is the prince of darkness, and Messer Francesco Valori [a leading Savonarolan] the archangel Michael' (419). By associating the Tito of the early chapters so closely with a false St Michael, George Eliot increases the depth of his eventual fall. In an earlier version of Tito's arrival in Florence, Nello advises him to retain the air of a 'faded prince' (of a man who has been shipwrecked) until he has attracted attention. George Eliot then decided to change the word 'faded' to 'fallen', possibly an oblique reference to Lucifer (35). At the execution of Bernardo del Nero, Pietro Cennini suspects Machiavelli, whose philosophy is closely allied with Tito's, of being in some way like Satan. For from being the 'severe' youthful Archangel, in perpetual war with evil, of Anna Jameson's description, Tito is rapidly overthrown by evil. As he shifts from a rescuing Bacchus to a deserting Theseus, Tito also moves from Archangel to fallen angel, from Michael to Lucifer.

George Eliot's decision to cast Tito in the role of a fallen archangel may have been provoked by her own researches in Florence. Another possible explanation presents itself, however. It in generally believed that George Eliot was influenced in writing *Romola* by Nathaniel Hawthorne's Roman novel, *The Marble Faun* of 1860, and that Hawthorne's use of works of art to define his own symbolic structures was taken over by both Eliot and Henry James.

One of the paintings which serves to underline that pattern of morality in *The Marble Faun* is Guido Reni's *Saint Michael the Archangel* of 1635, in the Capuchin Church of Sta Maria della Concezione in Rome (Fig. 10.3). The painting shows the youthful Archangel about to thrust his sword into the overthrown Lucifer, with an expression which Hawthorne thought one 'of heavenly severity, and a degree of pain, trouble, or disgust, at being brought into contact with sin, even for the purpose of quelling and punishing it'.[10] In *The Marble Faun* the artist, Miriam, shortly after playing a part in the killing of a man who has been her model and who may be a Capuchin friar, sees *Saint Michael the Archangel* in company with a group of friends. In her despair she mocks at 'the dapper' Archangel, 'is it thus that virtue looks the moment after its death struggle with evil?'[11] For Hawthorne Guido Reni's painting had a real religious appeal, a surprising response perhaps in a puritan from New England. George Eliot, on the other hand, like a true Ruskinian, disliked the work of Guido Reni, seeing it as pretentious, over-blown and lacking in true emotion: 'Guido is superlatively odious in his Christs, in agonized or ecstatic attitudes'.[12]

It is therefore unlikely that Tessa's Archangel in the Annunziata is by Guido Reni, but the parallel is nevertheless a striking one. Both writers turn to an image of the warrior saint and describe its effect upon a young woman. In both cases St Michael is evidently chosen for his traditional iconography, his association with a battle between good and evil, between the celestial and the fallen. Hawthorne's Miriam believes that Guido's St Michael is a fraud, but from what we know of the novelist's response to the painting, Hawthorne would not have agreed with her. Miriam's friends see a likeness between Guido's demon and the murdered man, but Miriam hotly disputes it. Is the dead 'model' a saintly monk or an emanation of evil? The reader is never sure. George Eliot's St Michael figure, Tito, on the other hand, is more clearly laid out for us. His angelic looks conceal a nature readily turned to betrayal and deceit. Perhaps George Eliot was responding to Hawthorne, even perhaps redefining morality in her own, more obviously 'human', terms.

Only the well informed would be aware of George Eliot's mingling of real and imaginary paintings in *Romola*. The writer does not signal a difference, but incorporates both into a carefully contrived and 'realistic' evocation of fifteenth-century Florence. Her self-immersion in the culture and history of the period results in a remarkably seamless collage of authentic and inauthentic. Although Eliot was not in a position to recognize it, much of her reference to real works is anachronistic: apart from the Fra Angelicos and the Piero di Cosimo *Venus, Mars and Cupid*, none of the specific paintings would have been found in Florence at the date of the novel.

George Eliot had a double purpose in introducing a multiplicity of art works into *Romola*. If one aim was to give authenticity to her own scene-setting, the other relates to her purposes in defining character. As the figure whose outward appearance is most insisted upon, it is not surprising to find that Tito is frequently defined through reference to the visual effect of works of art. Aspects of his character are brought into focus through these comparisons in the same way that Romola's conflicting roles of dutiful daughter and mature woman are captured when Piero di Cosimo, represents her, first as Antigone and then as Ariadne. The novelist (and the fictional painter) project a view of the character which is essentially fragmentary. It is noticeable that the only one of the major 'portraits' of *Romola* to be based upon an actual work of art is that of Savonarola. George Eliot resists the temptation, if she experienced one, to say that Tito or Romola *look like* a particular Florentine painting. Ultimately, the novel is an imaginative creation, and the faces of the leading characters remain free—the Leighton illustrations apart—for the reader to re-create.

Notes

1. I am grateful to Dr Marco Chiarini, to Dr Serena Padovani and to Professor Andrew Sanders for their help.
2. Andrew Sanders, notes to *Romola* (Harmondsworth: Penguin Books, 1980), p. 722.
3. Andrew Brown suggests in his notes to *Romola* that the reference here is to the *Coronation of the Virgin* in Cell 9 at San Marco rather than to the *Sacra Conversazione* in the corridor. While he is right to point to the representation of the Madonna 'crowned in her radiant glory' in the *Coronation of the Virgin*, there is no child in that fresco. The 'divine infant' looking forth 'with supernal promise' seems closer to the child in the *Sacra Conversazione*, who looks straight at the viewer with considerable nobility (like the child in the *Sistine Madonna*). Of course, since George Eliot had not seen the works, such considerations can never be more than speculations.
4. J. W. Cross (ed.), *George Eliot's Life as Related in her Letters and Journals* (Edinburgh and London: Blackwood, 1885), vol. 2, p. 220.
5. Ibid.
6. Hugh Witemeyer, *George Eliot and the Visual Arts* (New Haven: Yale University Press, 1979), p. 57.
7. Ibid., p. 58.
8. Anna Jameson, *Sacred and Legendary Art* (London: Longman, Green, and Co., 1888), vol. 1, p. 100.
9. George Eliot, *Silas Marner* (London, New York and Toronto: Oxford University Press, 1906), p. 144.
10. Nathaniel Hawthorne, *The French and Italian Notebooks* (Columbus, Ohio: Ohio State University Press, 1980), p. 521.
11. Nathaniel Hawthorne, *The Marble Faun* (Boston: Ticknor and Fields, 1860), vol. 1, pp. 230-31.
12. Cross, vol. 2, p. 49.

Figures

Figure 1.1   'The Blind Scholar and His Daughter'

Figure 1.2   'Under the Plane-tree'

Figure 1.3   'The First Kiss'

Figure 1.4   'Coming Home'

Figure 1.5   "You didn't think it was so pretty did you?""

Figure 1.6   'Escaped'

Figure 1.7   'Tessa at Home'

Figure 1.8 'Drifting Away'

Figure 1.9   'The Visible Madonna'

Figure 1.10 'At the Well'

Figure 10.1   Fra Angelico, *The Crucifixion*

Figure 10.2 Pietro Perugino, *The Virgin with Saint Michael, Raphael and Tobias* (detail)

Figure 10.3   Guido Reni, *Saint Michael the Archangel*

Contributors

Susan Bernardo, Associate Professor of English at Wagner College, has focused on Victorian fairy tales, the novels of Eliot and Brontë and, most recently, feminist science fiction. Her current work examines Oscar Wilde's *A House of Pomegranates*, Victorian versions of 'Beauty and the Beast' and Mary Shelley's *Mathilda*. She is also co-editing a collection of essays on women, culture and perversions.

Andrew Brown, editor of the Clarendon Edition of *Romola* (1993) and the World's Classics Edition (1994), is Director of Humanities and Social Sciences at Cambridge University Press.

David Carroll is Professor Emeritus of English at Lancaster University. Among his many publications on George Eliot are the Clarendon Edition of *Middlemarch* (1986), *George Eliot: The Critical Heritage* (1971) and *George Eliot and the Conflict of Interpretations* (1992). He is currently working on the Leverhulme electronic edition of the first volume of Ruskin's *Modern Painters*.

Julian Corner teaches at King's College, London. He has recently completed a PhD at Trinity College, Cambridge, entitled *The Beginnings of Geoge Eliot*.

Beryl Gray teaches for the Centre for Extra-Mural Studies, Birkbeck College, London, and is the co-editor with Dr John Rignall of the *George Eliot Review*, the journal of the George Eliot Fellowship. She is the author of *George Eliot and Music* (Macmillan, 1989), and has edited several of George Eliot's works, including *The Lifted Veil* (Virago Modern Classics, 1985) and *The Mill on the Floss* (Everyman Paperback, 1996).

Chris Greenwood, a graduate of Trinity College, Cambridge and a Kennedy Scholar, is currently writing a book for Scolar's Studies in European Cultural Transition Series, entitled *Adapting to the Stage: Henry James's Encounter with Theatrical Naturalism*. He has a second volume planned for the same series which will be a study of screen adaptations.

Caroline Levine is Assistant Professor of English at Rutgers-Camden. She has published a number of articles on Victorian realism, and she is currently completing a manuscript called *The Realist Experiment*. Her translation of Nicole Loraux's *Les enfants d'Athena* appeared as *Children of Athena* from Princeton University Press in 1993. With Mark Turner, she has recently edited a special issue of the journal *Women's Writing* (1996) devoted to George Eliot and gender.

Leonee Ormond is Professor of Victorian Studies at King's College, London University, and has published widely on Victorian and Edwardian literature and fine art, with books on George Du Maurier, J. M. Barrie and Tennyson. She is the author, with Richard Ormond, of a critical biography of Frederic, Lord Leighton and was one of the organizers of the 1996 Royal Academy Leighton Centenary Exhibition.

Shona Elizabeth Simpson received her PhD in English from Duke University where she held a Mellon Fellowship in the Humanities. While there, she won the Anne Flexner Award for poetry and the Benenson Prize in the Arts. She has published short fiction and poetry as well as criticism. She is currently Visiting Assistant Professor of English at Wake Forest University, in Winston-Salem, North Carolina.

Mark W. Turner is Lecturer in English at Roehampton Institute London. He is the author of *Trollope and the Magazines* (forthcoming) and has co-edited with Caroline Levine a special issue of *Women's Writing* on George Eliot and gender (1996). He is co-editor of *Media History* and has written on nineteenth-century periodicals and serial fiction.

Select Bibliography

Anderson, Patricia. (1994), *The Printed Image and the Transformation of Popular Culture 1790-1860*, Oxford: Clarendon.

Armstrong, Nancy. (1987), *Desire and Domestic Fiction: A Political History of the Novel*, Oxford: Oxford University Press.

Ashton, Rosemary. (1992), *G. H. Lewes: A Life*, Oxford: Oxford University Press.

Auerbach, Nina. (1982), *Woman and the Demon: The Life of a Victorian Myth*, Cambridge, MA: Harvard University Press.

Bär, Eugen S. (1974), 'Understanding Lacan', in eds Leo Goldberger and Victor H. Rosen, *Psychoanalysis and Contemporary Science: An Annual of Integrative and Interdisciplinary Studies,* vol. 3, New York, International Universities Press: 473-544.

Barrickman, Richard, Susan McDonald and Myra Stark. (1982), *Corrupt Relations: Dickens, Thackeray, Trollope, Collins and the Victorian Sexual System*, New York: Columbia University Press.

Barthes, Roland. (1977), *Image, Music, Text*, trans. Stephen Heath, London: Fontana Press.

_____. (1974), *S/Z*, trans. Richard Miller, New York: Hill and Wang.

Beer, Gillian. (1983), *Darwin's Plots: Evolutionary Narrative in Darwin, George Eliot, and Nineteenth-Century Fiction*, London: Routledge and Kegan Paul.

Bennett, Joan. (1962), *George Eliot: Her Mind and Her Art*, Cambridge: Cambridge University Press.

_____. (1986), *George Eliot*, Brighton: Harvester Press.

Berger, John. (1972), *Ways of Seeing*, London: BBC and Penguin.

Bersani, Leo. (1976), *A Future for Astyanax: Character and Desire in Literature*, Boston and Toronto: Little, Brown, and Company.

Bloom, Harold (ed.), (1986), *George Eliot: Modern Critical Views*, New York and Philadelphia: Chelsea House Publishers.

Bonaparte, Felicia. (1979), *The Triptych and the Cross: The Central Myths of George Eliot's Poetic Imagination*, New York: New York University Press.

_____. (1975), *Will and Destiny: Morality and Tragedy in George Eliot's Novels*, New York: New York University Press.

Booth, Alison. (1992), *Greatness Engendered: George Eliot and Virginia Woolf*, Ithaca and London: Cornell University Press.

Brooks Peter. (1984), *Reading for the Plot: Design and Intention in Narrative*, Cambridge, MA, and London: Harvard University Press.

Bullen, J. B. (1975), 'George Eliot's *Romola* as Positivist Allegory', *Review of English Studies* **26**: 425-35.

————. (1994), *The Myth of the Renaissance in Nineteenth-Century Writing*, Oxford: Clarendon Press.

Burckhardt, Jacob (1929), *The Civilization of the Renaissance in Italy*, trans. S. G. C. Middlemore, London: Harrap.

Carpenter, Mary Wilson. (1986), *George Eliot and the Landscape of Time*, Chapel Hill: University of North Carolina Press.

Carroll, David. (ed.), (1971), *George Eliot: The Critical Heritage*, London: Routledge and Kegan Paul.

————. (1992), *George Eliot and the Conflict of Interpretations*, Cambridge and New York: Cambridge University Press.

Conrad, Peter. (1973), *The Victorian Treasure-House*, London: Collins.

Cross, J. W. (ed.), (1885), *George Eliot's Life as Related in her Letters and Journals*, Edinburgh and London: Blackwood, 2 vols.

David, Deirdre. (1987), *Intellectual Women and Victorian Patriarchy*, Ithaca, NY: Cornell University Press.

Eliot, George. (1993), *Romola*, ed. Andrew Brown, Oxford: Clarendon Press.

————. (1992), *Selected Critical Writings*, ed. Rosemary Ashton, Oxford: Oxford University Press.

————. (1990), *Selected Essays, Poems and Other Writings*, ed. A. S. Byatt, London: Penguin.

————. (1981), *A Writer's Notebook, 1854-1879*, ed. Joseph Wiesenfarth. Charlottesville: University Press of Virginia for the Bibliographical Society.

Ermarth, Elizabeth Deeds. (1983), *Realism and Consensus in the English Novel*, Princeton: Princeton University Press.

Freud, Sigmund. (1991), *Case Histories II*, trans. James Strachey, ed. Angela Richards, Harmondsworth: Penguin.

Gilbert, Sandra M. and Susan Gubar. (1979), *The Madwoman in the Attic: The Woman Writer and the Nineteenth Century Literary Imagination*, New Haven: Yale University Press.

Girard, René. (1965), *Deceit, Desire and the Novel: Self and Other in Literary Structure*, trans. Yvonne Freccero, Baltimore: Johns Hopkins University Press.

Gordon, Lesley. (1994), 'Tito, Dionysus and Apollo', *The George Eliot Review* **25**, pp. 34-8.

Greetham, D. G. and W. Speed Hill (eds), (1996), *Text: An Interdisciplinary Annual of Textual Studies*, vol. 9, Ann Arbor: University of Michigan Press.

Guthrie, W. K. C. (1935), *Orpheus and Greek Religion*, London: Methuen.

Haight, Gordon. (1968), *George Eliot: A Biography*, Oxford: Oxford University Press.

Handley, Graham. (1990), *State of the Art of George Eliot: A Guide through the Critical Maze*, Bristol: The Bristol Press.

Hardy, Barbara. (1963), *The Novels of George Eliot: A Study in Form*, New York: Oxford University Press.

Harvey, J. R. (1970), *Victorian Novelists and their Illustrators*, London: Sidgwick and Jackson.

Heffernan, Thomas J. (1988), *Sacred Biography: Saints and their Biographers in the Middle Ages*, Oxford: Oxford University Press.

Hertz, Neil. (1985), 'The Notion of Blockage in the Literature of the Sublime', in *The End of the Line: Essays on Psychoanalysis and the Sublime*, New York: Columbia University Press: 40-60.

Holland, Norman. (1992), *The Critical I*, New York: Columbia University Press.

Holub, Robert C. (1991), *Reflections of Realism: Paradox, Norm, and Ideology in Nineteenth-Century German Prose*, Detroit: Wayne State University Press.

Homans, Margaret. (1986), *Bearing the Word: Language and Female Experience in Nineteenth-Century Women's Writing*, Chicago and London: University of Chicago Press.

Houfe, Simon. (1978), *Dictionary of British Book Illustrators and Caricaturists, 1800-1914*, Woodbridge, Suffolk: Antique Collectors' Club.

Hughes, Linda K. and Michael Lund. (1991), *The Victorian Serial*, Charlottesville, VA: University Press of Virginia.

Hutton, Richard Holt. (1888), *Essays on Some of the Modern Guides to English Thought in Matters of Faith*, London: Macmillan.

Irigaray, Luce. (1985), *Speculum of the Other Woman*, trans. Gillian C. Gill, Ithaca, NY: Cornell University Press.

Jameson, Anna. (1888), *Sacred and Legendary Art*, London: Longman, Green, and Co., 2 vols.

Kierkegaard, Søren. (1983), *Fear and Trembling; Repetition*, trans. Howard V. Hong and Edna H. Hong, Princeton: Princeton University Press.

Klein, Melanie. (1988), *Love, Guilt and Reparation*, London: Virago Press.

Knott, John R. (1993), *Discourses of Martyrdom in English Literature, 1563-1694*, Cambridge: Cambridge University Press.

Kuchler, Susanne and Walter Melion. (1991), 'Introduction: Memory, Cognition and Image Production', in eds Susanne Kuchler and Walter Melion, *Images of Memory: On Remembering and Representation*, Washington, DC and London: Smithsonian Press.

Lacan, Jacques. (1977), *Écrits: A Selection*, trans. Alan Sheridan, New York and London: W. W. Norton and Company.

_____. (1981), *The Four Fundamental Concepts of Psycho-Analysis*, ed. Jacques-Alain Miller, trans. Alan Sheridan, New York and London: W. W. Norton and Company.

_____. (1968), *Speech and Language in Psychoanalysis*, trans. Anthony Wilden, Baltimore: Johns Hopkins University Press.

Langbauer, Laurie. (1990), *Women and Romance: The Consolations of Gender in the English Novel*, Ithaca and London: Cornell University Press.

Lerner, Laurence (ed.), (1978), *The Victorians*, London: Methuen, 1978.

Linforth, Ivan Mortimer. (1941), *The Arts of Orpheus*, Berkeley and Los Angeles: University of California Press.

Martin, Carol A. (1994), *George Eliot's Serial Fiction*, Columbus: Ohio State University Press.

McMaster, Juliet. (1982), 'George Eliot's Language of the Sense', in *George Eliot: A Centenary Tribute*, eds. Gordon S. Haight and Rosemary T. VanArsdel, Totowa, NJ: Barnes and Noble Books.

Michie, Helena. (1987), *The Flesh Made Word: Female Figures and Women's Bodies*, Oxford: Oxford University Press.

Miller, J. Hillis. (1976), 'Ariadne's Thread', *Critical Inquiry* (Autumn), 57-77.

Mitchell, Sally. (1981), *The Fallen Angel: Chastity, Class and Women's Reading, 1835-1880*, Bowling Green, OH: Bowling Green University Popular Press.

Moi, Toril. (1994), *Simone de Beauvoir: The Making of an Intellectual Woman*, Oxford: Blackwell.

Nead, Lynda. (1990), *Myths of Sexuality: Representations of Women in Victorian Britain*, Oxford: Basil Blackwell.

Norris, Christopher. (1982), *Deconstruction: Theory and Practice*, London and New York: Routledge.

Oliphant, Margaret. (1863), 'Girolamo Savonarola', *Blackwood's Magazine* (June): 702.

_____. (1876), *The Makers of Florence: Dante, Giotto, Savonarola, and their City*, London: Macmillan and Co.

Olsen, Donald. (1986), *The City as a Work of Art*, New Haven: Yale University Press.

Poovey, Mary. (1988), *Uneven Developments: The Ideological Work of Gender in Mid-Victorian England*, Chicago: University of Chicago Press.

Postlethwaite, Diana. (1984), *Making it Whole: A Victorian Circle and the Shape of their World*, Columbus: Ohio State University Press.

Prochaska, F. K. (1980), *Women and Philanthropy in Nineteenth-Century England*, Oxford: Clarendon.

Rahner, Karl. (1961), 'On Martyrdom', in *On the Theology of Death*, New York: Herder and Herder.

Redinger, Ruby V. (1975), *George Eliot: The Emergent Self*, New York: Knopf.

Reed, John R. (1989), *Victorian Will*, Athens, Ohio: Ohio University Press.

Reid, Forrest. (1975), *Illustrators of the 1860s*, New York: Dover.

Rimmon-Kenan, Shlomith. (1983), *Narrative Fiction: Contemporary Poetics*, London and New York: Methuen.

Sadoff, Dianne F. (1982), *Monsters of Affection: Dickens, Eliot, and Bronte on Fatherhood*, Baltimore: Johns Hopkins University Press.

Sanders, Andrew. (1978), *The Victorian Historical Novel 1840-1880*, London: Macmillan.

Sanders, Andrew. (1980), 'Introduction' to *Romola*, Harmondsworth: Penguin.

Showalter, Elaine. (1987), *The Female Malady: Women, Madness and English Culture, 1830-1980*, London: Virago.

Stephen, Leslie. (1902), *George Eliot*, London and New York: Macmillan.

Thale, Jerome. (1959), *The Novels of George Eliot*, New York and London: Columbia University Press.

Trudgill, Eric. (1976) *Madonnas and Magdalens: The Origins and Development of Victorian Sexual Attitudes*, London: Heinemann.

Uglow, Jennifer. (1987), *George Eliot*, London: Virago.

Villari, Pasquale. (1896), *Life and Times of Girolamo Savonarola*, trans. Linda Villari, London: Fisher and Unwin.

Weeks, Jeffrey. (1981), *Sex, Politics and Society: The Regulation of Sexuality Since 1800*, London: Longman.

Weinstein, Donald. (1970), *Savonarola and Florence: Prophecy and Patriotism in the Renaissance*, Princeton: Princeton University Press.

Winnett, Susan. (1990), 'Coming Unstrung: Women, Men, Narrative, and the Principles of Pleasure', *PMLA* **105** (May): 505-15.

Winnicott, D. W. (1971), *Playing and Reality*, London: Tavistock Publications.

_____. (1975), *Through Paediatrics to Psychoanalysis*, London: Hogarth Press.

Witemeyer, Hugh. (1979), *George Eliot and the Visual Arts*, New Haven: Yale University Press.

Wolf, Robert Lee. (1977), *Gains and Losses: Novels of Faith and Doubt in Victorian England*, New York and London: Garland.

Index